Dostoevsky

DOSTOEVSKY

Language, Faith, and Fiction

Rowan Williams

continuum

Continuum International Publishing Group

The Tower Building	80 Maiden Lane
11 York Road	Suite 704
London SE1 7NX	New York, NY 10038

www.continuumbooks.com

First published 2008

Reprinted 2009, 2011(twice)

British Library Cataloguing-in-Publication Data
A catalogue record for this book is available from the British Library.

ISBN 9781441183880

Printed and bound in Great Britain

To the Georgetown Jesuit Community
with gratitude and affection.

Contents

Preface

The current rash of books hostile to religious faith will one day be an interesting subject for some sociological analysis. They consistently suggest a view of religion which, if taken seriously, would also evacuate a number of other human systems of meaning, including quite a lot of what we unreflectively think of as science. That is, they treat religious belief almost as a solitary aberration in a field of human rationality; a set of groundless beliefs about matters of fact, resting on—at best—faulty and weak argumentation. What they normally fail to do is to attend to what it is that religious people actually do and say—and also to attend to the general question of how systems of meaning, or "world-views," work.

Systems of meaning—philosophies of life, if you must, though the term sounds immediately rather stale—seem to operate by allowing us to see phenomena in connected instead of arbitrary ways. But this means the capacity to see things in terms of other things: it means abandoning the idea that there is one basic and obvious way of seeing the world which any fool can get hold of (and which some people then insist on dressing up with unnecessary complications), and grasping that seeing the world and being able to talk about what it is that we encounter, is something we have to learn, a set of skills that allows us to connect and to see one event or phenomenon through the lens of another. At the most severely pragmatic level, this leads to observational generalizations about laws; at a quite different but no less important level, it leads us into the world of metaphor. And in case anyone should think that these are radically separate, consider that "law" itself is a metaphor in the context of natural process. . . .

Metaphor is omnipresent, certainly in scientific discourse (selfish genes, computer modelings of brain processes, not to mention the magnificent extravagances of theoretical physics), and its omnipresence ought to warn us against the fiction that there is a language that is untainted and obvious for any discipline. We are bound to use words that have histories and associations; to see things in terms of more than their immediate appearance means that we are constantly using a language we do not fully control to respond to an environment in which things demand that we see more in them than any one set of perceptions can catch.

All of which is to say that no system of perceiving and receiving the world can fail to depend upon imagination, the capacity to see and speak into and out of a world that defies any final settlement as to how it shall be described. The most would-be reductive account of reality still reaches for metaphor, still depends on words that have been learned and that have been used elsewhere. So it should not be too difficult to see that a map that presents the intellectual world as a struggle between rival pictures, well-founded and ill-founded ways of describing things, literal and fanciful perspectives, or even natural and supernatural vision, is a poor one and one that threatens to devour itself in the long run, if the search is for the unadorned absolute. How shall we move the cultural discussion on from a situation in which religious perspectives are assumed to be bad descriptions of what can be better talked about in simpler terms?

This will involve the discipline of following through exactly what it is that the language of a particular religious tradition allows its believers to see—that is, what its imaginative resources are. When believers are engaged (as they routinely are, despite what may be assumed by the critics of faith) in society and politics and the arts in ways that are recognizable to nonbelievers, how are their perceptions actually and specifically molded by the resources of their tradition? This is not—*pace* any number of journalistic commentators—a matter of the imperatives supposedly derived from their religion. It is about what they see things and persons in terms of, what the metaphors are that propose further dimensions to the world they inhabit in common with nonbelievers.

Characteristically this repertoire of resources—in any religious tradition—is chaotically varied, not just a matter of a few leading ideas or doctrines. It includes the visual and the aural—what is sung and seen as well as said. It includes formative practices, rites, which leave their semantic traces in unexpected settings. And it includes the legacy of others who have engaged the world in the same ways, at various levels of sophistication. The forming of a corporate imagination is something that continues to be the more or less daily business of religious believers, and it needs to be acknowledged that this is a process immeasurably more sophisticated than the repetitive dogmatism so widely assumed to be the sole concern of those who employ religious language.

The way to demonstrate this is to lay out what it means in the practice of specific people; this series is an attempt to exhibit a common imagination at work—and in the process of further refinement and development—in the labors of a variety of creative minds. Because we are in danger of succumbing to a damaging cultural amnesia about what religious commitment looks like in practice, these books seek to show that belief "in practice" is a great deal more than following out abstract imperatives or general commitments. They look at creative minds that have a good claim to represent some of the most decisive and innovative cultural currents of the history of the West (and not only the West), in order to track the ways in which a distinctively Christian imagination makes possible their imaginative achievement. And in doing so, they offer a challenge to what one great thinker called the "cultured despisers" of Christian faith: in dismissing this faith, can an intellectually serious person accept confidently the simultaneous dismissal of the shifts, enlargements, and resources it has afforded the individual and collective imagination? What, finally, would a human world be like if it convinced itself that it had shaken off the legacy of the Christian imagination? The hope of the authors of these volumes is that the answer to that question will be constructively worrying—sufficiently so, perhaps, to make possible a more literate debate about faith and contemporary culture.

It seems to be customary for anyone writing a book about Dostoevsky to apologize for adding to the vast library that already exists, but
if some of the ideas expressed in the following pages—especially those
most indebted to Mikhail Bakhtin—are correct, there is never likely
to be a completely superfluous book on the subject, given Dostoevsky's
own assumption that the continuing of dialogue is what writing most
intends. So no apologies; and indeed, the writing of this book has been
so much of a stimulus and a delight that I would feel it both ungracious
and untruthful to say sorry for it.

Instead, I am very happy to record public thanks to all who have
made this book such a pleasure to work on. Stephen Prickett first
planted the idea in my mind, and I hope he will not regret it. Background work has accumulated steadily over a couple of years, but the
Church Commissioners, in agreeing that an Archbishop might be entitled to the occasional period of study leave, gave me the chance to do
some sustained writing in the summer of 2007. Without this opportunity, the final composition of the book would have taken a great deal
longer. Part of that leave was spent in the pleasant environment of
Georgetown University, where the President, John De Gioia, and the
members of the Georgetown Jesuit community, especially John Lan-
gan, SJ, Rector of the Jesuit Residence, made me abundantly welcome.
The dedication of this book expresses my gratitude to all who so kindly
made me part of their community life for several weeks in June 2007.

I am not by any standards a professional scholar of Russian literature and have gratefully relied on various friends to help me with
suggestions for reading and reflection. To them and to others who
have over the years shared, inspired, and deepened my interests in this
field, not least by the loan or gift of relevant books and articles, my
thanks,especially to John Arnold, Denis Bradley, Ruth Coates, Catriona Kelly, Robin Milner-Gulland, Stewart Sutherland, and Jonathan
Sutton.

I have not assumed a knowledge of Russian in readers of this book
(though I have included some Russian references in the bibliography)
and so have not referred quotations to the standard Russian edition of
Dostoevsky's works. This creates something of a dilemma: there is no
"standard" English translation, and the advantages and disadvantages
of the various versions on the market are not easy to assess compara-

tively. I have decided to make reference to what are probably the most widely available translations, those currently in print in the Penguin Classics, with the exception of *The Adolescent* (*Podrostok*, sometimes translated as *A Raw Youth*), where I have used the recent version by Richard Pevear and Larissa Volokhonsky. Page references to these editions are included in the text in square brackets. Very occasionally, I have modified published translations where I am unhappy with them or noted an ambiguity not captured in the version used. The transliteration of Russian words and names poses similar difficulties, given the different conventions followed by various translators; I have simply aimed to give a reasonably satisfactory phonetic equivalent.

Rowan Williams
Canterbury, August 2007

INTRODUCTION

Terrorism, child abuse, absent fathers and the fragmentation of the family, the secularization and sexualization of culture, the future of liberal democracy, the clash of cultures and the nature of national identity—so many of the anxieties that we think of as being quint-essentially features of the early twenty-first century are pretty well omnipresent in the work of Dostoevsky, his letters, his journalism, and above all his fiction. The world we inhabit as readers of his novels is one in which the question of what human beings owe to each other—the question standing behind all these critical contemporary issues—is left painfully and shockingly open, and there seems no obvious place to stand from where we can construct a clear moral landscape. Yet at the same time, the novels insistently and unashamedly press home the question of what else might be possible if we—characters and readers—saw the world in another light, the light provided by faith. The novels ask us, in effect, whether we can imagine a human community of lan-guage and feeling in which, even if we were incapable of fully realizing it, we knew what was due to each other; whether we could imagine living in the consciousness of a solidity or depth in each other which no amount of failure, suffering, or desolation could eradicate. But in order to put such a challenge, the novels have to invite us to imagine precisely those extremes of failure, suffering, and desolation.

This is the unresolved tension in the novels. But it is not—as it is too often portrayed—a tension between believing and not believing in the existence of God. Dostoevsky has been to some extent coopted into the service of an anguished agnosticism which he professed himself to have left behind; readers whose minds have been powerfully formed by a post-religious culture assume that the irresolution of the narratives shows us an author who is unable to decide the question for or against religious belief and—whatever his professions of faith in his public and private writing—was constantly drawn toward doubt and negation. An earlyish comment of his[1] has been cited in evidence, as has what is often seen as the failure of his last and greatest novel to deliver its supposed goal of defending or restoring the possibility of faith. William Hamilton, in an essay of the sixties, claimed that the study of Dostoevsky was a substantial influence in pushing him toward the "Death of God" school of theology, since the faith of the future, the faith that was supposed to emerge from the "crucible of doubt,"[2] was never given credible form in Dostoevsky's fiction, particularly in *The Brothers Karamazov*: "we can all receive Ivan with a terrible kind of delight . . . Ivan's picture of himself we immediately recognize as self-portrait; the God that is dead for him is dead for us; and his Karamazov-God of tension and terror is often the only one we are able to find."[3]

This is a curious judgment in many ways. It assumes, for example, that Ivan has a consistent position—whereas the novel represents him as exploring numerous positions, each with its own variety of mental agony for him. And if we ask what or who exactly is the God who is dead for him and for us, it is again far from straightforward to read off from the text a clear answer. It assumes, as do countless essays on Dostoevsky and faith, that Ivan's "mutiny" against the God who permits the torture of children stands almost independently within the novel and likewise that Ivan's "poem" about the Grand Inquisitor is a definitive and unironic statement, both within the novel and in terms of Dostoevsky's whole narrative strategy. And it assumes that the real energy of the novel is concentrated in the tension between Ivan and Alyosha. The body of the essay, much of it a very interesting discussion in its own right, also takes for granted that the religious sensibility represented by those figures who are supposed to represent the positive virtues of faith—especially Father Zosima and Alyosha—is at best residually Christian, let alone Orthodox. The critical lodestars by which Hamilton navigates tend to be the nonspecialist commentators of the first quarter of the twentieth century, D. H. Lawrence prominent among them,[4] for whom *Karamazov* was a site on which could be fought the standard battles of modernity or emancipation versus tradition.

Although there is nothing remotely like a critical consensus about—for example—the effectiveness of the treatment of Zosima or the relation of his teaching to Orthodox (and orthodox) Christianity, it would be hard to write an essay like Hamilton's today. We have become a great deal more sensitive to the need to read the *whole* novel, understanding that even a significant and concentrated "insertion" like the Inquisitor story is part of a carefully woven fictional construct. Too many views have been fathered on Dostoevsky as a result of isolating certain telling passages and even phrases and treating them as his personal philosophy. The massive importance of Mikhail Bakhtin's work on Dostoevsky, available in English since the 1970s, meant that every reader or critic worth his salt was now bound to give weight to the "polyphonic" dimension of Dostoevsky—the coexistence of profoundly diverse voices, making the novel itself a constant and unfinished interplay of perspectives: whatever Dostoevsky actually believed himself, he could not but put it into a *novel* as one perspective among others, since he was committed to a particular view of what authorship can and can't do (I shall be looking at this in detail in the third chapter of this book). This enforces a certain caution about any simple reading-off from the text of "what Dostoevsky thought." Instead of imagining a deeply divided authorial mind, half-consciously struggling with contradictory convictions or emotions and betraying this inner division in a confused text, we have a text that *consciously* writes out the to and fro of dialogue, always alerting us to the dangers of staying with or believing uncritically what we have just heard.

But as Bakhtin's impact spread and more critical work was devoted to him, the issues around faith in the novels came more directly into focus for many critics. These issues had tended to be the preserve of highly impressionistic, not to say sermonistic, essays in the earlier part of the century, not least those stemming from the Russian emigration—Berdyaev's well-known study, for example, or Konstantin Mochulsky's, or Shestov's extraordinary work on Dostoevsky and Nietzsche—or of directly theological studies from Protestant or Catholic thinkers.[5] The importance of Dostoevsky to the young Karl Barth and to the shaping of the ethos of "dialectical theology" was considerable.[6] But as a result, strictly critical discussion of this aspect of Dostoevsky, discussion that related the large themes to the detail of what is said in the fiction and how, was not in huge supply; and some of the essays devoted to religious aspects of the novel by serious literary critics were strikingly tone-deaf to the material.[7] However, a growing awareness of the complex relation of Bakhtin's thought to a hinterland of Russian religious philosophy and phenomenological speculation helped toward a deeper appreciation of Dostoevsky's connections to this world. From the mid-seventies onward, critical work in English on Dostoevsky became in general far more sophisticated, and part of that welcome development was a new seriousness of engagement with the religious aspect of the fiction.

This was further strengthened, of course, as the critical climate in Russia changed with the weakening and then the downfall of a Soviet regime that had never quite known what to do with Dostoevsky, an unmistakable Russian genius with (nearly) all the wrong ideas.[8] A fresh critical edition stimulated more and more interpretative work[9]; and the theological establishment in Russia also—tentatively—began to provide some useful resources for tracing the roots of Dostoevsky's religious sensibility and also the reception of his work by the Orthodox Church.[10] In recent years, the quality of critical discussion around these themes in a variety of contexts (not least in the exceptionally lively climate of North American Slavonic studies) has been unprecedented; several valuable symposia witness to the flourishing state of the discussion.[11]

In the present study, very much the work of a nonspecialist, but gratefully informed by this recent discussion, I have tried to sustain a focus on the question suggested earlier. That is, I have assumed that Dostoevsky is not presenting to us a set of inconclusive arguments about "the existence of God," for and against, but a fictional picture of what faith and the lack of it would *look* like in the political and social world of his day—an assumption articulated clearly by Bakhtin, and also one that shapes some of the most interesting philosophical discussion of Dostoevsky in recent decades (especially the work of Stewart Sutherland). Dostoevsky's intention of writing *for* the cause of faith need not, of course, limit the reader's response or conclusion as to how persuasively this comes over or how consistent its execution is. But I have taken it for granted that, to see what he is actually doing, we have to trace so far as possible the inner movement and coherence (I hesitate to use the word "logic") of the way he treats questions about how the life of faith is to be imagined—about the diabolical, about the kind of life that is able to resist the diabolical, about how what we encounter can be understood as a representative or vehicle of the holy. Perhaps the major point, though, is to do with the issues I have tried to raise about how far we can rightly see the perspective of faith as radically informing both Dostoevsky's sense of what it is to write fiction at all and his understanding of the interdependence between human freedom and human language and imagination. If I read correctly, he is committed to an understanding of both speech and fiction that is deeply rooted in a kind of theology. Acceptable or not to the reader, this is what we need to grasp if we are to read in a way that takes into account his own purposes.

This is to raise the question of how far and in what sense we should call Dostoevsky a Christian or indeed an Orthodox novelist. Such terms are fraught with problems: they will mean seriously different things as used of different writers, and a little clarification is needed. To take an obvious example: we think of Evelyn Waugh and Graham Greene (at least in much of his earlier work) as *Catholic* novelists, and we mean by this not that they are novelists who happen to be Catholics by private conviction, but that their fiction could not be understood by a reader who had no knowledge at all of Catholicism and the particular obligations it entailed for its adherents. Quite a lot of this fiction deals with what it is that makes the life of a Catholic distinct from other sorts of lives lived in Britain and elsewhere in the modern age. Some of it is about how dilemmas arising from the tensions between Catholic teaching and contemporary mores or personal crises of responsibility divide and even destroy individuals. Some of it is about how the teaching of the Catholic Church, difficult and apparently unreasonable as it seems, is obscurely vindicated as the hand of God works through chaotic human interactions. Some of it challenges us by refusing any such resolution and leaving us dealing us with the force of the conflicts generated.

But this is not the only way in which we can speak of Catholic novelists. Take four more cases, dramatically different in style, Flannery O'Connor, Walker Percy, Muriel Spark, and Alice Thomas Ellis.

Very little of their work is about the problems or dilemmas distinctive to Catholics as individuals in the contemporary world. It is rather about the possibility of any morally coherent life in a culture of banality and self-deceit. Their protagonists may or may not be Catholics by profession, but their narratives are those of people who encounter the effects of this banality or profanity or absurdity and are questioned by it—not in a way that necessarily leads them to profess orthodox Catholic faith, but in a way that leaves the assumptions prevailing in their environment under some kind of challenge. Their mode is essentially comic (not to say grotesque), in the sense that the persons of the fiction are caught in incongruities they do not themselves see or understand. We cannot expect an outcome that will "vindicate" any point of view; the novelist does not seek to depict—or to stand in for—Providence. O'Connor approaches the question of how grace works in the human world by portraying a world in which the variegated absences of grace—or sometimes the apes of grace—almost force the question, "What is wrong in this picture?" Percy's increasingly apocalyptic imagination displays an erosion of the possibilities of depth or consistency for human agents: their sense of time is distorted and they are caught in repetition to such a degree that only some kind of apocalyptic disruption offers hope. The ambiguity of his fiction lies in this simultaneous recognition that violence is the ultimate distraction for the lost self and that the violence of social, moral or mental collapse is the only tool that can break into the strongholds of the modern self. Spark and Ellis create characters whose comprehensive ironizing of their situations and relationships places the entire narrative within a framework of a kind of alienation; they have also played effectively with different strategies of fragmentation in narrative point of view, which has a similar effect. All four create a world in which the secular majority account of what is going on is severely relativized, but there is no simple alternative that anyone can step into by a single decision or even a series of decisions. The "religious" dimension of these fictions lies in the insistent sense of incongruity, unmistakable even if no one within the fiction can say quite what we should be congruent *with*.

The first kind of Catholic writer may introduce elements of the ethos of the second (Waugh especially, I think), but the basic structure of the narrative in my first category will still turn on tensions played out between clear rival accounts of what "congruence" demands, congruence with public teaching, congruence with social demand or personal fulfillment. These are narratives that *could* be written in substantial part by someone who was, as a matter of fact, not a Catholic but sensitively equipped to understand the tragedy of a person caught in these tensions. The second kind could only be written by someone whose concern was to provide a structured narrative space (a notion I'll elaborate later in this book) in which tensions were created for the reader rather than the characters—that is, in which we are invited not to contemplate the dilemmas of an individual which may or may not mirror our own, but to inhabit a narrative world whose center of gravity is hidden (as it is in all daily experience), but whose distinctive boundaries are capable of being sensed obliquely yet firmly.

Dostoevsky is obviously closer to the second than to the first category. He has no interest at all in the dilemmas of the Orthodox Christian as distinct from other people; for one thing, practically everyone in his world is at least nominally Orthodox anyway. Nor is he interested in *depicting* Orthodoxy. It was a gap in his writing that dismayed some pious readers in his lifetime and later; you will not find in him the affectionate sketches of Orthodox ecclesial life that characterize Leskov's work, or even the nostalgic vignettes scattered through the fiction of Tolstoy and Chekhov. The general environment is one in which, when Christian practice is mentioned, it is obviously Orthodox, and the scene setting in the monasteries is clear and credible. But anyone looking in the novels for any hint of exotic ritual, for "mysticism" or mystique, will be disappointed. Yet—and this will be argued in more detail later—the background against which his characters move and develop is extensively and deeply shaped by motifs in Orthodox Christianity. Like our second group of Catholic writers, he locates his narrative within an implied "order." But he is not primarily a comic artist in the sense defined a moment ago (though his comic and parodic skills are often ignored), and what prevents us from describing him simply as a comic artist is that even the clearest assertions and intimations of an authoritative moral and spiritual order are left open to fundamental question in the novels. The *presence* of order is visible, in verbal argument and in the lives of certain "iconic" characters (see chap. 5), but the authority of such presence, its capacity to establish itself as final or decisive for the characters in the fiction, is something which the novelist *strictly as novelist* will not settle for us by any obvious strategy of closure in the narrative. The reader's work remains to be done in this regard. Not a comic writer—the authorial withdrawal and obliqueness make this an inappropriate designation—yet in a sense clearly someone writing as an Orthodox believer, whose very Christian conviction seems to lead him to this withdrawal, this indetermination (see chaps. 3 and 4).

The tension between presence and (effective) authority will be a theme that recurs in different ways quite regularly as we reflect on the novels. And it may help us understand better why the question of the "existence of God" is not really at the heart of Dostoevsky's labors. In a passage that has been much cited to illustrate the indeterminacy of Dostoevsky's "real" feelings about faith, Alyosha Karamazov admits to Lise Khokhlakova [289], "It is possible that I do not even believe in God." It is a stark contrast to his response to his father's questioning a few chapters earlier ("'Alyosha, my boy: does God exist?' 'Yes, He does'" [179]), and we are told that Alyosha himself doesn't really understand what he has said to Lise. But the context of his remark is important: he has been speaking of the self-destructive strain in the *Karamazov* character that is leading his father and brothers to disaster; and he adds that "in addition to all that" his elder is dying, "the finest man in all the world, he is forsaking the earth" [289]. The latter comment is particularly significant, as it echoes the protests of Ippolit in *The Idiot* and Kirillov in *Devils* that the laws of nature (and thus of death) did not spare the greatest human being of all. And Alyosha's crisis of faith comes to a head when the operation of the laws of nature becomes all too obvious as the elder's body begins to decay after death.

The crisis is not so much, then, about whether God exists, but about what the nature is of God's relation with the world, and most of all with the human world. Alyosha's problem is in fact very close indeed to Ivan's—not in admitting the existence of God, but in the possibility of accepting God and the world and the problem of what sort of life such acceptance would entail. Alyosha's uncertainty about whether he "believes in God" is an uncertainty about whether the life he leads and the feelings he has are the life and the feelings that would rightly follow from belief in God. "God exists but I'm not sure whether I believe in him" may sound an absurd statement, but it reflects a serious spiritual perception.[12] If I live like this, can I really claim to believe? Simone Weil, in a much-quoted *pensée*, wrote that she was absolutely sure that there was a God, in the sense that she did not believe her love was based on an illusion, and absolutely sure that any God her mind could conceive could not exist (because of the innate corruption of the finite imagination).[13] We do not have to take on board all of Weil's passionate pessimism about the nature of all individual human subjectivity to see the point, and it is a point very close indeed to what Alyosha is saying. He knows the difference between self-destructive activity and the life of genuine belief (as he sees it in the elder), but he cannot truthfully say that he is yet committed unreservedly to the latter.

When he is first introduced to us, we are given several hints of what lies ahead. He is in the monastery partly because of a revolt against other options, partly because belief in God and immortality has simply taken hold of his imagination and he cannot believe that anything less than visibly wholehearted commitment in the form of the monastic life can rightly and credibly express this faith. "But Alyosha said to himself: 'I cannot give up two roubles instead of "all"'" [40]. But the decisive factor is meeting Father Zosima, and Alyosha is convinced that the elder possesses a "secret" that can renew the world [45]. However, he is also at this stage still wedded to an idea of what this might mean that is bound up with how the elder will bring "glory" to the monastery: he envisages Zosima, in other words, as the focus of a great and inspiring *cultus*.

So it is entirely in character that he should be anxious about the genuineness of his faith at a point when he is deeply aware of his kinship with his family's destructive heritage, recognizing that he is not "innocent" [286], and when he is suffering from the prospect of the elder's imminent death—a point at which he is also finalizing his abandonment of monastic life through his engagement to Lise. He has to undergo a set of purgatorial trials so as to arrive at a different kind of faith. The elder's death and decay forces him to abandon the idea of a triumphalist cult of Zosima as sage and wonder-worker; the encounter with Grushenka shows him that God can be at work in the least act of generosity from a flawed and sinful person; the vision of "Cana of Galilee" which overtakes him as he dozes by the elder's coffin declares that it is not only heroic "maximalism" that genuinely expresses faith—precisely the vision he will communicate to his brother Mitya later on. God will value and work with the least sign of movement toward him. Alyosha has sensed a divine abundance and liberty that exceeds human standards of success and failure; his belief has been transformed—but not in the sense that he has become convinced of God's existence. It is rather that he now sees clearly what might be involved in a life that would merit being called a life of faith.

"For Dostoevsky, the true synthesis," writes Stewart Sutherland, "the final reply of belief or unbelief, can only come in a statement that conforms to the demands of art and reality."[14] Sutherland is not persuaded that such a fusion of art and reality can be found even in *Karamazov*, despite Dostoevsky's best intentions, and he has written compellingly about Dostoevsky's exemplary failure in depicting Christ-likeness, in Prince Myshkin as in the saints of *Karamazov*, contrasting him with Kierkegaard, for whom there could—more or less by definition—be no decisive visible form of holiness, given the essential anonymity, or at least utter ambiguity, of incarnation itself.[15] He reminds us that this failure is itself a theological matter, a way of illustrating Weil's point that what we can successfully conceive as a representation of the divine will inevitably be a falsehood in some crucial respect. But to some extent, Dostoevsky knows what he is about, knows what kind of failure he has condemned himself to. What he does in *Karamazov* is not to demonstrate that it is possible to imagine a life so integrated and transparent that the credibility of faith becomes unassailable; it is simply to show that faith moves and adapts, matures and reshapes itself, not by adjusting its doctrinal content (the error of theological liberalism, with which Dostoevsky had no patience) but by the relentless stripping away from faith of egotistical or triumphalistic expectations. The credibility of faith is in its freedom to let itself be judged and to grow. In the nature of the case, there will be no unanswerable demonstrations and no final unimprovable biographical form apart from Christ, who can only be and is only represented in fiction through the oblique reflection of his face in those who are moving toward him. And the question will never be resolved as to whether faith's capacity to survive disillusion and apparent failure (Zosima's body decaying) is a mark of the power of resourceful self-deceit or the power of truthfulness. A good *novel* will not pretend to answer this; a novel written for the sake of the credibility of Orthodox Christianity can only set out the (necessarily incomplete) narrative and invite the reader freely to indwell it and discover whatever is to be discovered.

There will be a fair amount of discussion in later pages about freedom. Some of it has to do with Dostoevsky's actual depiction of varieties of freedom in the personages of the novels, and particularly the terrifying profiles of "revolutionary" freedom sketched in *Devils*. Here we have a diagnosis of the pathology of fantasies of absolute freedom comparable (indeed quite closely comparable) to Hegel's in the *Phenomenology*: "the freedom of the void" is the dream of a liberty completely without constraint from any other, human, subhuman or divine; because it has no "other," it can also have no content. But this means that the hunger for such freedom can only manifest itself in destruction, flinging itself against existing limits; and when those limits are destroyed, it has to look around for more "others" to annihilate, culminating in self-destruction. "Since limits make us what we are, the idea of absolute freedom is bound to be terroristic," says Terry Eagleton in an exceptionally penetrating essay on the political pathologies of the contemporary West.[16]

But deeper than that is the notion of freedom that is outlined in the very method of Dostoevsky as narrator. As we shall see, it is crucial to his understanding of what he is doing that he sees language itself as the indisputable marker of freedom: confronted with what seeks to close down exchange or conflict, we discover we can always say more. This is emphatically and evidently a liberty that *depends* on otherness. It is generated by what is other to the mind or self or will; it is through response to—including contradiction of—what is given that we develop as subjects. And this means, of course, that when we have nothing with which to engage, we stop speaking and stop developing. It is in one sense true that we can say what we like; in another sense, manifestly not true, since we are performing linguistically within a world in which we have to make ourselves recognizable to other speakers, as they are to us. Some of Dostoevsky's most intriguing and teasing fugues of obsessive reflection—as in *Notes from the Underground*—explore the balance between the liberty to say what we like, protesting about the reduction of language to mathematical clarity or certainty, and the necessity to say what can be heard. And Dostoevsky in effect argues that this necessity of saying what is recognizable is finally grounded in the order established by a creator: recognition is possible because we are all at the most basic level of our being made to resonate with the interdependent life of a universe that is addressed and sustained by a Word from God. Our problem—if we believe this—is how to live so as to allow that resonance to shape what we say and do. And if we do not accept such a premise, we shall need to work rather hard, so Dostoevsky assures us, to explain why this does not leave us with the destructive vacuity of "absolute" freedom, with the void. And this means the death of language: either the malign silence of apathy and the absence of desire ("you've lost your eloquence completely" says Lizaveta to Stavrogin—or, "now you've fallen silent," as another translation has it) after they have failed to consummate the romance they both vainly hoped for [518] or the stream of empty words that seek nothing except power—of which the demonic chatter of Pyotr Verkhovensky is Dostoevsky's most chilling example.[17]

The Dostoevskian novel is, as we shall see in chapter 2, an exercise in resisting the demonic and rescuing language. It does this by insisting on freedom—the freedom of characters within the novel to go on answering each other, even when this wholly upsets and disappoints any hopes we may have for resolutions and good endings, and therefore also the freedom of the reader to reply, having digested this text in the continuing process of a reflective life. It enacts the freedom it discusses by creating a narrative space in which various futures are possible for characters and for readers. And in doing so it seeks—in the author's intention—to represent the ways in which the world's creator exercises "authorship," generates dependence without control. The twist in the apologetic is that it is precisely the possibility of refusing to acknowledge that representation, or to acknowledge that something real is being represented, that constitutes it as a veridical representation. The fiction is like the world itself—proposed for acceptance and understanding but unable to compel them, since compulsion would make it impossible for the creator to appear as the creator of freedom.

All this is a fairly long journey from the deceptively straightforward question of whether Dostoevsky is a Christian or Orthodox novelist, but the exploration of these issues about belief, unbelief, and liberty has made clear, I hope, why Dostoevsky can only be the *kind* of Christian novelist he is because he leaves this level of ambiguity about whether faith can offer lasting, sustainable resolution in his narratives. The extent to which, similarly, he can only be the kind of *Orthodox* novelist he is in virtue of certain narrative strategies is less clear-cut, and debate on this is unlikely to ease off in the foreseeable future. But I shall be offering some reasons for not dismissing this as a serious possibility: there are undoubtedly emphases in his understanding of Christ which are strongly echoed in his approach to novelistic method, as Bakhtin stresses; but there are also aspects of his treatment of how the holy is represented that are more readily intelligible in an Eastern Christian than in a Western (Catholic or Protestant) framework, and the fifth chapter of this book attempts to trace this in detail.

My judgment overall is that Dostoevsky's distinctively Orthodox frame of reference, especially in regard to this last point about the understanding of images, is a deeply significant element in the construction of his fictional world—not simply at the level of stage-setting, as if we were to imagine onion domes painted on a backdrop, but at the level of basic theological perspectives on creation and incarnation—and also in regard to what he understood by the Church. His opposition to Roman Catholicism is often as intemperate as it is ill-informed, but he is consciously drawing on a peculiarly nineteenth-century Russian Orthodox set of polemical concerns, going back to mid-century religious philosophers and essayists like Kireevsky and Khomyakov, and echoed in the early work of his friend Solovyov.[18] What these writers have in common is that they fiercely attack what they see as a *secularizing* move in Catholic thinking and practice, one that seeks to resolve religious doubt by appealing not to the free consensus of persons united in the Body of Christ but to a supreme executive authority, the papacy, which, simply by being a supreme executive, becomes a monarchy on the model of other monarchies, and so sets itself up as a rival *political* power.[19] The point for our present discussion is that, on this basis, Dostoevsky might well have claimed that a good Catholic, by his definition, could not write a good novel: such a writer would not be able to understand how religious uncertainty could be represented as held or healed within a narrative of the interaction of persons, a narrative that left unresolved precisely how and why the process *should* be seen as authoritatively pointing to a mended universe, yet inviting a commitment to this process on the basis simply of what the narrative had made morally and imaginatively possible.

Roman Catholicism was one of those subjects on which Dostoevsky could be spectacularly pigheaded, and the claim I have just ascribed to him is not to be taken too seriously in just those terms. What matters is that we see his thoughts about liberty and what we have learned from Bakhtin to call "polyphony" to have been bound up in a general sense of what was different about Orthodoxy, a sense which he shared with some of the most innovative Orthodox minds in his milieu. It was neither a mark of Westernizing liberalism, as some charged it with being, nor simply—at the other extreme—a reflection of Slavophil romanticism about the communal vision of Old Russia. It was part of what linked him with the monastery at Optina and the thinking that had developed there and among some of the literary and intellectual friends of the monks. Certainly for him the *Russianness* of this vision was a matter of obsessive conviction, underpinning his ambitious claims for the Russian people as the only nation with a genuinely universal mission.[20] But its foundations lay deeper than nationalist or racial mythology.

In these pages, we shall be trying to discern something of these foundations. At the beginning of this introduction, I summed up the central question posed by the various moral crises to which Dostoevsky was seeking to respond as "What is it that human beings owe to each other?" The incapacity to answer that question coherently—or indeed to recognize that it is a question at all—was for Dostoevsky more than just a regrettable lack of philosophical rigor; it was an opening to the demonic—that is, to the prospect of the end of history, imagination, and speech, the dissolution of human identity. The question does not seem any less pressing in the new century, and the incapacity or unwillingness to answer it is even more in evidence. If Dostoevsky's fictions still arrest the reader with their diagnosis of the most acute human crises, as they unquestionably do, it will not be a waste of time to clarify some of the vision out of which he worked—whether or not our labors in dealing with these crises finally bring us where he wants us to be.

I

CHRIST AGAINST THE TRUTH?

In February 1854 Dostoevsky—just released from the prison camp, but still living under legal restriction in the military settlement at Semipalatinsk—wrote to Natalya Fonvizina, who had given him the copy of the New Testament which he had used in prison, a statement of personal faith that has continued to challenge and puzzle ever since. He describes himself as "a child of unbelief and doubt" and says that he expects to remain so until his death; he speaks of the burning *desire* to believe and its cost to him; and, perhaps most famously, he claims that "if someone were to prove to me that Christ was outside the truth, and it was really the case that the truth lay outside Christ, then I should choose to stay with Christ rather than with the truth."[1]

It is a statement that confirms the suspicions of those who see in Dostoevsky a great literary imagination distorted by irrational and self-tormenting religiosity, which he clings to in the face of the evidence of a nightmare world; he knew—such a critic might say—that there was no possible way of supporting his Christian conviction by argument, and implicitly acknowledged this in Ivan Karamazov's great parable. Like Milton, he is of the Devil's party without knowing it, or at any rate without honestly acknowledging it, and his professions of faith are at best poignant testimony to his nostalgia for impossible certainty, a nostalgia expressed by a bare irrational insistence on his *choice* to believe.[2] On such a reading, religious conviction—given the character of the world we live in—can only be such an obstinate self-assertion; a rather paradoxical matter, given the Christian and Dostoevskian insistence on self-abnegation.

A more sympathetic reading would link it to the whole intellectual drift, from the late eighteenth to the twentieth century, toward a distinction between objective and subjective in religious language, between the deliverances of historical inquiry and the self-commitment of faith. Dostoevsky is here seen as part of the story that begins with Lessing's "ugly ditch" between history and the utterances of faith, that proceeds by way of Kierkegaard's analysis of faith as subjectivity, and that finds diverse twentieth-century expression in Rudolf Bultmann's Christian existentialism[3] and, most radically, Don Cupitt's antirealist theological programme. The confession of faith is just that: a risky self-projection in the face of a void or a world of manifest meaninglessness, faith and not "justifiable assertion." Religious truth is not ordinary truth, a reporting on publicly available and testable realities. It is in one sense or another something *created* by human freedom.[4]

Given the centrality of freedom to all that Dostoevsky wrote—and there will be much more to say about this later on—this looks like an attractive reading. Dostoevsky becomes the ally of a particular kind of religious modernity in which an aesthetic of self-definition through the option to entertain a religious mythology replaces any residual metaphysic, any suggestion that religious utterances purport to tell the truth about the universe. But I want to suggest that this is a hasty and inadequate reading, which finally leads to a seriously mistaken understanding of many other aspects of Dostoevsky's work. That this is so becomes apparent when we pick up some of the echoes of the Fonvizina letter elsewhere in his writing, and also when we think through more carefully the actual phraseology of the letter; it is also worth bearing in mind that Dostoevsky wrote these words at a point when he was a good way from the beliefs of his literary maturity, and was still attempting to come to terms with the enormous mental and imaginative upheavals of his prison experience. In prison, he had—so he later claimed in *A Writer's Diary*—received Christ into his soul in a new way, because of his contact with the faith of the ordinary Russians around him.[5] But it is clear that he did not at this point resume regular Orthodox worship. He seems to have made his Communion on occasions in Siberia during his imprisonment, and even at the time of his most direct involvement with the radical movements of the day had not completely abandoned church practice, but the evidence is of very infrequent contact with Orthodox sacramental life in the years after his release.[6]

It would be a mistake, then, to take the words of the Fonvizina letter as some sort of immutable testimony: he is slowly evolving a religious idiom and practice and still uncertain of how to relate it to the Orthodox tradition. Yet the letter undoubtedly represents significant strands in his thinking and cannot be written off as a passing aberration. Fortunately we have a good deal of evidence that he himself in later years wanted to make better sense of these ideas, and we shall be examining four places in his later work where they seem to be in his mind and where his reworking of the themes offers some critically important interpretative light.

First, in 1864, there is the whole discussion in *Notes from the Underground* of the arbitrary element in the human mind. The "Underground Man," the tormented, savage, ironical and absurd first person of this text, directs some of his most concentrated venom at a philosophy of rational self-interest. The right-minded liberal world of his time assumes that when human beings are authoritatively shown what is good for them, they will want it and choose it; but the fact is that human beings are not so constructed. Demonstrate that two plus two is four, and there will be someone who will simply assert that it is not so. People will not readily accept any would-be definitive account of what is in their interest. "A man can consciously and purposely desire for himself what is positively harmful and stupid," and will insist on the right to want it [36].[7] As Edward Wasiolek notes in his introduction to Dostoevsky's fiction, even some of the pre-exile pieces, such as *Mr Prokharchin*, already portray people determinedly ignoring or subverting their own interests.[8] What the rational administrator decides is best for us may appear of derisory insignificance in the face of this or that compulsive passion—which may be a passion for truth or love, or a passion for damaging and destructive experience.

In other words, part of the distinctively human is the capacity for perversity, addiction, self-sacrifice, self-destruction and a whole range of "rationally" indefensible behaviors. Remove this capacity and two things result: the distinctively human disappears and is replaced by a pattern of ordered but mechanical interaction; and violence is canonized as the means of social rationalization—because the amputation of irrational human needs or wants can only be effected by force. Dostoevsky's fierce polemic against Mikhail Saltykov-Shchedrin in 1863 and 1864[9] brings out this theme very starkly: if human beings turn out to desire what they ought not to, the only solution for the consistent rationalist is the removal of whatever part of them is involved in the desiring. If someone wants to dance, cut off his legs. But, Dostoevsky insists, the freedom to refuse what is claimed to be rational is part of an integral or complete account of human existence; its denial is thus an act of violence, even if it is done in the name of peace or welfare.

Many later pages of Dostoevsky cast their shadow before them here. But the specific context is significant. The Underground Man is someone who refuses to be *reconciled*: it is no use saying that the world is thus and not otherwise and has to be accepted, because he experiences it as both challenge and offence. The "thereness" of the world and its processes, whether of mathematical calculation or physical regularity, does not yield any meaning that would make possible a "reconciled" life, an intelligent acceptance of things as part of a coherent moral policy. The givenness of the world is felt, says the Underground Man, as a "stone wall" [23], inviting efforts to break through it and causing all the more pain as those efforts are renewed and fail. And in that process of hurling the mind and soul against the unyielding surface of things, the frustrated self increasingly takes the blame for the situation: it is inner weakness that makes the wall impenetrable—as if, by sheer force of will, it might be possible to break through into a world where two and two did not make four. If all there is really to know is that two and two make four, there is "nothing left to do, much less to learn" [41]. The "derision" with which the Underground Man regards the Crystal Palace of a future in which all needs are rational and can be rationally satisfied is the expression of a desire for a world in which human needs were not reduced to what could be rationally satisfied; if that is all there is, the palace will in reality be a "henhouse." And it is a proper matter for derision if the powers that be are constantly trying to persuade us that these squalid surroundings are actually splendid. If only we could really be convinced of that, these deeper desires could be forgotten, but the very existence of the desires begs the question, "Can I have been made for only one thing, to come at last to the conclusion that my whole make-up is nothing but a cheat?" [43].

What we have here, in fact, is remarkably like a highly dramatized version of the Hegelian Unhappy Consciousness, with a few extra refinements: the self's ideal existence is unattainable, and what is actually experienced in self-awareness is failure and finitude, finitude itself as a form of humiliation. We experience a "demand" to be reconciled with what simply is (and thus to accept a situation in which we no longer have anything to learn), and when that demand cannot be met, there is guilt and resentment. When the demand is concretely made by an other possessed of or at least claiming power—the rationalist social organizers dreamt of by the social theorists who are in Dostoevsky's sights here—their project can only appear as violent, and so provokes the verbal counter-violence of the Underground Man's rantings. Reason, presented as the triumphant exercise of rationalizing power, power to reshape and reduce the human experience, appears invasive. In one of the great paradoxes of modernity, which Dostoevsky was among the first to recognize, the idea that reason could provide nonviolent ways of resolving the essentially *un*reasonable conflicts of the human world is turned on its head. The amputation of unmanageable desires for the sake of peace becomes the quintessential form of "modern" violence. And, if we can presume to keep in view the Hegelian parallels, reason as defined here represents a basically *pre*rational set of strategies in that it refuses to work with its "other."

It is highly unlikely that Dostoevsky had Hegel even remotely in mind when he wrote the *Notes*. But the parallels are illuminating: the Underground Man is neither a ludicrous irrationalist, though his exaggerated rhetoric invites the charge, as he well knows, nor a trial run for some Sartrean rebel or voluntarist, glorying in the refusal of the world as it is. As the passage referred to puts it quite plainly, this is a state of consciousness that is deeply miserable and painful, and has no glory about it. The Underground Man's savage depiction of his own ridiculous behavior when he tries to demonstrate to his snobbish friends how little he cares for their (supposed) contempt shows that he has no illusion about being a developed or mature specimen of advanced nineteenth-century humanity; his whole essay (including the sad and self-loathing anecdote of the second part) is a demolition of any claim that either he or those he castigates could be thought of as having solved the problem of how to live in the world.

What is especially interesting is that Dostoevsky originally intended to include in *Notes* reference to religious faith as the only way of resolving the tensions he had evoked—the supreme case of a refusal of the bullying of "reason," but one that did not end up in a world of resentful and ludicrous self-assertion. He wrote to his brother[10] that he had meant to speak of Christ and the immortality of the soul in this connection, but was warned off by the censors. It sounds as though he had envisaged a kind of apologetic based on the instinctive denial of reductive pictures of human capacity, the denial most clearly evident in the perverse refusals of self-interest, for good *and* evil purposes, that characterize human behavior. Ten years after the Fonvizina letter, Dostoevsky has turned what was originally perhaps little more than a rhetorically extreme insistence on the compulsion which Christ exercised on his imagination and affections into the beginnings of a very serious literary and theological strategy—even if he would have demurred from being described as a theologian. It is literary as well as theological, because, as we shall see, what he is doing becomes fully explicable in the context of grasping how he sees language itself, including the language of fiction.

But for now we can at least recognize how the rhetoric of the Underground Man elucidates the 1854 declarations. What at first sight appears a deeply perverse and problematic affirmation of Christ's priority over "truth" takes on a somewhat different cast. The interpretation of the remarks to Mme Fonvizina is, of course, complicated a bit further by the absence of the definite article in Russian: to set Christ over against truth itself sounds even worse than setting him beyond the truth. But it seems from the *Notes* that we must understand "the truth" as "what is the case" in the world, as the sum of rationally and evidentially demonstrable propositions independent of human desire and indeed human self-description. It is the empirical world as it confronts human awareness as an impenetrable surface, with no "readable" pattern. In the *Notes*, the focus is on those who are trying to map out plans for human improvement on the grounds of what is obviously best for all (or for most) in terms of their material needs. But as Dostoevsky's fictional imagination matures, the world that resists the individual will comes to include the obstinate givenness of moral outrages—the horrors of which Ivan Karamazov speaks. And the basic point is the same, only so much sharpened in the latter case: how do we continue to live intelligently and without despair in a world that so deeply pulls against our ideals? How are we to be reconciled—if at all—to meaninglessness, not only as the neutral processes of a material environment but as the moral nightmare of a history of irreversible evil and sadism?

We shall be returning at length to Ivan Karamazov's "mutiny." But before that, we shall look briefly at a second text from the later Dostoevsky which refers us back very directly to the language of 1854. This comes in the very long first chapter (significantly titled "Night") of the second part of *Devils*. Nikolai Stavrogin, the darkly enigmatic figure on to whom so many people have been projecting messianic hopes, is visiting some of his "disciples," including Shatov, recently returned from a prolonged spell abroad (in America) in which he has been extending his experience of the brutalities of nineteenth-century capitalism. Shatov has become more than ever a fanatical partisan of the sort of extreme Russian nationalist views that were often associated with Dostoevsky himself; indeed, he is a very good example of one of Dostoevsky's most disconcerting habits, that of putting some of his own views in the mouth of a character with obvious flaws and blind spots. Shatov developed his convictions about Russia as the one and only "God-bearing" nation under Stavrogin's influence a couple of years earlier, but has now realized that Stavrogin no longer believes this—if he ever did. Stavrogin is beginning to emerge in the narrative as someone who can repeatedly draw others into his own world by his personal magnetism; but that world is a series of almost randomly varying possible points of view, none of which he actually owns for himself. The tragedy of his associates is that they become his "creations": they take on varied and contradictory aspects of his thoughts and commit themselves uncritically.[11]

Shatov reminds Stavrogin of what he used to say—how no Russian can be an atheist, how Catholicism had succumbed to the temptations Christ refused (a significant anticipation of Ivan Karamazov, of course)—

asking, "Didn't you tell me that if it were mathematically proved to you that truth was outside Christ, you would rather remain with Christ than with truth? Did you say that? Did you?" [255]. Stavrogin does not reply directly, and Shatov insists that he is repeating what Stavrogin claimed to believe, "only a dozen lines, just the conclusion" [256]. The preferring of Christ to the truth has become the foundation for a sort of national-ist metaphysic: what shapes the destiny of nations is an affirmation of corporate identity against death, a desire, says Shatov, that is identical with the "pursuit of God." National integrity depends on having a God who is the God of that nation only; "The more powerful a nation, the more individual its god" [257]. It is impossible for a nation to share its vision with others. Insofar as God is the actual form of a nation's self-assertion as free and distinct, as called to lead all other nations to "sal-vation," the nation becomes a sacred thing, incapable of compromise.[12] "The people is the body of God" [257]. Does Shatov then believe in God, asks Stavrogin, and Shatov replies incoherently that he believes in Russia and Orthodoxy and that the Second Coming will occur in Russia—"But in God? In God?" "I—I shall believe in God" is all that Shatov can say [259].

This is a notoriously difficult section to interpret; but one thing that can be said unequivocally is that it makes it impossible to treat the Fonvizina statement as a simple defense of pure voluntarist faith. It is as if Dostoevsky is attempting to clear his own system of something—the 1854 letter was not, of course, on the public record. But with a very typical eye for the possible shadows around his most strongly held convictions, he sets out what might be done with an apparently vol-untarist phrase and warns against such a strategy. If choosing Christ over the truth means that the most significant element in religious commitment is the sheer power of the will to hold to whatever it likes, we are once again in the territory of violence. A nation's surge of will to identify itself as the unique bearer of God's purpose within history is, as Shatov readily grants, a recipe for exclusion and for competi-tion without mercy. And the paradox is that there is no God yet for Shatov: he is trapped within a voluntarist politics and metaphysics that demand a primary willed act for which there is no foundation. We have to commit ourselves to being God-bearing while knowing at some level that the God whose purpose we "bear" is our own projection. And it is clear that this is intolerable: Shatov is fully aware, as he admits, that he is recycling stale nationalist (Slavophil) rhetoric which has for foundation only a sheer empty self-assertion. And when he looks at Stavrogin, he discovers that he is looking into a mirror: Stavrogin, whose only consistent affirmation is to do with the power of the will, has no way of discriminating between good and evil. It is all the same whether he asserts himself or humiliates himself, whether he preserves life or destroys it. Confronted with this, Shatov's despair is intelligible: if this is the basis of his religion of national self-assertion, it is both vacuous and potentially self-destructive.

Shatov is, of all the would-be revolutionaries in the book, the one who exhibits the most convincing signs of something like ordinary humanity. We see him later on in the novel [III.5] attending his wife in labor: he is well aware that the child is in fact Stavrogin's, but his response of wonder at the birth, and unquestioning generosity, followed by reconciliation with his wife, are marks of a sort of prosaic—but nonetheless miraculous—goodness not in large supply in the feverish moral atmosphere of the novel. As if to highlight the contrast, Dostoevsky has Shatov briefly visiting his neighbor and fellow radical Kirillov; Kirillov, whose metaphysical adventures are even more tortuous and bizarre than Shatov's, wants to talk about the sense of the "eternal harmony" he experiences intermittently. Shatov is concerned for Kirillov's health, and almost cheerfully dismissive of his vision: this is how epilepsy begins, and Kirillov needs to be careful [587].

For Kirillov, who believes that suicide is the supreme and logical climax of human maturation into God-like power, the future is irrelevant. "What do you want children for, what do you want mental development, if your goal has been attained?" [586]. The moment of cosmic acceptance that bursts upon him represents a "reconciliation" beyond love or forgiveness; there is no labor left to undertake. And at this moment, Shatov's preoccupied anxiety directed toward the very specific future of his wife and her child is clearly to be understood as not only a saner but a more transformative thing than Kirillov's ecstasy. Yet again, Dostoevsky puts his own experience and thought in the person of another so as to subject it to criticism; the moment of visionary clarity preceding epileptic trauma, which he describes elsewhere in words almost identical to Kirillov's here and with which he was so familiar, is "judged" by the sheer fact of ongoing life, the risks and human celebration of a new birth.

But the point is that Shatov has been liberated from the need to create God through his own will by the invasive presence of joy; the midwife and Shatov's wife suspect him of running out onto the stairway to pray while she is in labor, and after the birth, as he and his wife talk aimlessly and affectionately together, we are told that one of the things Shatov speaks about is "the existence of God." Earlier, in the conversation with Stavrogin, he has urged the latter to "kiss the earth" in penitence and to find God by work ("everything is in that" [262]). Kissing the earth and washing it in tears are standard Dostoevskian tropes, of course, but the surprisingly "Tolstoyan" injunction to work is less so. Only when we see Shatov at his wife's bedside is it plain that the work involved is not necessarily (as Shatov himself at first seems to think) a return to the soil; it is simply the labor of conserving life in small particulars, a commitment to human history not as a grand project but as the continuance of a vulnerable localized care. And the vulnerability is hideously underlined as Shatov's murder follows the birth almost immediately—as harsh a dissolution of unexpected promise as the end of *King Lear*.

Shatov is the chosen victim of the revolutionary cell because it is assumed by the others that he is going to inform the authorities about their illegal actions, and they are manipulated by their conscienceless leader, Pyotr Verkhovensky, into murder. But in one sense they are right to see Shatov as threatening: the practical needs of a human birth relativize the generalities of the various revolutionary philosophies so passionately and ineffectually discussed in the group. One of the pervasive themes of *Devils*, to which we shall be returning, is that certain kinds of radicalism, in Dostoevsky's eyes, are in fact a denial of recognizably human futures, and it is a point not unrelated to the Underground Man's apologia for human difficulty and perversity as part of a concrete human distinctiveness that resists reduction.

So the allusion back to the Christ-and-truth axiom of 1854 leads us into a complex Dostoevskian scrutiny and glossing of the original remark. Taken initially as a charter for voluntarism, for understanding religious commitment as the will's adherence to its own projection, it breaks down into absurdity and violence. It is not Shatov's Russian

Christ or Russian God, the manifestation of a corporate self-will, that brings about actual and specific reconciliation in the world; nor is it the all-embracing but therefore empty reconciliation of Kirillov's cosmic vision. The unplannable and unpredictable emotion around the baby's birth, the conviction of something *having been made possible* by agency other than the will, is the pivot of change. Certain sorts of action and event open the way to reconciliation, though they still demand of us the labor of making the possibilities actual. What is coming into focus gradually is the idea, not that Christ is in some sense to be created by the will, but that reconciliation with the unyielding and superficially meaningless processes which we confront becomes possible because of some event which reconfigures those processes as manifestations of gift or of beauty. And the response to such a moment is, in the nature of the case, not a matter of compulsion, not anything resembling a "mathematical" proof, but an act of *appropriate* freedom, recognizing its capacity to act so that there will be reconciliation.

Dostoevsky defends freedom against all comers, and his Underground Man insists on the right freely to refuse to cooperate in what we are told is good for us. But that does not mean that Dostoevsky is proposing a valuation of naked will as being in itself good. Stavrogin is put before us as an example of will arbitrarily exercised, and the effect is that of a black hole into which those around him are drawn, an ultimately self-consuming void. It is essential to recognize that the relation between the world and the motions of the human mind or soul is not that of cause and effect—as would be the case if a wholly clear and comprehensive account of what was in our interest automatically produced rational and harmonious behavior. But that hiatus between world and soul is not a way of claiming that the will is the source of good or that reconciliation with the world is impossible or undesirable. Living without reconciliation—like the Underground Man or Shatov in his first long conversation with Stavrogin—is not presented as anything other than hellish, a self-tormenting.

In other words, Dostoevsky's confession of 1854, whatever exactly it meant to him at the time of writing, comes to mean something like this. "Truth," as the ensemble of sustainable propositions about the world, does not compel adherence to any one policy of living rather than another; if faith's claims about Christ do not stand within that ensemble of propositions, that is not a problem. It means that they cannot be confused with any worldly power that might assume the right to dictate a policy for living or impose a reconciliation upon unwilling humanity. This does not mean that they are irrational in the sense of contradictory or in the sense of being arbitrarily willed; they represent something that can make possible new motions of moral awareness precisely because they are not generated by the will. But these new motions generated by the recognition of the claims of faith are a response that moves "with the grain" of things, at least to the extent that it does not lead to literal and spiritual self-destruction. At this level, response to Christ connects with a "truth" that is more comprehensive than any given ensemble of facts.

The truth of faith is thus something that cannot be reduced to an observable matter of fact: it is discernible when a certain response is made which creates the possibility of "reconciliation," and is fleshed out by way of the specific engagements of loving attention. But a serious question remains, the question which is uppermost in the third of Dostoevsky's later texts which we are examining for help about his understanding of faith. Briefly put, the issue is this: if the claims of Christ represent an order of reality quite independent of the ensemble of facts in the world, if they are not simply part of what happens to be the case, how exactly do they connect with that world? Are they not bound to be in significant ways detached or ineffectual in any sphere outside that of the personal moral motivation? If Christ and "the truth" are outside each other's realm (and the territorial resonance of Dostoevsky's choice of the word "outside," *vne*, is important), are we not bound to admit that—even if faith preserves us from self-destruction—there can be no ground for thinking that Christ can make a difference in the world of specific historical interaction? The vision of faith can transform the local and personal world of a Shatov; but Shatov will be murdered and the moral chaos of the narrative is not redeemed.

Effective compassion for humanity, it seems, requires more; this moral chaos cannot be left to be regarded with suffering resignation. Hence the most powerful of all Dostoevsky's self-critical meditations on Christ and the truth, Ivan Karamazov's "Grand Inquisitor" fantasia.

The Underground Man has protested at the assumption that we can be ordered to surrender our liberty, even when it is liberty for perverse contradiction; but the Inquisitor has an answer. "There is for man no preoccupation more constant or more nagging than, while in a condition of freedom, quickly to find someone to bow down before" [*Karamazov*, 331]. Freedom in respect of discerning between good and evil is a burden and a terror; Christ offers not a comprehensive scheme of conduct but simply "your image before him to guide him" [332]. By refusing the temptations of the Devil to the varieties of manipulative power and control, Christ has indeed acted according to his divine nature, but has set before human consciences an impossible ideal. He respects humanity too much, the Inquisitor says, and this kind of respect is at odds with compassion. "In respecting [man] so much you acted as though you had ceased to have compassion for him . . . Had you respected him less you would have demanded of him less, and that would have been closer to love" [334].

Love is what the Inquisitor can claim to show, a love based on what humanity actually is and specifically needs. Without the management of the Inquisitor's covert despotism, there is only the violent "slavery and confusion" [337] to which humanity is condemned by the freedom Christ gives; the Inquisitor can guarantee the prosaic happiness of the ordinary and weak, the humble who are left without hope by the impossible demands and promises of the gospel, a gospel that could only ever make sense to a tiny minority of spiritual athletes. Like Plato's governing class in the *Republic*, he sacrifices any hope of personal and interior reconciliation, any spiritual integrity, by governing through a deliberate fiction, using the name of Christ to bring about a regime wholly alien to Christ's words: "only we, we, who preserve the mystery, only we shall be unhappy" [338].

The Inquisitor is, in fact, caught in a peculiarly paradoxical stance: the alienation between Christ and the truth leads to a defense of the truth through pretending that there is no such alienation. Christ becomes, in the hands of the inquisitorial elite, part of the unquestionable and unchangeable system of the world, a sanction for benevolent power which can manifest itself in "miracle, mystery and authority," in the successful management of the social and material environment. He is the source of rewards and punishments in the context of a sacralized society which can persuade its members that they are in fact truly free because the conditions under which they live and act are secure. The truth is that no one *really* wants liberty, yet people want the semblance of it; they want to fantasize that they are free, and this can be provided through the illusions of control that are managed by the Inquisitor. Faith is thus no longer a response jolted out of the self by the irruption of something that makes possible what had seemed impossible; it is assent to religious power as simply another face of the power that manages and secures the world.

At the end of the Inquisitor's colossally potent and emotionally charged apologia, there is silence, and then the famous and bewildering climax: Christ kissing the Inquisitor "on his bloodless, ninety-year-old lips," and the Inquisitor opening the door to banish the stranger, as he hopes, forever [342]. Does this or does it not suggest any sort of resolution? In an influential and well-argued study of Dostoevsky's religion posthumously published in 1973, A. Boyce Gibson underlined the problems both of fitting the Inquisitor narrative into the argument of Ivan's whole polemic against the God who tolerates unimaginable human cruelty and suffering in his world, and of reconciling it with what we know of Dostoevsky's personal faith. He rightly dismisses the notion that the narrative is a tacit admission of ideological defeat, but observes that the Inquisitor passage represents "an anarchist Christ . . . confronted by a solidarist church"[13]—whereas we know that Dostoevsky's commitment to Orthodox solidarity, to a real and concrete Christian *culture*, was unquestionable. He concludes that the Inquisitor belongs to Dostoevsky's *past*. Ivan is speaking for the Dostoevsky of decades earlier, in fact for the Dostoevsky of the Fonvizina letter to the extent that the letter speaks of unresolved doubts, of a Christ who cannot be accommodated within the world and who exists essentially as the object of a desperate private passion. In other words, the conclusion of the Inquisitor narrative is quite deliberately unresolved, but the rest of the novel, especially what is presented through the figure of Father Zosima, provides the needed correctives.

If Boyce Gibson is correct, the narrative is precisely a conscious embodiment of the principle of Christ over against "the truth"—leaving us with a Christ who is transcendent but more or less powerless in the real world. It is a picture that connects very obviously with one popular reading of Dostoevsky's view of sanctity, a reading found most eloquently in the unfairly neglected work of Paul Evdokimov on the novelist: the Dostoevskian saint is like an icon in the room, a "face on the wall," a presence that does not actively engage with other protagonists but is primarily a site of manifestation and illumination. Others define themselves around and in relation to this presence.[14]

There are two very substantial points here. First, it is definitely true that the Inquisitor narrative is not meant to be a last word in the novel and should not be abstracted from the rest of it. Dostoevsky himself conceived the sixth book of the novel, detailing the life and teaching of Zosima, as a riposte to Ivan's polemic, and—though this is less often discussed—Ivan's encounter with the Devil in chapter 9 of book 11 represents a significant revisiting of several themes in the Inquisitor chapter.[15] And second, it is true that the characteristic mode in which holiness appears unconditionally in Dostoevsky's novels is at least as much presence as agency—though it is misleading to suggest that this leaves holiness inactive or wholly silent: Tikhon in *Devils* has crucial things to say, as does Zosima in *Karamazov*, and we shall return to this topic at length in the fifth chapter of this book. Both contribute to the action of the novel overall in essential respects. But recognizing the importance of the insights of both Gibson and Evdokimov should not oblige us to accept that the conclusion of the Inquisitor narrative can be seen simply as a perspective that has been left behind or transcended: Dostoevsky's insistently dialogical idiom does not allow us to think of the novel's development as an advance from less to more adequate ideas. And, crucially, the echo of Christ's kiss for the Inquisitor in Alyosha's kiss for Ivan brings the Inquisitor passage directly into the main narration.

It is more accurate to see the Inquisitor as a culmination of the kind of implied argument that Dostoevsky has been conducting with his 1854 self in the course of all the texts we have so far been discussing. For the Underground Man, the exclusive affirmation of a "truth" detached from both meaning and will leads to a lethal reduction of what is human, to an ideological or indeed literal violence against the full range of human experience and the radicality of human desire. For Shatov, confronted with Stavrogin, the further and very tempting reduction of meaning itself to will has finally to be resisted; if it is will alone that creates the object of faith, the most fundamental reality in which we live is going to be the arbitrary struggle for power between different kinds of exercise of the will. There is no conversation possible between moral policies (or antipolicies, as we might characterize Stavrogin's approach). And now, in the Inquisitor's great monologue, we see that a "truth" which seeks the definitive exclusion of Christ for the sake of the compassionate management of human affairs can only be maintained by deliberate falsehood: by the denial that freedom is anything more than the choices enabled for reasonable beings in a state of security, by the persuasion that these choices are the same as real freedom, by the appeal to a clear system of rewards and punishments, so that moral choices are constrained by imagined consequences, and finally by the appropriation of religious rhetoric to sanction the static and controlled society that all this implies. From the Underground Man to the Inquisitor, the persistent theme is that truth "outside" of Christ requires lying about the human condition.

Yet the answer cannot be in terms of an assimilation of Christ to the world's contents, to the ensemble of true propositions. This is in effect what the Inquisitorial elite are doing, in full awareness that both truth and Christ are sacrificed in the process. To accept Christ's claims, or the Church's claims for Christ (we shall need to return to the differences and convergences between these two sorts of claim), is to recognize an interruption that introduces a new element into the moral world. Christ is apprehended when something not planned or foreseen in the contents of the world breaks through, in an act or event that represents the *gratuity* of love or joy. And such an event alters what is possible by offering the will what might be called a "truthful" or appropriate direction for desire. It does not compel and cannot be treated in the framework of causes and effects; if the possibility is not activated, if the will is not "caught," nothing can make it. But ultimately Dostoevsky invites us to acknowledge that unless such a response is made, there is no reconciliation with the unyielding world that confronts us and no possible way of engaging it without one or another kind of illusion, at worst the deliberate fictions of a power, like the Inquisitor's, that seeks ultimate control of others.

In this light, the conclusion of the Inquisitor narrative—and Alyosha's echo of it—is intelligible. Christ's response to the Inquisitor's delineation of the "real" world is an act of gratuitous compassion—not the Inquisitorial compassion that seeks to remove the suffering by force, but a bare recognition of the Inquisitor's imprisonment in the tragic contradiction of falsehood for the sake of truth. It changes little, if anything—except that the Inquisitor lets Christ go free. There is, it could be said, a tacit acceptance that Christ cannot be overcome by the Inquisitor's violence; and although the Inquisitor commands Christ not to return, we have already, at the beginning of the narrative, been told that he does in fact return to the world in hidden form again and again throughout history "to visit his children at least for an instant" [324]. The kiss establishes *Christ's* freedom; it literally secures freedom from the prison and it represents the freedom to refuse the argument over power and tragic necessity. Thus Alyosha is able to make the same gesture [343] in response to Ivan's conviction that his philosophy is bound to put him beyond Alyosha's understanding or love. Alyosha's attitude toward Ivan is no more constrained by Ivan's thoughts than Christ's compassion for the Inquisitor is constrained by the Inquisitor's hostility. The unexpected has broken in; the issue is not just about human freedom but about the freedom that exists beyond the world of cause and effect and is intermittently permitted to break through. "The miraculous gesture explodes [Ivan's] script," as Maria Nemcova Banerjee puts it in an excellent recent discussion, and Alyosha's *imitatio Christi* "transforms Judas's signal of betrayal into a sign of healing."[16]

So Christ's place "outside the truth" becomes in effect Christ's place in or with or as the reality of a freedom beyond the systems of the world, Christ's place in or with the *protest* of a desire that is without final historical satisfaction but moves confidently through history as if tracing a fundamental rhythm grounded outside the mechanism of the world's details. Human freedom is enabled to respond as it needs to in order to be itself when this nonworldly freedom becomes apparent. Is this what Ivan Karamazov thinks he is saying? Apparently not; but it is what Alyosha hears him saying. Ivan has already explained to Alyosha [307] that he accepts an "eternal harmony" grounded in God as a true account of the universe; but, as he will set out at length in the chapter that follows ("Rebellion"), he will not accept in any other sense than this. He will not be reconciled. He wants to "return his entry ticket"; "I decline the offer of eternal harmony altogether" [320]. He is afraid that, confronted with the overwhelming evidence for God's supreme justice at the end of time, he, with everyone else, will join in the hymn of praise. But from his present vantage point he can only see this as a betrayal of the actuality of unforgivable cruelty and pain in the world as it is. Like the Underground Man, but in a far more morally acute fashion, he is protesting at the amputation of some aspect of human awareness and aspiration for the sake of universal harmony—in this case, the outraged and unconsoled awareness of the horrors he describes. Can harmony be built on a foundation of unforgivable atrocity?

Alyosha's reply to this is what prompts Ivan's Inquisitor narrative. The younger brother insists that the expiation for human cruelty that Ivan has declared to be impossible is in fact a reality because the voluntary suffering of Christ establishes him as the one who has the right to forgive; by identifying with all sufferers, he can offer absolution to their tormentors as if he stood precisely in their place as victims. It is clear, then, that Ivan's narrative needs to be read as—in his eyes—refusing this theological way out from his problem. Christ's coming into the world is the visitation of a divine agent—both at his first coming and in the subsequent manifestations of his presence, as that in sixteenth-century Seville which forms the starting point of the Inquisitor story. What is being underlined by Ivan is precisely that Christ does not share the suffering of the human condition, and that his indifference to the actual constraints felt by finite and weak mortals is the heart of the trouble. He asks inhuman things of human beings because he is irremediably an alien. The final kiss "glows" in the Inquisitor's heart, but the Inquisitor is not changed: how could he be? His analysis is unanswerable. So Ivan's narrative is deliberately designed to undermine Alyosha's appeal to incarnation.

However, Alyosha's kiss gives the entire story a new twist. Gratuitous acceptance in the face of rejection has become possible because of Christ; he has not, after all, asked the impossible but has changed the scope of what is possible, and Alyosha acts so as to demonstrate this. While it would be wrong to overemphasize the doctrinal substrate of Dostoevsky's argument,[17] we cannot miss the characteristically Eastern Christian insight that, by taking human nature, the divine person of the eternal Word transforms that humanity and communicates something of his own capacity and liberty to it. If Alyosha can show Ivan such a transformed humanity, Ivan's case fails: Christ is indeed truly human, and his humanity is manifest in the effects of his life and work upon human beings now. And so Alyosha's original point, that the incarnation somehow permits Christ to absolve on behalf of all, is not simply dismissed.

Neither is it wholly endorsed, of course. Alyosha's initial argument is uncomfortably close to the kind of guaranteed harmony that Ivan is protesting against, and the challenge that emerges is whether there is any way of giving due weight to the incarnational point that does not still invite Ivan's returning of his ticket. How far the rest of the novel might spell out such a strategy is a hard question, which will merit some later discussion. But what stands, from the complex exchange between the brothers at this stage of the narrative, is that the presence of Christ before the Inquisitor and his world may be "iconic" in the sense that Christ plays no decisive public role, but is not passive or ineffective. Unwittingly, so it seems, Ivan's intended dismissal of Christ's effectiveness gives Alyosha the opportunity to prove his brother wrong.[18]

The general issue about the nature of sanctity in Dostoevsky will need some more detailed treatment. Boyce Gibson sees both Tikhon in *Devils* and Myshkin in *The Idiot* as instances of characters who somehow fail in the test of effective sanctity; they are, so to speak, all-too-close imitators of Ivan's silent Christ. But both cases are far from straightforward and require some close reading, to which we shall be coming back later. In any event, it looks as though the role of Christ in the Inquisitor narrative cannot be described simply in terms of unworldly passivity. Nor is it just a matter of a model for behavior being prescribed. The earlier Dostoevsky, even at the time of composing *Notes*, was evidently much less of a clear believer in the traditional doctrine of Christ's dual nature as divine and human. In the poignant reflection written at his first wife's deathbed in April 1864, we find some of the roots of what is being outlined in *Karamazov*. "Christ alone could love man as himself, but Christ was a perpetual eternal ideal to which man strives and, according to the law of nature, should strive,"[19] but this highly moralistic account (an account which also, confusingly, seems to see Christ-like self-sacrifice as the culmination of a "natu-ral" moral evolution) is somewhat qualified as these jottings proceed. First there is the appeal to immortality as the necessary solution to the problem posed by our failure to attain selfless love on earth; Christ himself warned in the gospel that his teaching would not find ready acceptance within history, and we need a dimension beyond history to grow into full understanding and full actualization of our nature. So, "if you believe in Christ, then you believe you will live eternally."[20] Then there is the recognition that the ideal embodied in Christ is experi-enced as contrary to humanity's earthly nature; our failure to sacrifice ourselves radically in love for the other, our unwillingness to give up our ego, becomes the source of suffering, and this suffering is the state we call sin. The joy experienced in sacrificial love balances this suffer-ing. This is the equilibrium that makes sense of life on earth; but it is moving toward the full and final synthesis of all human experience in an ultimate future when the law of Christ is realized in everyone.[21]

This is a difficult and far from coherent text. It is hard to avoid the conclusion that "Christ" here remains the name of an ideal briefly realized in history, opening up a new level of imperative but not actu-ally exercising personal transforming power over human selves. This Christ is not a source of grace, despite having "entered entirely into mankind";[22] it is for us to transform ourselves in response. All of this is not, in fact, very different from what we know of Dostoevsky's under-standing of Christ in the pre-exile days—a passionate personal devo-tion to a human ideal. And there is also confusion about whether the life of sacrificial love is genuinely natural to us or at odds with our nature; Dostoevsky's language is wildly imprecise. All in all, this is a strong statement both of some kind of intrinsic impulse in human beings toward sacrifice and of the gulf between ideal and concrete his-torical possibility. But setting it out in this way may help us see the continuities and the differences in relation to the Christ of *Karamazov* (and indeed of other later works).

For one thing, Dostoevsky goes out of his way in the Inquisitor narrative to show a Christ fully recognizable as the Jesus of the gospels. The depiction is deliberately naïve, celebratory, full of verbal echoes from the Bible; it is plain that this is not simply an abstract and ideal figure, pronouncing the laws of sacrificial morality, but a Christ recapitulating exactly what the historically specific record shows. Notably, he does not *teach*; he works wonders (interestingly, in the notebooks for *Devils*, where we see Dostoevsky taking immense trouble to get the conversation between Shatov and Stavrogin right, there is a point at which Stavrogin makes just this point about the inadequacy of seeing Christ as teacher; and it is also found in Dostoevsky's own personal testimony.²³) The climax of the story, as we have seen, is a gesture, not a word; and Alyosha's imitation of the gesture is something rather different from obedience to a command. Implicitly, Dostoevsky has moved some distance away from the "ideal man" model, and there is a stronger, though still elusive, sense of Christ as giving fresh capacity to the moral imagination, not merely furnishing it with fresh imperatives.

However, this becomes clearer if we look at the pivotal scene of Alyosha's dream or vision at Zosima's coffin in chapter 4 of book 7. As Father Paissy reads the gospel narrative of Jesus' first miracle at the wedding in Cana, Alyosha, half-asleep, recalls Zosima's words, "Whoever loves human beings, loves their joy" [466]. "Lover of humankind" is a liturgical epithet of Christ, used at every Eucharistic celebration in the final prayers, and thus very familiar to Dostoevsky and his Orthodox readers. And as the lover of humankind, Christ shares in the ordinary joys of human beings, the celebrations of the poor. The Inquisitor has depicted him as hostile to the needs of everyday humanity, as having nothing to say to anyone except the spiritual elite; Alyosha reflects that, although Christ has come to earth "for the sake of his great and terrible deed" [467], this cannot mean that he denies or turns his back on the joys of the most needy—especially not when the specific form of that joy involves hospitality toward himself. Just as Shatov is brought closer to the reality of God by the "routine" joy of seeing a newborn child, so here Alyosha begins to be reconciled as he sees Christ accepting the inadequate and elementary hospitality of the near-destitute and affirming and intensifying their celebration. He is on earth for a purpose; but that does not make him an enemy of the gratuitous overflow of human warmth and companionship.

Zosima speaks to him, picking up the anecdote Alyosha has just heard about the onion—the woman offered the chance of salvation because of her one generous action, giving an onion to a beggar: Christ will gladly receive the most inadequate service (the poorest hospitality) from any who approach him. He has made satisfaction for all sin and therefore is free to dispense mercy to each and all. The fact that he has really only one great work to do on earth, to accept the consequence of human evil by his death on the cross, means not that he repudiates everything else, but that any and every human situation can be open to his gift, and the smallest move toward him, even through the medium of instinctive human joy, can be met with the overflow of welcome.

Like the haunting speech of the drunken Marmeladov in part 1, chapter 2 of *Crime and Punishment*, evoking the welcome of Christ at the end of time for all the broken, the failed, and the humiliated [29–30], the reflections of Alyosha and the invitation of Zosima to "Come and join us" are unmistakably rooted, once again, in the liturgy—this time in the well-known words of the Paschal homily ascribed to St John Chrysostom which is read at the first Matins of Easter in the Orthodox Church. This homily invites all to share on the celebration of Pascha, "those who have fasted and those who have not fasted," that is, the pious and the worldly alike: as Zosima implies, because the great work is done for good and for all, there is a sense in which all human effort is relativized and no one has a greater "claim" on heaven than anyone else. Here we are some way from the notes of 1864 and the tragic tensions around the fulfillment of our spiritual ideal; all this has been overtaken by the awareness of pervasive gift. And the chapter ends, significantly, "Three days later [Alyosha] left the monastery, something that was also in concordance with the precept of his deceased Elder" [469]. The commitment to the everyday world, to work and sexuality and the processes of time, has been enabled by the vision of Christ's commitment to the world, a commitment expressed not only by his performance of what he is sent to do but by his day-to-day solidarity with human beings. Read in this light, the vision at Zosima's coffin fills out the perspective hinted at in Shatov's evolution in *Devils*, as we have noted: the labor which Shatov urges on Stavrogin is the work of attentive love in small particulars, a work which, from the vantage point of the rationalist reformer, is going to be full of unnecessary things and casual griefs and joys.

One point to note in passing: Alyosha shrinks from looking directly into the face of Christ when Zosima bids him do so ("do you see our sun, do you see it?") [468], and this has encouraged some commentators[24] to go along with the view of a number of Orthodox critics that the whole ethos of Zosima's teaching and persona is less than properly Orthodox.[25] We shall need to discuss Zosima's portrait more fully later on; but in this context, too much should not be read into Alyosha's fear to look at Christ. Jones speaks of this fear as unconnected with "any theological impediment." But it is difficult to see quite what this means. Fear is a frequent response in the Bible to divine manifestation—not least to the appearances of the risen Christ, and it falls to Zosima to repeat the words of Christ, "Do not be afraid." This is, so far as it goes, a perfectly "Orthodox" exchange. It also echoes, uncannily, as Jones himself observes, the very well-known conversation between St Serafim of Sarov and his disciple Motovilov:[26] as the two of them talk together in a snowy forest, Serafim asks Motovilov why he is not looking at him, and Motovilov says he is afraid because the monk's face is shining like the sun. This narrative was not published until well after Dostoevsky's death, so that it is in the highest degree unlikely that he had ever come across it; it is just possible that Motovilov or his editor may have shaped the wording to echo the text of *Karamazov*. But that is pure speculation. However, the point stands that Dostoevsky's wording has nothing about it that is alien to his tradition.

As Steven Cassedy has emphasized in a lively recent study of Dostoevsky's religion,[27] the novelist is not presenting us with a religious system, not even with a unique personal synthesis of various traditional ideas, though it is not too difficult to find something like that in the works; rather, he is presenting some of the ways in which human beings experience and speak about faith. And, since his writing is unquestionably one of the ways in which he explores and challenges his own faith, we can expect to find internal argument and tension in the work, and—when things are moving well—some sense of advance and clarification. So far, we have been trying to follow some of the ways in which the confession of half-faith in the Fonvizina letter is probed, explicitly and implicitly, by Dostoevsky in several of the major fictions. Voluntarism remains a real temptation, it is clear: if the truth about Christ as understood in traditional credal orthodoxy is not a fact among other facts, how is it different from the mere choice to hold this particular attitude to Christ? Increasingly, the answer to this emerges in terms of two themes. Negatively, to accept that faith is no more than an act of self-assertion leaves human subjects with a meaningless world-process in the face of which they make a quite arbitrary resolution, which is no more morally intelligible than someone else's resolution to give rein to their private passions. In making this resolution, they are not delivered from the question of whether there is any sense to be made of humanity in its entirety. Positively, if I recognize faith as generated from outside, by events in which the world appears unpredictably as grace and above all by the phenomenon of Jesus, what I do in the light of this irruption becomes a witness to the authenticity and independence of the source of faith—and thus to a reality that is not an item within "the truth" about the world but is the context within which this "truth" is fully illuminated.

Dostoevsky would not suggest that this is an intellectual solution to the question of atheism. His concern is not to argue at this level, but to show that the response of faith claims a cognitive or objective (though the word is not a happy one here) character, and that the believer's free and willed adoption of faith is understood by him or her as something independently made possible, not as willed *into* existence. And in the most developed exploration, in *Karamazov*, this entails some clarity about what has previously been obscure in the works: awareness of the givenness of the new dimension of moral vision and capacity unites with the celebration of the natural world—the "sticky leaf-buds" celebrated by Pushkin, which Ivan admits to loving [301]. Those who are inclined to dismiss Zosima's or Alyosha's words and gestures as "nature mysticism" rather than anything specifically Christian have perhaps missed the connection between the embrace of the material world and the encounter with a very particularly Christian and liturgical sense in *Karamazov* of an act of divine welcome.

This acceptance is not for Alyosha the embrace of a finished universal order—any more than it is for Ivan. The leaves are what they are, not simply manifestations of rational harmony. And this is why the atrocities detailed by Ivan are likewise not to be dissolved in a rational harmony at the end of time. There is no third-person answer to this challenge. Ivan recognizes that it is possible that in some unimaginable future the victims will forgive the criminals, but he insists that they have no right to do so, least of all on behalf of any other person. We have the freedom to refuse *equally* consolation, revenge and reconcili-

ation. Because what has happened simply should not ever have happened, and a world in which it can happen is unacceptable and not to
be made acceptable by any future at all [320].

The world remains a set of particulars, to be seen and valued as
such, not as aspects of a supposed harmony; allow them to be seen in
the light of an imagined whole, and they become derealized—which is
an intolerable outrage where the nightmare sufferings of children are
concerned. But Ivan is also insisting on the freedom to opt out of the
passage of time: the refusal to accept a world in which atrocities happen is also a refusal to accept the actuality of healing or forgiveness.
And while this is in many ways an appropriate aspect of the human
response to atrocity—as in the memorial inscription at Auschwitz, "O
earth, cover not their blood"—the shadow side of it is the denial of
any future freedom to alter relations or transform memories. Does the
protest end up paralyzing freedom itself? Ivan's reluctant willingness
to go on living—even living with a degree of joy in the world—suggests
that he has not in fact surrendered the future. But what the protest
leaves us with is an absolute clarity that this kind of reference to the
future cannot and must not be the projection of a *necessary* reconciliation, and that the confusion of faith's perspective with any such idea
is something that has to be resisted. Alyosha's faith, which is still significantly untested at the point when he hears the Inquisitor story, will
not turn out to be an affirmation that cosmic process will necessarily
justify or heal; all he will really know is that change happens and that it
is not dependent on human resource. There is, we have seen, no "third-
person" reply to the lament over unconsoled pain; there is equally no
simple third-person account of what the character is of the reconciliation claimed by the believer.

But this is not to appeal to mysterious and arbitrary private convictions; Dostoevsky is concerned as a *writer* to show what belief and
unbelief are like rather than either to conclude an argument or to take
refuge in the unfathomables of subjectivity. Given that he has repeatedly stressed the liberty of human beings to refuse what is put before
them, he leaves us with the necessary nonresolution of statements and
behaviors within the interaction of the narrative—the "polyphony" so

famously discussed by Bakhtin, about which there will be more to say in the third chapter of this book. And in this connection, there is a fourth and final later text to consider in relation to the Fonvizina letter before we leave the subject, a text that has not received quite the degree of attention that it deserves. Dostoevsky himself regarded (or said that he regarded) book 6 of *Karamazov* as the reply to Ivan's protests; but some have seen the real reply as chapter 9 of book 11, "The Devil. Ivan's Nightmare." It is not simply that the Devil who appears to Ivan in this chapter refers back to the Inquisitor text: the whole of the Devil's discourse is shot through with intertextual allusion to earlier themes[28] and, as we shall see in the next chapter, draws on the variety of ways in which the diabolical is imagined in the whole course of the novel. It is in some ways the most extraordinary chapter in the novel, treating as it does not only the theme of religious belief and unbelief but the nature of the novelist's own imagination.

It is made clear to us that this is not the first time that Ivan has been faced with this diabolical interlocutor; and the conversation begins with a casual reminder to Ivan about something he has forgotten. Ivan rounds on the Devil and accuses him of trying to prove his existence to him by this reminder: his visitor is attempting to show that he knows what Ivan does not know. And this becomes a recurring theme, almost a game: can the Devil persuade Ivan that he is saying anything other than what Ivan himself has already said or thought?

The issue in this conversation, one of Dostoevsky's masterpieces both of comedy and of dramatic tension, is what might be called the last frontier of the anxieties around belief and will that have been aroused elsewhere in the novel. Does *anything* come to the mind from beyond itself, or is the appearance of the world a creation of the ego? The Devil's rhetoric has the Escher-like quality, landscapes turning inwards on themselves in visual but plausible absurdity, that can characterize this kind of discussion. Thus the Devil suggests that even if he does say things that Ivan has not thought of, this doesn't mean he is not a hallucination: "In dreams, and especially nightmares, oh, the kind that are caused by indigestion or whatever, a man sometime witnesses such artistic conceits, such complex and realistic scenes . . . as, I swear to you, Lev Tolstoy could never write" [817]. So is he admitting that he is not real? Surely his purpose is to persuade Ivan that he is? But no, this is the Devil's "new method" [824]: he wants to keep the mind in suspense, knowing that as soon as there appears to be conclusive proof of his own nonexistence, the skeptical self will rebel against the compulsion of proof (the Underground Man's liberty for perversity).[29] He is also playing on Ivan's self-disgust and desire to disown the "vulgarity" of diabolical cynicism and satire; this surely cannot be the "real" content of the philosophical mind.

The ingenuity of the Devil's argument is that it addresses precisely the longing for a simplified and purified rational consciousness that haunts the minds of people like Ivan. If the Devil is real, the "underground" thoughts of the mind are not native to it; if the Devil is unreal, his appearance of reality is one of those aberrations of the mind that make us unreliable judges of reality or truth. But if the Devil is real, what does that imply? That God also exists [813]? To this, the Devil can offer no decisive response, because he, as one who shares the skeptical and enlightened mindset of his human interlocutor, naturally doubts the objectivity of what he sees and has to entertain the possibility that it is all the effect of his own transcendental I [821]. So to prove himself real to Ivan, the Devil must persuade him that he guarantees the alien origin of irrational and "underground" elements in the mind. But by thus affirming the indestructibility of the underground self, untouched by reason, he confirms the impotence of reason and the endless possibilities of untruthfulness in self-understanding.

And so it goes on, a sadistic teasing of Ivan (and the reader) which moves Ivan inexorably closer to mental breakdown. Only at the very end of the encounter, when Alyosha breaks in with the news of Smerdyakov's suicide, is there what seems like a kind of closure: Ivan instantly claims that the Devil has already told him of the suicide. As Ivan, in the chapter that follows, descends rapidly into incoherence, this "proof" of the Devil's reality becomes implicated in his torturing self-doubt as to whether he should admit his complicity in Smerdyakov's murder of their father, because the Devil has told him of his impure motives; and as the chapter proceeds, and Ivan's self-castigation becomes more and more violent, we realize that Ivan is now "quoting" things that the Devil has not said in the preceding chapter. It is in fact not clear that the news of Smerdyakov's death has been given to Ivan before Alyosha's arrival, whatever Ivan says; the Devil's decisive triumph is this terminal confusion, in which Ivan attributes to the devil thoughts and utterances that are really his own.[30]

Right at the beginning of the conversation, the devil dismisses material proofs of an "other" world—evidence from spiritualism, for example (Dostoevsky had been following the public discussion of this with interest, as the *Writer's Diary* makes plain).[31] But the paradoxical point he proceeds to labor is that, as a disembodied spirit, he is not capable of belief, and looks wistfully at the historical and physical beings whose history he helps to advance: "I would renounce all this empyrean existence, all these honors and ranks just in order to be able to take fleshly form in the person of a seven-pood merchant's wife and set up candles to God in church" [821]. Meanwhile, "as for all the rest of what surrounds me, all these worlds, God and even Satan himself— for me it remains unproven whether all that exists in itself or is merely a certain emanation of mine, the logical development of my *I*, which has a pre-temporal and individual existence" [821]. Again, offering a different sort of reason for refusing God, the devil, as he witnesses the ascension of Christ, is sorely tempted to join the angelic host in their hosannas ("I am, after all, you know, very sensitive and artistically impressionable" [827]), but refrains. Should he join in the chorus of achieved cosmic harmony, time would come to an end (he has already explained, in a passage that will need discussion later on, that he is responsible for the continuance of "events" [820]). It is difficult not to read this as a kind of commentary on Ivan's refusal of "harmony" at the end of time, "when all that is in heaven and under the earth flows together in one laudatory voice" [319]. Here, the devil refuses what you would think to be indubitable evidence for God because his task is to go on making things difficult, sustaining the possibility of error and failure in the universe so that some may be "saved"—i.e., may make a free choice for God. "I mean, I know that in the end I shall knuckle under . . . and discover the secret," he says [828]. But for now there is a secret that he is not being told: he is aware of two competing truths, "theirs" (God's), which is obscure to him and is connected with the continuance of history and choice, and his own simple desire to "do good." He would, he tells Ivan, be happy to be annihilated [820]; he does not at all relish his role as agent of perpetual negation (Goethe's Mephistopheles has it wrong).

In all this, the devil appears as both a more complex and a cruder version of Ivan as we have encountered him earlier in the novel. But the underlying point is this: history continues, and individual spiritual struggle continues, precisely because we do not know whether the devil is real or not. We do not know what it is that emerges from our own fantasy and intelligence and what it is that is given to us and required of us from beyond ourselves—both the vision of God and the vision of total meaninglessness. The only advance toward any solution of this is in time, in the history of struggle and self-purification. The radical and destructive temptation is to halt time itself, which can be done in a variety of ways. We saw earlier that Ivan's refusal of any possibility of final healing or forgiveness has the effect of refusing certain sorts of future as morally unthinkable. But equally the Devil—quite convinc-ingly—argues that it was right for him not to assent *prematurely* to the universal hosanna. There will be a final reconciliation, or at least a sur-render, but so long as God's secret is not uncovered for him, a hosanna drawn out by emotion and feelings of solidarity is a temptation to be resisted. Neither the Devil nor the reader can at this point define what would be needed to recognize the appropriate moment of reconcilia-tion. It is not enough to be confronted with "evidence" for the triumph of God's love or justice; Ivan and the Devil agree on this. But what if the assent required is not a capitulation to the unanswerable—just the sort of slavery which the Underground Man rightly fights against—but something else? That something else is a "secret" to the Devil in the sense that he is locked out from the self-commitment of bodily and temporal life and thus from the self-risking of love.

So Ivan's Devil embodies virtually the entire argument we have been examining. He is indeed the irrational in us, in the sense that he negates (however reluctantly) the strategies we devise to take our-selves out of time—out of *narrative*, it is tempting to say. To settle for "the truth" in the sense of that ensemble of finished propositions we can securely defend is one of the ways of removing ourselves from the narrative continuum of our lives; to opt for Christ in the face of this is to accept that we shall not arrive within history at a stage where there are no choices and no commitments to be made. The truth of defen-sible propositions, a truth demanding assent as if belief were *caused* by facts, generates a diminished view of what is human; it educates us in ignoring aspects of human narrative that we disapprove of or find impenetrable. Meaning comes by the exercise of freedom—but not *any* sort of exercise of freedom. By taking the step of loving attention in the mundane requirements of life together, something is *disclosed*. But that step is itself enabled by a prior disclosure, the presence of gratuity in and behind the phenomena of the world: of some unconditional love. The narrative of Christ sets that before us, and the concrete historical reality of Christ is what has communicated to human nature a new capacity for reflecting or echoing that love.[32] Yet to see even this "from outside," to see the triumph of Christ simply—as the Devil does—in terms of a Baroque apotheosis drawing out sentiments of warmth and togetherness in praise, is something other than the invisible and radical act of commitment. To believe in the triumphant Christ in such a way is something less than belief—it is indeed another variant of trying to stop history.

Throughout this chapter, we have been seeking to trace how Dostoevsky thought through his early and inchoate profession of willed faith. All kinds of considerations have worked against simply reading it as a defense of voluntarism or "nonrealism" in matters of religious belief, but this does not mean that we reach a final account of Dostoevsky's faith which will work as a system that has passed beyond trial and contention. At the very end of his life, he could write words that are remarkably similar to the 1854 confession. In his final notebook, he would say: "Christ was mistaken—it's been proved! . . . but I would rather stick with a mistake, together with Christ."[33] The tone is far more self-consciously ironical than in 1854, but there is the same defiant declaration that faith in Christ stands in opposition to what can be compellingly proved as part of the world's rational fabric. And while in 1854 he can say that he expects to be a "child of unbelief and doubt" to his dying day, in 1881 he writes (with a curious verbal echo of the reference to childhood in the earlier text): "it is not as a child that I believe in Christ and confess him. My hosanna has passed through a great crucible of doubt."[34] "Passed through": this undoubtedly sounds as though he thinks of doubt as a thing of the past. But the phrase, as Dostoevsky himself notes, is one that he has already used in the Devil's conversation with Ivan. A hosanna is not enough: it must "pass through the crucible of doubt, etcetera, etcetera" [820, but my translation]. Dostoevsky, in his note of 1881, is responding angrily to K. D. Kavelin's criticisms of his Pushkin lecture and other aspects of his thinking, underlining (with, as Frank points out,[35] an unusually aggressive affirmation of his own integrity) that his faith is not as infantile as his critics want to make out. But the very phrase he quotes as embodying his profoundest conviction is one that he has allowed the Devil to use in a bored and dismissive way, as if it were a rather stale phrase.

It is a clue of some significance. There is, for Dostoevsky, no form of words about faith that is beyond criticism; sincerity is not enough. Just as Ivan is forced by the Devil to question the motives of his most riskily generous action, so his creator is obliged to relativize even his most intense utterance about faith. To refuse to do this would be to suggest that a point had been reached where there was nothing more to be said—which would be to take refuge in the escape from time which undermines true faith. So long as language remains possible, so does contradiction. There is nothing sayable that cannot be answered or continued or qualified in some way or another.

This is, we should note, definitely not the same as saying that no utterance is truthful as far as it goes, or that every statement of faith is simply flawed and unreliable, a human construct with no proper claim to communicate what is real. It is rather that every new statement of faith has to issue into a linguistic world where it may be contradicted, ignored, parodied or, as here in *Karamazov*, trivialized as a cliché. Dostoevsky can only demonstrate the intensity and integrity of his own formulation by at once himself exposing it to these uncontrolled and potentially destructive reactions. He had written in 1876, quoting Tyuchev, that "a thought once uttered is a lie,"[36] but this does not imply that we should stop talking, only that we have somehow to build into our talking that awareness of what, by saying this and not that, we have stopped saying or started concealing.

Thus there is no end to writing. The endless turning on itself of the Devil's conversation with Ivan is analogous to the writer's self-interrogation. And when it is God that we are talking about, the need for such self-interrogation becomes more urgent, since the dangers of avoiding it are so dramatic. All that we have seen of the destructive and self-destructive potential of the language of faith, the various ways in which we can reduce it either to the willed and subjective or to the descriptive and worldly, with the suicidal consequences of both, means that we have to *go on* speaking/writing about God, allowing the language of faith to encounter fresh trials every day, and also fresh distortions and refusals. In writing fiction in which no formula is allowed unchallengeable victory, Dostoevsky has implicitly developed what might be called a theology of writing, specifically of narrative writing. Every fiction is at its most fictional in its endings, those pretences of closure and settlement. Every morally and religiously serious fiction has to project something beyond that ending or otherwise signal a level of incompletion, even in the most minimal and formal mode, indicating an as yet untold story. This is what Dostoevsky does at the end of *Crime and Punishment*, and he attempts to do the same, less directly, with *Karamazov*. The endings of *The Idiot* and *Devils* can be read as at least leaving marked trails of unfinished business.

This means that for Dostoevsky the discourse of fictional creation as he pursues it becomes one of the strategies of resistance to a world where—as the Underground Man fears—what is said or thought is always at risk of being reduced to what is strictly reflective of existing states of affairs, the effect of those causes that are "out there" in the supposedly real world. Faith and fiction are deeply related—not because faith is a variant of fiction in the trivial sense but because both are *gratuitous* linguistic practices standing over against a functional scheme of things. The gratuity of faith arises from its character as response to the freedom of the creator as unexpectedly encountered in the fabric of the world. The gratuity of fiction arises from the conviction that no kind of truth can be told if we speak or act as if history is over, as if the description of what contingently *is* becomes the sole possible account of language. A fiction like Dostoevsky's which tries to show what faith might mean in practice is bound to be both inconclusive in all sorts of ways, and also something that aspires to a realism that is more than descriptive.[37] How precisely this is worked out in characterization will be the concern of the third chapter.

There is one further point to be made in connection with this. If the process of writing is as I have suggested for Dostoevsky, it is not surprising if the notebooks often seem somewhat at odds with the novels in their final form. Sergei Hackel observes[38] that the preparatory notes about Zosima seem to contain more "mainstream" Orthodox reference than what is found in the text, and reads this as a deliberate toning-down of the specifically Orthodox location of the piety of Zosima and Alyosha. He is not by any means wholly wrong about this, but what matters is that the actual writing has brought Dostoevsky, for whatever reason, to a point where such explicit reference does not make novelistic sense for him. For good or ill (Hackel would say the latter in this case), the notebook is left behind in the commitment of writing the fiction itself.

But the most spectacular case of this is the relation between notebook and fiction in *The Idiot*. Much critical confusion has been caused by an uncritical reliance on the notebooks to illuminate the text: hence the continuing arguments about who or what Myshkin is "meant to be," specifically whether he is a Christ figure. The increasing critical consensus is that he indeed a failed Christ figure, but because of Dostoevsky's statements in the notebooks and in his correspondence that he is trying to create a "perfectly beautiful man," and the apparent "Christ-Prince" equation,[39] discussion continues about how far the Prince's failure as a protagonist should be read theologically, as a statement about—once again—Christ's relation to mundane worldly truth or the effectiveness of grace in the actual world of human relationships or Dostoevsky's capacity to sustain his surface Christian conviction in the actual process of writing. What we are seeing in the novel, certainly, is not the outworking of a theological strategy but the effect that the writing itself has upon the original purposes of the writer. It is more or less inevitable that Myshkin should emerge as a seriously confused and confusing figure. To the extent that a fiction cannot reproduce the gratuity of the once and for all particular existence of Jesus, any "Christ figure" is bound to be ambiguous. The theological interest of the novel is not in the question of how successfully Dostoevsky has embodied one or another of his (wildly diverse) *idées maîtrises* for this novel,[40] but in what precisely happens as Myshkin takes shape in the process of being written, and how the writing, not the planning, shapes what is possible for him as a character.

The result, for those familiar with notebooks and novel, is a kind of counterpoint between a projected saint and a particular written char-acter, and this in itself produces some theological insights. Michael Holquist, in an intriguing chapter on *The Idiot* in his 1977 study of *Dos-toevsky and the Novel*,[41] agrees that Christ—as fully theologically under-stood—cannot be a character in a novel. But his emphasis is on the fact that Christ is incapable of change, always wholly defined by his eternal origin and his saving purpose; he cannot have a narrative evo-lution. I shall be arguing something rather different—that it is Mysh-kin's own changelessness that prevents him from being a "savior" in any sense, and that the gulf between him and Christ is to do with the fact that the Prince makes no adult choices. Despite Holquist's thesis, it remains true that the Christ of the gospels is in fact presented as making such choices—resisting temptation in the desert, struggling to accept the divine will in Gethsemane. It may not be possible to represent the historical Christ in a real novel (one that is to do with narrative and linguistic definition of character), and the sheer particu-larity of that figure means that creating a Christ *figure* will always be a doomed enterprise. But this does not mean that Jesus of Nazareth has no narrative, no history of formation, and some of what Holquist objects to in a novelistic rendering of Christ would be applicable to any historical figure, any personage whose destiny was known *outside* the novelistic framework.

Undoubtedly, Dostoevsky wants to tease his readers in this context. Myshkin's physical appearance is plainly modeled on the traditional Orthodox iconography of the Savior, and when Nastasya has the vague impression that she has seen him before [123], it is almost certainly this that is meant to be in mind. Yet the point that has been made about the Christ of the Inquisitor fable applies far more strongly here: if this is a Christ figure, it is one who has no "hinterland," no God behind him. He is vague when asked if he believes in God [255 ff.], though he responds with a very Dostoevskian catalogue of moments of religious insight; he is unfamiliar with Orthodox liturgy [682]—unsurprisingly, given that he has been away from Russia for so long. He comes onto the Petersburg scene as unannounced as the Jesus of St Mark's gos-pel—with the significant difference that Myshkin has nothing to say or do when he arrives. In the first few encounters recorded, we do, however, see what happens when he is around: his own unprotected naivety draws out of others both an intense exasperation and hostility and an unexpected tenderness and openness. Myshkin may not be a protagonist, a character involved in directing the agon of the novel's action through his own self-venturing, but he is a catalyst for hidden or latent feeling and so in that mode a shaper of action in others.

Myshkin is an epileptic, and the unforgettably vivid description of the pretraumatic "aura," the sense of harmony and luminous clarity, foreshadows Kirillov's ecstatic vision, as we have already observed. Significantly, the Prince quotes [265] from the *Revelation of John* in the New Testament the phrase "time will be no more" (Rev 10:6; modern versions tend to translate, "There will be no more delay"). The ecstatic vision is of a state beyond time and so beyond choice and action. But perhaps even more significantly, the same phrase is quoted by Ippolit in his desperate ramblings as he prepares for suicide [447]. The connections with Kirillov in *Devils* are too close for comfort. There is some sense in which the ecstatic vision of harmony is bound up with *death*. For all the compelling beauty of what is experienced, and the overpowering feeling of having *really* grasped the nature of things, the outcome is destructive.

Myshkin's language about it is interesting. He speaks of the vision as "full of reason and the final cause . . . proportion, reconciliation and an ecstatic, prayerful fusion with the highest synthesis of life" [264]. If we read this against the background of all we have been considering in this chapter so far, it sounds as though what Myshkin—and Dostoevsky—perceive in this state is actually the world against which both the Underground Man and Ivan Karamazov rebel, the world of causal completeness, where we have no option but "reconciliation." For the rebels, this world is a terrible, mechanical thing, threatening liberty, but the references to the timeless moment of ecstasy prior to seizure simply oblige us to recognize that the vision can also be overwhelmingly attractive. After all, even the language in which Ivan imagines the whole creation crying "You are just, O Lord" at the end of time makes it clear that it is a consensus which will be hard to resist.

The language of causality and of reconciliation should in fact make us very wary of Myshkin at this point and of whatever spiritual perspective he may represent. If Dostoevsky began in the hope of depicting an unequivocally "beautiful" character, the pressure of the writing is pushing this intention out of shape. Clearly, Dostoevsky hoped that by making the Prince a man effectively without hinterland, orphaned and exiled and recovering from severe mental disorder, he could short-circuit the difficult issue of how to depict the processes by which beauty is actually generated in time-bound human persons. But as the narrative advances, it becomes obvious that this timeless virtue has no resources of memory and critical self-awareness to make it effective in the world of human relations. It illuminates and, as we have seen, catalyses, but it is shot through with a radical vulnerability which is more disturbing than the silence of the Inquisitor's prisoner and not simply to be explained by reference to the Russian valuation of passive suffering and self-emptying, kenosis. Finally it collapses into itself. Myshkin goes back into the darkness out of which he emerged at the start of the narrative. For him, at least, the future has been erased, and for several other characters too, it has been ruined or destroyed or corrupted. The premature embrace of harmony turns out to be an act of violence in its own way—including violence, suicidal violence, to the self.

Is this the context in which we should read Myshkin's approach to other characters? His openness and simplicity can indeed bring out good in others, but at the same time we have to ask whether his approach to others is not also shadowed by the will to believe of them less than is actually true. He sees Nastasya Filippovna's portrait and immediately *wants* her to be good [43]. Throughout the narrative, his response to her is consistently to pity her, to see her as an innocent victim, to imagine happy futures; what he does not and cannot do is to *attend* not only to her sense of violation but to her willful self-punishing, her manipulation of her identity as victim, and the virtually suicidal impulse that carries her toward the fatal union with Rogozhin. There is, we might say, no "talking cure" here, no speaking and listening about what Nastasya's actuality is. It is very telling that, when she writes to Myshkin of her feelings about him, she says that he appears to her as loving solely for the sake of the loved one, not for himself, but this means that he cannot be he equal, because he has no "investment" in her actual reality such as might cause him to feel "shame or anger" about her. She imagines him in relation to a sentimental picture of Christ with a child, in which, significantly, Christ's hand rests "unconsciously, forgetfully" on the child's head, while "a thought as enormous as the whole world rests in his gaze" [530]. If this is selfless love, it is also, troublingly, love that seems not to relate to the one loved. Finally and understandably, she is bound to rebel against Myshkin's timeless pity, which leaves her frozen in the role of a wounded innocent in need of the unquestioning generosity of another. If, as has been observed,[42] Myshkin is a man with no history, he equally tends to reduce others to the same state. And the effects are fatal.

It may be objected that Myshkin does challenge Nastasya: "You're not like that, not like the person you pretended to be just now," he protests when he meets her [138]. But, while he is right to see Nastasya as constantly dramatizing her condition and so concealing something, he does not see either how this arises or what might heal it. The issue is well expressed by Simonetta Salvestroni in her study of Dostoevsky's biblical allusions: Myshkin belongs in an unfallen world (comparable to that of *The Dream of a Ridiculous Man* or Stavrogin's dream as reported in his confession to Tikhon),[43] so that he can see "the points of departure and arrival but has no knowledge whatsoever of the transit from one to the other. He knows nothing of the obstacles and limits of the everyday: not only the external perils but more particularly the still more insidious dangers that spring up out of the deepest places in every human being."[44] Beauty in the human world is ambivalent: Myshkin's instant attraction toward Nastasya's beauty, as Salvestroni notes,[45] takes no account of the ways in which beauty has been a burden for her; it is seen simply as the manifestation of an inner spiritual quality. So the truth that Myshkin sees and sometimes uncovers in others is a very shadowed matter. To see the truth in someone is not only to penetrate behind appearances to some hidden static reality. It also has to be, if it is not to be destructive, a grasp of the processes and motors of concealment, a listening to the specific language of a person hiding himself. It is perhaps the difference between "seeing through" someone and understanding him.

Thus Myshkin's relationship with Nastasya never moves within the narrative; nothing changes, and it is this fundamental lack of development that is partly responsible for Nastasya's despairing option for Rogozhin. The Prince offers her a profound compassion which at first seems transforming. Nastasya is not used to being valued in this way, without either condemnation or acquisitive desire, and her first reaction is a sober conviction that the Prince is the only man she has met capable of being "truly devoted," loyal to her [181]. Indeed, if we follow one possible translation of her parting words to as she leaves her party in Rogozhin's company [part 1, chap. 16, 204], she believes that in Myshkin she has seen a real human being for the first time (though the Russian can also mean that she has seen for the first time what human beings are really like, i.e., what degradation they are capable of). But because that valuing does not issue in anything further, because it does not *learn*, it finally fails to transform.[46] We could discuss in similar terms Myshkin's relations with Ippolit or indeed Rogozhin; and in the latter case, there is the unsettling possibility that the Prince actually prompts Rogozhin's murderous instinct, especially in the dramatic episode [part 2, chap. 5] where he—do we say "deliberately"?—puts himself in the way of Rogozhin's violence by failing to leave Petersburg for Pavlovsk and drifts back toward Nastasya, knowing and not knowing that Rogozhin is waiting and ready to kill him. As Wasiolek says, "The prince creates, or helps to create, the attack upon himself,"[47] as he also creates or helps to create the nightmare conclusion of Rogozhin's murder of Nastasya.

One recent critic has said[48] that Myshkin treats other characters as though he were their author. It is a valid insight: and, as we have noted, it is in the actual writing of Myshkin's character that this kind of ambivalence becomes plain. It turns out to be impossible to depict a beautiful character without giving him a history that will enable him to understand the changes and processes of growth or repression or whatever that occur in temporal beings. Myshkin's timelessness is what prevents him being a savior. It could even be said that it brings him close to being diabolical, as has been plausibly argued.[49] Bakhtin says of the Prince that "[i]t is as if he lacks the necessary *flesh of life* that would permit him to occupy a specific place in life (thereby crowding others out of that place)."[50] But, although Bakhtin associates this with the atmosphere of "carnivalistic play" that he claims surround Myshkin—and incidentally allows him to penetrate what others do not—he does not seem to give weight to the negative side of all this. Where Myshkin appears, it is not as if we find nothing but carnival and overturning of hierarchies; the carnival effect is, as Bakhtin rightly observes, a distinctive aspect of Myshkin's impact on individuals and groups, but the incapacity to occupy a place is precisely what, in Bakhtin's own terms, makes it impossible for Myshkin to be involved dialogically with others. To say that nothing obscures Myshkin's "pure humanness"[51] is in fact to deny the Prince what is most crucially human—growth, memory, the capacity to listen and *change* place—which you cannot do if you don't have a place to begin with. Bakhtin (untypically) allows a certain sentimentality about Myshkin's compassionate penetration of appearances to obscure the features that make the Prince incapable of a proper Bakhtinian unfinishedness and interdependence. Although he assimilates Myshkin's anarchic carnivalesque impact to the carnivalesque effect of Nastasya's emotional excess ("the 'idiot' and the 'madwoman,'" carnival heaven and carnival hell), this is to miss the seriousness of Nastasya's located and wounded humanity; she has exactly what Myshkin does not have in this connection.

There is one significant image in the novel which might—though this is speculative—throw a little more light on Myshkin's ambiguity. The reproduction of the younger Holbein's picture of the dead Christ which hangs in Rogozhin's lodgings and makes so devastating an impression on both the Prince and Ippolit [254-55, 475-76] is a kind of anti-icon, a religious image which is a nonpresence or a presence of the negative. This is true in a purely formal sense: in classical Orthodox iconography, the only figures ever shown in profile are demons and—sometimes—Judas Iscariot. The icon seeks to confront the viewer/worshipper with a direct gaze informed by the divine light. Holbein's painting shows (though this is not explicitly described in the novel) a corpse seen from alongside—not only a dead man fixed at a moment in the past (there are Orthodox depictions of the dead Christ and his entombment), but a dead man in profile, a double negation of the iconographic convention. In a fairly literal sense, this is a "diabolical" image.

The Prince describes it as an image that could make one lose faith [255]; later on, Ippolit sees it as representing the defeat of goodness by eternal darkness and unreason ("Nature appears, as one looks at that painting, in the guise of some enormous, implacable and speechless animal or, more nearly, far more nearly, . . . some enormous machine of the most modern devising, which has senselessly seized, smashed to pieces and devoured, dully and without feeling, a great and priceless being,—a being which alone was worth the whole of nature and all its laws" [447]). As commentators have noted, his perception is like Kirillov's agonized picture in *Devils* of the three crosses, on one of which hung the supreme example of human goodness: "if the laws of nature did not spare even *Him*, . . . then the whole planet is a lie and is based on a life and a stupid mockery" [614]. The question is whether the Holbein image, focusing so sharply the issue of whether incarnate goodness can live effectively in the mechanical world of violence and counterviolence, is meant to be in some way an image of Myshkin himself. Diane Oenning Thompson has suggested that Myshkin's final collapse leaves him "as impotent in the living death of his incurable idiocy as the Christ of Holbein's painting"[52] and Leatherbarrow[53] rightly sees the analogy between the painting of a Christ "emptied of divine content" and Myshkin's character. It is not only a question about Myshkin at the end of the book. The significant confrontation of the Prince and the painting relatively early on might be taken as indicating that the lethal weakness of Myshkin is already in view—even intuited by Rogozhin at some level. At the very least, the picture tantalizingly puts before us an image of Christ that is—in Orthodox terms—no image at all, as if to alert us to the novel's central paradox, that the person who is presented as innocent and compassionate in Christ-like mode is in fact unwittingly a force of destruction.

This is perhaps why the relationship with Rogozhin is so important for the structure and logic of the book. At the simplest level, Dostoevsky is doing what he regularly, almost compulsively, does with his characters, "doubling." But the relation seems more intimate and complex than that. Certainly it illustrates the Girardian thesis that we learn to desire by imitating the desire of the other and so create rivalry at the very heart of our desiring: both Myshkin and Rogozhin are trapped in their different but intertwining desires for Nastasya because of each other. And thus we have to recognize the *complicity* of Myshkin in the distorted, finally murderous desire of Rogozhin. Their exchange of crosses in what is apparently a simple rite of brotherly bonding, takes on a more somber character (we shall be discussing this in detail later on, in chap. 4). Innocence and guilt are "exchanged"; Myshkin takes on the responsibility of Rogozhin, responsibility *for* Rogozhin. We have already seen how he half-consciously pushes Rogozhin toward murderous violence. And the ending of the novel takes on added significance, as George Steiner points out: "When Rogojin is taken away from him, the Prince collapses once again into idiocy. Without darkness, how should we apprehend the nature of light?"[54] Yes; but the symbiosis is in fact stronger and darker in character than this straightforward opposition implies.

None of this is meant to suggest that we reverse one kind of conventional reading of *The Idiot* and treat Myshkin as simply an "evil" force. He is never that. But—in contrast to the Goethean devil so much disapproved of by Ivan's diabolical visitor—Myshkin is a "good" person who cannot avoid doing harm. And this is not to do simply with any sort of fatalist or Calvinist notion that, because of our mixed motives and so on, all human virtue is ultimately false or empty: it is to do with a very specific aspect of Myshkin's character, the absence of a position that has been shaped by experience and choice. Dostoevsky begins with something like a thought experiment: imagine a human subject devoid of the defensive mechanisms produced by a history of hurting and being hurt, of choices and therefore of exclusions; imagine someone who has never had to make a choice that excludes an option or disadvantages another. In other words, imagine unfallen humanity, as it is imagined in the various Utopian dreams and fictions with which Dostoevsky toyed in general terms in a number of his fictions. And then, imagine what impact this would have upon human beings who had made such choices and experienced such giving and receiving of hurt; imagine such a person caught up, without really knowing it, in the systems of rivalrous desire. The narrative then has to do the work of discovering what would be the fate of a "perfectly beautiful" character, and what is discovered is both the apparently miraculous renewal of vision that comes in the presence of someone without rivalry or pride—the sense of carnivalesque celebration and delight that sometimes attends Myshkin, to which Bakhtin draws attention—and the disastrous effect of relationship with someone who has never "learned how to learn."

Thus Myshkin's tragedy sheds a clear light on the whole of Dostoevsky's implicit Christology. In classical theological debate, there is a question as to whether the humanity taken on by the eternal Word in the Incarnation is fallen or unfallen. It seems at first like a typically abstract and unhelpful issue to consider, but in fact it touches a number of important theological points. If the Word takes on a fallen humanity, does this mean that he is born into a humanity that is—in Augustine's language—incapable of not sinning? In which case, how can he restore it? But if the Word takes on unfallen humanity, in what sense does he undergo precisely the experience of fallen beings faced with potentially tragic choices? If he does not, once again, how can he restore it, healing all that he has assumed, in the vocabulary of the fourth-century Gregory Nazianzen? The question is really about the nature of God's identification with us in the life of Christ. And in the context of the literary and narrative imagination of Dostoevsky, it poses the problem of how anything like spiritual and moral transformation can be represented in his fiction. With increasing clarity, he turns away from any suggestion that the position of Christ "outside" the mundane truth of the world means a simple standoff between ideal humanity and achievable historical virtue. Myshkin is, in a way, the *reductio* of such a view, following through to its tragic conclusion a view that tries to remove any tragic shadow from the person of the saint or redeemer. And the identification of the reconciliation that God seeks to bring about with a timeless order and harmony, such as is glimpsed in the epileptic aura or fantasized about in dreams of the Golden Age, is dismissed—not without profound nostalgia (the pathos of Dostoevsky's writing on both subjects is unmistakable). The restoration of humanity is to do with "labor" (Shatov is correct), including the labor of choice and self-definition.

How exactly this would have to be clarified in the language of the traditional theological debates is a long story: one way of putting it is that the Word takes on the *consequences* of the Fall so far as they affect the circumstances in which human beings exercise their freedom, but does not take on the impaired judgment which distorts created freedom. For Dostoevsky, these would be impossibly abstruse issues, compared with the specific challenges of writing a narrative. But it is not unimportant that the Inquisitor fable turns upon that gospel story in which the specific liberty of the incarnate Word is most plainly set out, the story of the temptations. As we noted earlier, the biblical narrative of Jesus is not one from which tension and decision are absent (and their presence caused considerable headaches to the theologians of the early and mediaeval Church). But for Jesus to be human at all, this narrative implies, is for him to be faced with choices not simply between good and evil but between options that *might* arguably be good but also bring with them incalculable costs. The options that confront actual historical agents are not like self-contained items on a shelf or rack awaiting buyers; they are part of a continuum of human policies that may be flawed and damaging, and they will already be constrained by what has happened. This is the concrete meaning of embracing the consequences of fallenness. Even a subject whose desires are creative and altruistic has to enact those desires in a context where their objects will often appear obscure and ambiguous, so that good outcomes cannot be tightly and causally linked to good intentions.

Thus the temptation story is bound to be a narrative of real risk: either a yes or a no could produce destructive results, and the Inquisitor narrative unsparingly details the negative effects of a decision to avoid what could be coercive means of attaining justice or enlightenment. What then matters, morally and spiritually, is not whether the result of a choice creates pain or loss but whether there remains the possibility of acting so as to change the situation further. The Christian claim is that Jesus' refusal of coercion or violence is the refusal of a path that would close off such further and potentially life-giving change, and we have seen how, in the "afterlife" of the Inquisitor story in the novel, it turns out that possibilities have indeed been generated. The alternatives are not unqualified guilt or frozen innocence. Myshkin faces no temptations of this order, and so remains impotent. We shall see later how a character who seems to be Myshkin's polar opposite—Stavrogin—ends up in a very similar place, and for comparable reasons.

Dostoevsky's working out of what might be meant by the possibility of having to opt for the Christ who is "outside the truth" turns out to be closely connected with an entire rationale (if that is the right word in this context) for fiction itself. At the simplest level, the writing of fiction is, as we have noted, one of those things people do in order to affirm something other than the world of plain facts and obvious accounts of them, the world of mathematical closure. In that world, given the evidence or the argument, the future is clear and there are no significant decisions to be made. In the world of the novel, when all this has been said, everything is still to play for. And the attempt to approach human affairs as if they belonged to the world of evidence and determined outcome is bound to end in violence—ideological violence to the understanding of what humanity is, literal violence toward those who will not be convinced. The novel, in its narrative indeterminacy, is a statement of "nonviolence," of radical patience with the unplanned and undetermined decisions of agents.

For a critic like Lukacs,[55] the novel, whose history begins with that text so important in *The Idiot*, *Don Quixote*, has its origins at the point where secularism also takes its origin. When it is no longer possible to plot the significance of human lives against the unquestioned backdrop of what is agreed to be the one universal narrative, the writer begins to create ordered narratives for individual imagined lives, possible trajectories for readers to explore as they try to make sense of their own. Dostoevsky, however, marks a more radical phase in secularization itself, the questioning of the sacredness of enlightened individuality. He represents the first stirrings of a new and more challenging sense of what the novel is and achieves. Holquist, in the conclusion to his study of the ways in which Dostoevsky reshapes the idea of the novel, observes how he dissolves the tidy endings and the unitary personalities that were once the currency of the novel. And Malcolm Jones appositely quotes[56] a character of Aldous Huxley saying of *Karamazov* that "It makes so little sense that it's almost real"; it is hardly a "novel" at all on the old model of fiction that takes for granted "unity" and "style."

But the interweaving of theological and literary themes that we have been tracing may suggest something more than this, something that might look like a kind of postsecularism about the novel. Dostoevsky's fiction undoubtedly makes a major contribution to the collapse of the enlightened "modern" subject; through its suspicion of easy harmonics, it puts in question the simple narrative resolutions of an earlier age. But by doing so, it ranges that kind of narrative naivety alongside the "truth" that threatens to turn into violence. To some degree or other, the novel is going to be on the side of the Underground Man, on the side of a profoundly suspicious and critical liberty. As such, it does not promise to be edifying or positive: it is easy to understand why Dostoevsky was such a trial to Soviet critics, who, like their nineteenth-century forebears, complained about the "unhealthy" atmosphere of his books.[57] But by being on the side of the Underground Man, the novel is also, in Dostoevsky's hands, on the side of faith, whether it likes it or not, whether it "approves" of it or not. Instead of being the ultimate stage of narrative secularity, Dostoevsky's fiction draws us back firmly toward a theological problematic.

Human subjectivity seeks, in the chaotic exchanges of speech and action, definitions that are continually renegotiated, sometimes with radical breakage and change of direction. What is unavoidable is the risk involved in this; as Myshkin's case underlines, turning away from the business of self-definition does not get rid of the risks but may intensify their tragic quality. The fact that Christian faith regards a particular human narrative as basic allows us to think that the processes of choice and self-definition that impose themselves on human agents may be not just open in a general way to grace or hope, but effective enactments of divine purpose. Yet that divine purpose does not lend itself to being "narrated" in a way that would foreclose the possibilities of failure or cost. What the perspective of God's purpose contributes is the conviction that there is something that makes it worthwhile *continuing* the narration—and thus the processes of self-defining which narrative works with—because divine purpose cannot be extinguished even if it can be defeated in any one measurable time span. As Jones hints, what we have is sort of narrative translation of the principle of "negative theology"—the principle that whatever is specifically said of God has also to be un-said as soon as it seems to offer the seductive prospect of a definition of the divine essence.[58]

If this is a possible reading of what Dostoevsky is taking for granted, then he is indeed reshaping the novel, not in a more but in a less resolutely secular direction. This is by no means a move toward the novel as straightforward religious apologetic; everything in his fictional achievement tells unequivocally against that. But if the novel's narration is sustained in some way by a religious narrative that *does not require* the closures of conventional early modern fictional texts, the way is open for a much less controlled, less morally balanced, more psychologically and verbally unresolved writing. It is as if grace could be shown in fiction only under the form of a systematic turning away from certain kinds of moral closure. A reader of some of the more theologically literate fictions—the work of Bernanos, Flannery O'Connor or Patrick White, occasionally Updike—of the last century might recognize the signs. But there is a discussion to be had about the theological resonance in this particular key of writers without theological commitment—an A. S. Byatt or an Ian McEwan.

Evdokimov wrote[59] of the eschatological perspectives of Dostoevsky's fictions, a perspective, he says, that becomes sharper as the possibilities of human and humanistic spiritual resources become thinner. Eschatology is often conscripted by ideology, when the latter claims to be able to determine, advance or control the former. (One of the ways in which it can be expressed and sometimes distorted is, of course, in association with *apocalyptic*; and Dostoevsky's prose writing frequently succumbs to this. Despite the regular apocalyptic *reference* in the novels, however, they are not themselves vehicles of apocalyptic imagination.) In the light of what we have been considering in this chapter, the novel ought to be a stout defender of the independence of eschatology in its most robust sense—that is a defender of the apparently obvious but actually quite vulnerable conviction that the present does not possess the future. Whether or not we say, as earlier believers in eschatology would have done, that God is in possession of the future, the one thing we can agree on is that we are not. The open, ambiguous, unresolved narrative insists on this, which is why novels are never popular with ideologues and do not flourish in climates where eschatology is excessively realized. You do not find fundamentalist novelists (only what you would have to call fabulists, writers of narratives with closed significance).

But to go back for a moment to Ivan's conversation with the Devil: it will be recalled that the Devil claims to be the necessary condition for "events" to go on happening. In the light of our subsequent discussion, it sounds as though you could therefore say that the Devil was responsible for what makes novels possible. And this would be a typically Dostoevskian thought. Once you have elaborated a serious theological thesis about how the narrative of the Word incarnate might be the cornerstone of a theory of the novel, Dostoevsky insists that you think about the inverse of this. Is fiction really made possible by incarnation, or should we ascribe it to the perpetual restlessness of the Devil—who is, as he himself tells us, an agnostic? In less heavily freighted terms, is fiction driven by convictions (explicit or not) about an endless resource that underlies and in varying ways permeates all finite activity, or by the sheer possibility of "answering," countering, anything that can be said, and of following any narrated event with another one? The Devil keeps events moving because he feels obliged to, but has no image or concrete expectation of the "reconciliation" he dutifully gestures toward. If the novel can be a witness to the openness of complex and ambivalent action to grace, it can also be a witness simply to the ambiguity. And that, Dostoevsky might say, is exactly what you would expect if you turn away from both ideological manipulation of your world and the sentimental, individualized eschatology of conventional early modern narration; exactly what you would expect if a novel is to be a novel in the way that he conceives it must be.

2

DEVILS
Being toward Death

The role of the Devil—and of devils in general—needs some
more discussion. As has already begun to become clear, Dostoevsky sends out some very mixed messages about this. Ivan's Devil is
a benign and—as Ivan says—somewhat vulgar source of complicated
motivation and unreasonableness; the Inquisitor's Devil is "wise and
terrible," representing the immense force of rationalism. Devils occur
in various guises, folkloric, sinister, literary and biblical, in all the major
novels. W. J. Leatherbarrow's recent monograph on the demonic in
Dostoevsky argues very strongly that his evocations of the Devil are
anything but decorative elements in the whole concept of his fiction;
and he notes particularly that *Karamazov*, preoccupied as it is with the
nature of its own storytelling (a point argued brilliantly and at length
by Victor Terras),[1] shows from the start a concern with "lying, telling
a tale, and devils."[2] Behind a good deal of the narrative of *Karamazov*,
says Leatherbarrow, lies the theological suspicion that any sort of fiction is a challenge to God's sole "authorship."[3] If the analysis of the
preceding chapter is accurate, then part of what Dostoevsky is trying
to do is to create a fiction that will be closer to the truth God intends
than any kind of factual reporting. It need not be a challenge to the
one creator, but to establish this, he has to make us see more clearly
what is and what is not the province of the Devil in the business of
storytelling. And, while these themes are pervasive in the novels, it is
undoubtedly *Karamazov* that offers the most extensive reflection on

them, and thus the most extensive "diabology." Before turning else-where, then, we shall spend some more time with his most developed thoughts on the subject.

✠ ✠ ✠

Lebedev's caution in *The Idiot* against supposing that you have dis-missed the Devil by dismissing the lurid folkloric images that haunt the popular mind is a good place to start [437]. This kind of folklore is alluded to several times in the novels, sometimes mockingly, some-times by those who take it seriously, and it usually indicates some sub-stantial thematic notes. In *The Brothers Karamazov*, the devils of legend and popular imagery are referred to with some frequency in particular connection with certain characters. The very first time we encounter Fyodor Karamazov directly, rambling in his own unmistakable voice [book 1, chap. 4], he is deriding popular pictures of hell, at the same time as arguing that anything other than the most crudely literal hell is not worth believing. The monks (Alyosha is about to enter the monas-tery) are bound to indoctrinate him in these crudities ("those fellows over in the monastery no doubt believe that hell has a ceiling"—for the hooks to hang from which the devils use in their tortures [37]). Alyosha's mild denial that any such nonsense is taught is ignored by his father. A little later, we hear Fyodor speaking less extravagantly but still satirically about a rather less metaphorical kind of devil. Dur-ing his baroque monologue of surreal buffoonery at the monastery, he speculates that he may be possessed by an evil spirit—but "one of small proportions" [59]. He is a liar but not the father of lies—"well, the son of it, the son of a lie" [63] (in a novel deeply preoccupied with father-hood and sonship, this is a phrase to note). The narrator ironically con-firms Fyodor's self-analysis, since we are told that, at dinner with the abbot of the monastery, the "stupid devil" which possesses him makes him once again come out with a malicious and absurd attack on his hosts [119]. Fyodor's last observation on the subject occurs when he is sitting "Over Some Cognac" (the title of chap. 8 of book 3) with Ivan and Alyosha: Ivan denies both God and the Devil, and the old man asks, "Then who is laughing at man, Ivan?" Ivan "smiled, ironically," and answers, "The Devil, probably"—who does not, of course, exist. "What a pity," says Fyodor [179].

The diabolical is a stage prop for Fyodor, an occasion for mockery or satire, an alibi for his own anarchic cynicism and clownishness. It is "a pity" that there is no Devil, presumably because it would be good to have a cosmic prototype for this anarchy. At the same time, even Fyodor himself seems to acknowledge that the attitude of systematic mockery is not necessarily truthful: his absurdities are regularly exposed as such, and—at least in Zosima's presence—he admits their falsity. It would not be too far wrong to see his self-description as possessed by a small devil as being close to the judgment that Dostoevsky invites from the reader: Fyodor is a largely worthless man, greedy, selfish, casually cruel and abusive, hiding behind his clownish mask, yet it is hard to see him as a major focus for real evil in the novel. He belongs in spirit with the riotous crowd around Rogozhin in *The Idiot*, the "devil's vaudeville"—figures whose chaotic and shameless amoralism is more a symptom than a cause of serious corruption. These are indeed "sons of the lie," characters who literally cannot distinguish truth from falsehood. Interestingly, Zosima speaks "with a smile" to Fyodor, and his advice is direct and robust: he should stop telling lies, not least because lying to your self makes you easily offended, which is a great seduction [62–63]. Despite Fyodor's attempts to provoke the elder, Zosima seems to regard him with more of dismissive amusement than moral horror; though later episodes portray him in rather darker colors.[4]

Zosima in fact is presented as skeptical or at least unworried about "small devils." When Father Ferapont breaks in to the room where vigil is being kept over Zosima's body, one of his charges against the elder is that he "rejected the devils" [434]; we are told the anecdote of how Zosima, confronted by a monk suffering from diabolic fantasies, eventually suggested medicine rather than exorcism. Ferapont, of course, is an expert on devils in the most unequivocal and literal sense. His conversation with the "little monk" from Obdorsk in chapter 1 of book 4 shows him as a stout persecutor of the diabolical inhabitants of the monastery. The failure of his fellow monks to practice extreme forms of fasting leaves them in bondage to the Devil, and so it is not surprising that devils are to be seen everywhere, hiding under the cassocks of the brethren. Ferapont's description of catching one unfortunate devil by slamming the door on his tail and then destroying him by making the sign of the cross ("He died right then and there, like a squashed spider" [223]) is exactly the kind of story Fyodor might have expected the monks to take seriously. But it is very clear that Ferapont does not speak for the monastery or its ethos. It is left to the Obdorsk monk to take him as a spiritual hero—though Dostoevsky suggests very skillfully some of the difficulties even this rather stupid visitor has in believing Ferapont's fantasies; it is a fine comic episode, though already suggesting the pathos underlying Ferapont's aggression, the pathos that comes through in the scene over Zosima's body.

It may be as well to note in passing that the repeated statement in some of the critical literature that Ferapont stands for "traditional" asceticism over against the more humane and progressive theology of Zosima will not do. Ferapont's obsession about fasting is the sort of thing regularly condemned by the mainstream of Eastern monastic literature as excessive and individualistic, and, quite simply, it is clear that he is seriously mentally disturbed. His illiteracy is made plain in this first episode with the Obdorsk monk (he has somehow managed to invent a distinction between the *svyatodukh* and the *Svyatyi Dukh*, often rendered in English translations as a distinction between the Holy Ghost and the Holy Spirit) [223]. At Zosima's coffin, his resentment pours out against those who have patronized his ignorance: "in my time here I've forgotten what I did know" [435]. And he laments the fact that Zosima—a priest-monk who has taken the "great habit"[5]— will have a more spectacular funeral than he will. He may be a focus for other resentful and silly people who are suspicious of the role of the elders, but he is not and is not designed to be a spokesman for any sort of traditional theology or practice.

For Ferapont, power over these highly physicalized evil presences is a compensation for being excluded from the religious elite, the educated and ordained, who, for him, lack true spiritual integrity such as he has, confirmed by his visions and ecstasies. Zosima, who did not see the diabolical in this external and material way, is being properly punished by the premature corruption of his body. Though it has not always been noted by critics, it is significant that Ferapont's description of the body of the trapped devil ("He must have rotted in that corner, and stunk, but they've never seen him, never smelt him" [223]) is directly echoed in his tirade against the dead Zosima ("He used to give folk purgatives to keep the devils away. So now they've bred and

multiplied among you like spiders in the corners. And even he himself has gone and stunk the place out" [434]). Zosima, in his eyes, is
a straightforwardly diabolical presence, threatening Ferapont's own
spiritual authority by playing down the physical reality of his demonic
foes, over whom Ferapont has clear and indisputable power. And so
Zosima is appropriately punished by a cruel and physical manifestation
of God's judgment: "In this we see a great sign from the Lord," says
Ferapont of Zosima's premature decomposition.

But of course, as we have seen in the first chapter of this study,
the material manifestations of spiritual realities are always ambivalent,
and the idea that anything can be proved by such manifestations is
mocked by no less an authority than Ivan's Devil. Even the disturbing
sign of physical corruption is questionable. Smerdyakov, the murderer,
bears a name which suggests an association of smell with evil, yet he
is so named by Fyodor in derisive commemoration of his unfortunate
mother, "Stinking Lizaveta" [book 3, chap. 2] who is unmistakably
a "holy fool." And there is a throwaway line in chapter 6 of book 4,
describing Alyosha's first visit to the Snegiryov family, where the hypersensitive Mrs Snegiryov speaks about visitors who accuse her of having
bad breath; "And why are they so interested in my air, anyway? A corpse
would smell worse" [265]. Smells, including the smell of the dead, cannot be taken as a moral indicator. We have been warned in passing not
to pay too much attention to Father Ferapont's judgments.

So, if Fyodor Karamazov's devils are not much more than semi-
serious projections of his casual untruthfulness and insistent mockery,
Ferapont's are projections of his urge to demonstrate a spiritual power
that eludes him within the sophisticated framework of the monastery.
They are more serious than Fyodor's because, instead of just representing a corrosive but not very consistent undermining of any claims
to dignity or moral integrity, they are far closer to a real refusal of the
good. Father Paissy accuses him of doing the Devil's work by his fanatical hatred [434]. And his breakdown in tears of self-pity tells us a good
deal about his sense of impotence in the actual world of human skills
and relations. Perhaps then what can be said about devils in the narratives of both Fyodor and Ferapont is that they provide stories to
tell about the circumstances where ordinary human narrative is too
embarrassing or humiliating to manage. Certainly they are vehicles

of untruth—untruth about the situation, untruth about the two men themselves, vehicles of lying to oneself, but as such they are also, in the narrative structure, ways of glimpsing truth. Here are characters whose references, serious in one case and frivolous in the other, to the diabolical indicate their hiddenness from themselves. In Dostoevsky's narrative art, telling certain kinds of stories about demons is a sign of something substantially wrong in the teller.[6]

But—and here is the twist in the tale—this is not because the demonic is an inappropriate or fabulous category. To be seduced by the attractions of "diabolic" narration, as Ferapont is, is a mark of having *really* succumbed to diabolical temptation, to be doing the Devil's work, as Paissy accuses Ferapont of doing. The false register of language about the demonic—externalized, physicalized, the language of the invasion of a human spirit by a nonhuman one—alerts us to something true about those who claim physically to see devils. These figures who appeal to the devils of folklore are missing the genuinely diabolical problem of self-deceit. As we shall see, this becomes clearest when we look at the two major references in *Karamazov* to the Devil, both in relation to Ivan. It has been suggested[7] that Ivan stands to Ferapont as Alyosha does to Zosima; both Ivan and the monk see the demonic as external, both are locked in an isolation that ends in madness. Is Ivan (metaphorically) Ferapont's spiritual son as Alyosha is Zosima's? The parallels are slightly strained, but there are genuine connections here: in some degree, Ferapont is at least part of the preparation for Ivan's visions of the demonic.

But before turning to this, there is one other character in *Karamazov* who is briefly but tellingly associated with the demonic. Lise Khokhlakova, the teenaged girl to whom Alyosha becomes engaged, is from her first appearance a puzzling and unsettling figure. We are repeatedly told that she is "hysterical" and so are left uncertain as to whether she has indeed been healed by Zosima as is claimed. Her obsession with Alyosha is signaled at her first entrance in the scene at the elder's cell [book 1, chap. 4]. Despite her virtual proposal to Alyosha [book 3, chap. 11], it becomes clear that she has a complex emotional attachment to each of the brothers in different ways. In her last substantive appearance, chapter 3 of book 11, she is designated in the title as "A Little Demon" (*Besenok*): she begins by repudiating

Alyosha on the grounds that he is liable to behave like Myshkin—"if I married you, and suddenly gave you a letter to take to the one whom I loved after you, you would take it and unfailingly deliver it, and bring the reply back, too" [741]. She has, she says, no respect for him. But the truth is that she is dangerously close to the mentality of Nastasya Filippovna—the conviction that she is condemned to unhappiness and deserves the worst of suffering. She confides in Alyosha that she longs to burn down the house; a page or so later, this has become a desire to tear down everything. And then "They will all stand round me and point their fingers at me, and I will look back at them. I like that idea. Why do I like it so much, Alyosha?" [744].

She is in love with destruction, her own and that of her world; she wants to be found guilty and to be looked at by her judges, divine and human, and to laugh in return; she insists that everyone—like her—is secretly in love with evil, including parricide, and she repeats her longing to be annihilated. It is at this point that she describes a recurrent dream of devils, "In every corner, and under the table," like Ferapont's devils in the monastery, approaching to take hold of her. She crosses herself and they retreat; she is overcome again by blasphemous thoughts and they advance; she crosses herself and they retreat again. Alyosha admits to having the same dream. Lise then confides to Alyosha a hideous sadistic fantasy, based on the slanderous stories about Jews crucifying Christian children at Easter ("Is it true?" she asks Alyosha; and Alyosha, in this respect as poisonously and unpardonably prejudiced as his creator, replies, "I do not know").[8] She has shared this also with Ivan and asked if he thinks this is "good," as she does; "He suddenly laughed and said that it really was good" [743–44].

What exactly is going on in this unpleasant chapter (which ends with Lise—not for the first or last time?—inflicting an injury on herself)? Ivan's generalized contempt for humanity, in his own person and in others, has mutated into a real pathology in Lise. The diabolical with which she flirts in her dream, as in her waking fantasies, is here bound up with terror and hatred of her body and her sexuality and that of others: the crucified child is repeatedly described by Lise as having had his fingers cut off, in a blatant castration image (it is worth remembering too that, on Alyosha's previous visit he has had his finger bitten, and Lise insists on dressing the wound—as if Alyosha is a safe "suitor" as long as his sexuality is damaged or blocked). She is inviting Ivan and Alyosha to confirm her self-loathing by their contempt. For a modern reader, the layers of implicit reference to cycles of abuse seem unmistakable; we cannot but ask questions, questions which Dostoevsky would have well understood, about Lise's history. Her devils are not strategies for concealing or displacing the truth about herself, as with Fyodor and Ferapont, but representations of what she believes to be the worst about herself. They are in pursuit of her: they are urging her to self-destruction, and part of their method is (so the progression of the chapter suggests) to persuade her to say that everything is "good"—her self-hatred, her sadism, her humiliation at that sadism and self-hatred, and so on.

Ivan and Alyosha are called upon in different ways to reinforce the work of the devils. Lise is asking them to tell her that she is indeed committed to equating good and evil (i.e., treating everything as good), that the devils have in fact come to control her. For Ivan, this equation of good and evil is the "right" conclusion (so she thinks; presumably Ivan's response is ironic, a recapitulation of his earlier "mutiny" which assumes that if you accept the world of unspeakable cruelty and pain, especially the abuse of children, you are in effect saying that all this is good), and it leads simply to his despising her as he despises everyone. For Alyosha, it is the sinful conclusion, which should, she believes, lead to Alyosha despising her for her criminal perversity. Alyosha refuses to play along; she extracts from him the promise to weep for her, but we are given no further sign of any release from her diseased emotions, and are left with the image of her crushing her finger in the door. At this point, she is in thrall to the diabolical—not in the "possession" mode of which Fyodor and Ferapont speak, but as someone who has for that moment accepted a verdict on herself that condemns her to irreconcilable alienation from any economy of grace or mercy. According to the definition offered by Zosima in the last of his recorded discourses [book 6, chap. 3(i)], she is experiencing hell in that she is unable to love ("There is no one whom I love. Do you hear? No one!" [748]).

So the demonic in this instance is a complex matter, involving both a vision of the world as morally indifferent, so that sadistic cruelty is on a par with any other behavior, and a vision of the self as condemned to unqualified humiliation, pain, and rejection because of its acceptance of this vision of the world. There is no God to pass judgment, and the world is morally neutral (and thus terrible), but if there is no God to pass judgment, there is no acquittal or release either, and the sense of nausea and revulsion at the self's passion for pain and destruction is beyond healing. The chapter as a whole can be read a gloss on Zosima's meditations on judgment and hell. If God does not exist, it is not simply that everything is permitted—the slogan which is so often repeated in *Karamazov*, though, significantly, it is never heard directly in Ivan's mouth; the devastating truth is that there is no escape from the diabolical, that is, from the immobilizing of the self in humiliation and self-hatred. The triumph of the diabolical is when we cannot bear to see what we cannot deny is the truth, in ourselves and in the world—the systemic cruelty and the humiliating world of inner fantasy and revolt against "good."

Lise's devils are agents of truth, but they are evil because that truth can only be heard or read as an incentive to self-destruction. To what extent she is indeed trapped in this is left an open question, one of the many at the end of the novel. But this episode is an important stage in the clarification of the nature of the demonic which is going on throughout the book, and it ought to help us read both the Inquisitor narrative and Ivan's nightmare with more illumination. The demonic is not simply the perversity which makes Fyodor a buffoonish and irresponsible critic of his monastic hosts and more generally a man at the mercy of destructive impulses. Fyodor is a liar, but one who is still not incapable of recognizing his lies, even if he is incapable of doing anything about them (because of the delights of pretending to offence and claiming attention, as the elder tells him). Ferapont is a liar, who does not recognize how deeply he is meshed in untruthfulness because he cannot own and express his deepest resentments; the demonic is here a more serious level of untruthfulness than in Fyodor's case, as it allows him indefinitely to postpone self-knowledge. But there is a self-knowledge that is demonic as well, and this is what Lise endures: to know the self's fantasies of destruction or perversity and to feel there is no escape or absolution from them, to know that you are part of a world that is irredeemable. The sense of the demonic moves from Fyodor's conscious lies to Ferapont's unconscious lies to Lise's conscious truthfulness, but because this is a truthfulness divorced from love of self or others, it is in fact, of the three cases, the most pronounced instance of diabolical power.

How then does this help us with understanding Ivan's nightmare? As we have noted in the first chapter, the Devil whom Ivan encounters is presented as a force that makes for good to the extent that he holds us back from premature reconciliation. By continually keeping us aware of our complex motivations and of the ambiguity of appearances (ourselves to ourselves, as well as the world to our minds), he is the energy that drives history to continue. "If everything on earth were reasonable, nothing would ever happen. Without you there would be no events, and it is necessary that there should be events"; so the Devil reports the task given him by higher authority, complaining that he is thus made the scapegoat for an irrationality he would gladly see disappear [820]. There is always another question to be asked, even when every apparent requirement of "reason" has been met—the question that comes from "Underground," we might say, from the freedom that is both endless opportunity and endless curse.

But we should be a little careful about taking the Devil at face value only. All we have just said is true so far as it goes, but we have already been warned through Fyodor and Ferapont that we cannot expect truth from the Devil; indeed, if we take the Devil's own methodology seriously, we should have to ask questions of all he tells us. The telltale element is the Devil's ignorance of a "secret" about the unfolding of events that is known only to the unnamed "them" who have determined his course. All he can do is speak of the endless and, as far as he knows, purposeless succession of history through suspicion, conflict and the negotiations of varying sorts of self-deceit—through the lives of various Fyodors and Feraponts, in fact. He presents himself as the defender of what we might call a narrative integrity, the possibility of telling one's own story and that of others without foreclosing their meaning or distorting the telling in the interests of a false reconciliation, a harmony between particular and general that is simply not given in the flow of events. Ivan's Devil, as we have noted, is the patron saint of (Dostoevskian) novelists. But—just as Fyodor and Ferapont have warned us to be cautious about what the Devil claims for himself—

Lise's dreams and fantasies have also warned us that the recording of events as a continuum without value and differentiation leaves us with a mangled idea of freedom and even of truthfulness. If all we have before us is a continuum which includes equally horror and beauty, the horror is worse than it would otherwise be because there is no way of putting it into a context where it can be in any way healed or modified. It just happens. And if what I recognize in my own self is horror, the horror of sadistic or parricidal desires, as well as aspiration and compassion, how is the disgust at that horror to be managed without the urge to self-destruction?

The Devil, of course, quotes to Ivan his own poem, "The Geological Upheaval," in which Ivan has argued that the destruction of the idea of God will liberate truly disinterested love for the first time ("Very charming," says the Devil [830]). But, he adds, what if the period never arrives when all will agree on this? What if all that happens in the interim is the steadily growing recognition that without God there is nothing to regulate or make sense of the human will? The ego moves in to the vacant place of God. "Everything is permitted"—which means not simply that all crime is legitimate but that all valuation must come simply from the willing self. As Evdokimov notes,[9] if *everything* is permitted in a world without God, so is the love of God and neighbor, but what cannot be sustained is any sense of the anchorage of such a policy in the nature of things. And if that self is conscious of its own complicity in a cruelty from which it shrinks, what then? Ivan, remember, is undergoing this nightmare as he wrestles with his own complicity in Smerdyakov's murder of their father. As with Lise's despairing self-awareness, there is no place for the ego to stand in making judgments of value because it is self-condemned already.

It is in thus insisting on a radically and incurably divided and shamed ego that the Devil of Ivan's (and Lise's) dream emerges as more than a benign rascal who is permitted to exist in the created order simply to keep events moving. He is the source of a self-alienation that paralyzes or pushes toward suicide; this has already, in fact, been spelled out in the characterization of Stavrogin, but here in *Karamazov* it is embedded in the fullest typology Dostoevsky has so far attempted of the demonic. Leatherbarrow, in his excellent discussion of some of these themes, says of book 6 of the novel, the Zosima dossier, that its inadequacy illustrates the incapacity of the "realistic novel" to witness to divine grace.[10] But part of Dostoevsky's technique is repeatedly to demonstrate what realism without grace looks like. Whether or not the Zosima chapters can be defended (and we shall be examining them at greater length in the concluding chapters of this book), the signals are clear that a diabolical narration, a narrative that simply records the supposedly bare phenomena of a world imbued with horror and a self entrapped by almost unmentionable desire will collapse upon itself. That kind of speech, that kind of representation of what is "real," finally silences itself: as we have noted, it cannot bear what it sees, within or without, and so resigns from speech, in insanity or suicide. Dostoevsky's own narration, on the basis of what was argued in the first chapter, is generally a sustained attempt to avoid that conclusion. It is not just that loose ends are deliberately left and facile resolutions rejected; it is also that a future is projected in which insanity or suicide are not the inevitable prospect, because what has been allowed in the narrative from some other perspective, call it grace if you will, remains at work. It has to be granted straight away, of course, that *The Idiot* strains this to breaking point, leaving practically no imaginable future for any of its chief characters; but this is perhaps Dostoevsky's most deliberately extreme assault on the twin enemies of a religious "realism"—timeless ecstatic acceptance on the one hand and neutral reportage of the world's "being-toward-death" on the other.

As was suggested above, part of the secret that the Devil does not know is to do with incarnation; he thinks of the bodily state as somehow giving access to a simplicity of response of which he knows nothing. Bizarrely—at first sight—he seems to associate bodiliness with a more wholehearted affirmation of belief in God, the devotion of the sixteen-stone merchant's wife. The significant clue in this is something to do with the body as expressing shape and limit, and thus challenging the fiction of the omnipotent mind and/or will. The Devil's skepticism about the existence of anything outside his mind is clearly an effect of his disembodied nature. Solipsism is easier if you habitually encounter no limits and no surprises, such as the embodied life brings with it.

So we might expect that one of the things in these narratives which represented symbolic defeat for the Devil would be encounters with physical limit, including unexpected physical suffering. Alyosha's first encounter with Ilyusha Snegiryov [book 4, chap. 3] culminates in his having his finger bitten severely by the boy. Alyosha responds with dignity and kindness; but he has been forced to ask what sort of complicity he might have in the boy's humiliation and violence, even to ask about what he later explores with Lise, [281–84], the ways in which kindness itself humiliates. He has discovered the material costs of risking engagement with injured people, and it is a significant moment in Alyosha's movement into the world from the monastery. In its way, it is like the physical experience of the stench of Zosima's corpse, a shock which underlines the uncontrollable otherness of the material environment. And of course when Lise jams her finger in the door at the end of her last conversation with Alyosha, it is an attempt at exorcism, in the way that self-harm is always a desperate effort to connect with one's body, even through pain, when the inner world is distorted and frightening.

Encounter with the surprises of the material world does not have to be painful. It is important that what keeps Ivan still wedded to the world he longs to reject is the "love" he feels for "the sticky little leaves." The physical world not only shocks, it can also compel a sort of loyalty. The struggle against the Devil is bound up with the struggle against what some (like the American novelist Walker Percy) have called "angelism," the aspiration toward a state of radical disconnection with the body, for the sake of a more unqualified control of the environment. Thus the defeat of the Devil is the triumph of a commitment to the physical. This may sound odd to those who suppose that religious faith is inherently uneasy about materiality; less odd to those familiar with a thoroughgoing sacramental theology, especially the theology of the Eastern Church with its insistence on the indwelling of divine activity in matter, an indwelling brought to light (literally) in the making of icons.[11] And for Dostoevsky, this commitment to the material world is most simply to be seen in the commitments of practical compassion. The episode [book 11, chap. 8] where Ivan returns after his third and final interview with Smerdyakov to rescue a peasant in danger of freezing to death is connected directly with Ivan's resolve to give evidence on his brother's behalf at the trial the next day: he is committed to a world in which decisions for the good can be made, and in which future purposes can have an impact on present attitudes.

The tragedy is that by this stage the insidious self-doubt and endless questioning which the Devil proceeds to exploit in the nightmare of which we read in the following chapter of the novel is a more compelling habit.

Narratives that represent the defeat of the Devil—and that therefore say something, however obliquely, about the presence of grace—are narratives that exhibit their characters in a state of commitment to something other than their own will and their own self-image. A story of grace can be a story about some sustained physical engagement no less than a story about compassion between persons. Dostoevsky might not have been quick to agree, but you could read something like the narrative of Levin's day mowing with the peasants in *Anna Karenina* as a story of "grace" in this sense. But undoubtedly the paradigm for Dostoevsky would have to be the narration of love. What this means is most comprehensively defined for him by the thoughts he puts into Zosima's mouth, but it is at least as illuminating to consider how, in the actual process of his fiction, love is made the subject of narrative. In the first chapter above, we considered the importance in *Devils* of Shatov's experience of his wife's childbearing, and how his extremely specific and prosaic concern was deployed in the narrative to relativize Kirillov's suicidal fantasy. As in the story of Ivan's reluctant helping of the drunken peasant in the snow, what matters is not a general and sustained feeling of benevolence but a liberty to respond attentively to present need—which is also why Myshkin appears as someone whose love is flawed, since, at crucial moments like the confrontation between Nastasya and Aglaya near the end of the book, he cannot see what Aglaya needs, or indeed what Nastasya truly needs (he persists in identifying her need for love with a need for pity).

Ivan responds reluctantly because in theory, as he has told us, he cannot believe that love of the human neighbor is possible. "In order to love a person it is necessary for him to be concealed from view; the moment he shows his face—love disappears" [309]; this comes at the beginning of the chapter on "Mutiny," and offers a good deal of insight about how we read the pages that follow. For Ivan as a theorist, the only love that is possible is for humanity in the aggregate—a theme that will be developed at length in the Inquisitor fable. Love is therefore always "discarnate." Confronted with specific human

objects, it is impossible because it cannot be rational; it must be qualified by the universal culpability of human beings. It is reasonable
only where children are concerned—they do not share the corruption
of adults. From Ivan's perspective, there could be no "realistic" stories of love except love for children—and these would be odd narratives, since they would never move beyond the stage at which the real
interactions of desire and conversation arise. They would be as near
as you could get to the prenarrative world of timeless harmony. Think
back to *The Idiot*: Myshkin's idyllic relationship with the wronged and
scorned Marie in Switzerland and with the local children whom he
persuades to love her is a perfect illustration of the only kind of narrated love Ivan would admit [part 1, chap. 6]. And this is of a piece
with Myshkin's enthrallment to a prehistory, a world without adult
memory or differentiation, with Nastasya's association of him with
the picture of an absent-minded Christ both blessing and ignoring
the child leaning at his knee [*The Idiot*, 530].

If children alone can be loved "rationally"—that is, in a way that
does not fly in the face of evidence—it is possible to see why the abuse
of children becomes for Ivan the most devastating and unanswerable of
crimes. If this is possible, let alone prevalent, it threatens any reasonable account of the world; or rather, if reason turns out to demand the
acceptance of this for the sake of longer-term harmony, reason itself
must be perverse and morally intolerable. And so we end up with Ivan's
peculiar aporia: the Devil is the force that makes events go forward in
their contingent or irrational way, and so makes narrative possible; but
the Devil is also the force that requires us to accept that contingency
without hope or love. He is thus also the force that can drive us to the
desperate attempt to police the world of contingency in the name of
a generalized love, but can offer no reconciliation in regard to the fate
of individuals.

Very gradually, the connections between the Devil of the Inquisitor text and the Devil of the nightmare come into focus. The Inquisitor's Devil, as we have noted, is "terrible and clever," "wise and terrible"
[*Karamazov*, 328, 333]. The questions he puts to Jesus are more than
the ordinary human mind can imagine for itself: they come from "the
eternal and absolute [mind]" [329]. Yet this spirit is also "the Spirit of
self-annihilation and non-existence" [328]. The fundamental paradox

of the Inquisitor's address is that the deepest wisdom is to recognize ultimate nothingness. As Evdokimov observes,[12] talking in this connection about absolute nature, ego, Spirit, and so on is simply a way of finding verbal substitutes for this nothingness. The Devil's temptations are made in the name of this, inviting Christ to acknowledge that the creativity he assumes in humanity is illusion. On the face of it, he is inviting Jesus to forswear exactly that valuation of unpredictable liberty which, in Ivan's dream, he claims to be enabling. If there is nothing fundamental, nothing that grounds human meanings, no course of action is inherently more worthwhile than any other. Yet the reality of suffering—whether rationally or not—still causes agonized pity, and this can be dealt with only by a systematic policy of minimizing suffering, denying it and educating human beings to look for swift and unambiguous solutions where it appears.

Thus the Devil's aim is what could be described as a massive *rewriting* of humanity's capacity and future: the Devil, it has been said, desires authorship,[13] and the Inquisitor's world is *his* narrative. In this world, humanity is given roles to play, songs to sing, even emotions to enjoy or tremble at; it is allowed the dramas of sin and expiation, strictly on the Inquisitor's terms; it will, very importantly, "have no secrets" from its masters [338]. Even rebellion against the system is foreseen and catered for in advance [337]. In other words, it will have in relation to its rulers the kind of transparency that might be expected in a fictional character's relation to an author. It is another version of Myshkin's ambivalent compassion, which unconsciously looks to shape the other in his own image. In this world, as in the world of fiction, there is no sin except that of the author ("and as for the punishment of those sins, very well, we shall take it upon ourselves" [338]). And the result is that every human being (except for the inquisitorial class) becomes a child again, and is guaranteed the "sweetness" of childlike happiness and innocence. All are loveable because they are guiltless, guiltless because they will make no real choices. Their faces are "concealed" just as Ivan has said they should be.

In the light of all this, when we come to read Ivan's nightmare, we read it with extra care. As Ivan recognizes, the nightmare devil is a crude reduction of the tragic nobility ascribed to the demonic in the Inquisitor narrative. But he is also the voice of what Ivan cannot explicitly "own" in his conscious voice, and part of that is the recognition that contingency repeatedly escapes control. The story slips away from its author and demands to be written differently. And the Devil's role as embodying negation has the undesired effect of upsetting his aspiring authorship. In theological terms, his nothingness is "real" only as the shadow of something solid. The image of the ultimate void, the "nonexistence and self-destruction" of the Inquisitor text, is literally a blank, literally beyond speech; it is speakable, narratable, only as it appears in contention with movement and actuality. Diabolical authorship, as we have seen, ends in silence and death. It persists only because it is in dialogue with actual contingency. Thus the Devil's negations have the effect of pushing forward an uncontrollable history; he cannot perfect his own authorship, because that would mean the dissolution of creation itself.

It is this knife edge between negation and creation that the diabolic mythology of *The Brothers Karamazov* is meant to illuminate. Actual authorship, the writing of a specific human writer, like actual choice, is both a response to the seductive lure of negation (as defined in the Inquisitorial world) and a negation of that negation. It is a protest against premature closure and an act that makes such closure more difficult by further complicating the human narrative. And in the light of the Inquisitor fable, we can see that what the Devil of the nightmare says about his good intentions needs questioning: he wants harmony, not complication, he says; he doesn't enjoy making things difficult. But it is that "making things difficult" which is the guarantee of that freedom he fears; his desire to spare us the complications of contingency is only another form of the Inquisitorial Devil's more overt programme to subdue guilt and responsibility and secure a protracted childhood for us. It is possible too that his confidence in final reconciliation for himself and all beings is not to be taken too much *au pied de la lettre*; naturally, his hopes are still to do with a final deathlike harmony. And if that is what lies at the end of time, his puzzlement at being obliged to provide the raw material for continuing "events" is intelligible.

The Inquisitor, as we have seen, is committed to what amounts to the hiding of the human face under a mask of childlike acceptance. Those who have been tempted to see the Inquisitor fable as some sort of covert statement of Dostoevsky's own views have seriously underrated the ways in which Dostoevsky signals the Inquisitor's corruption, and the telltale references to this perpetual childhood, combined with the goal of making every human being transparent to authority should make it clear that we are not to think of the Inquisitor as anything other than an enemy in the author's metaphysical campaign. Narrative resistance to the "terrible and wise spirit" means both removing the veils that hide authentic humanity and restoring to humanity that *intrinsic* hiddenness which belongs to free agency—the mysterious and sometimes arbitrary dimensions of self-determination which are so central to Dostoevsky's fictions. We shall see in the next chapter how the different ways in which human beings become or fail to become visible to each other shapes Dostoevsky's whole vision of what human maturity and indeed human salvation might look like.

But a crucial element in that vision is *immortality*. Repeatedly, belief in God and in immortality are bound together in Dostoevsky's writing—as they are explicitly in the conversation between Fyodor Karamazov and his two younger sons in book 3, chapter 8.[14] Ivan rejects even the faintest hint of immortal life, and his fable takes it for granted that immortality is an illusion. The ruling elite will use the mythology of heaven and hell, of course, as part of the mechanics of control. But "if there were anything in the other world, it goes without saying that it would not be for the likes of them" [338]. Because the mass of humanity has never taken human choices, never elected to determine who they shall be, there is nothing for them to be in any future life. The only ones who deserve immortal reward are the two opposing elites, those who have followed Christ's radical commands and saved their souls, and those who have ignored Christ, sacrificed their happiness and integrity, and saved others.

In other words, immortality—if there is immortality—is for those who have deliberately constructed a meaningful narrative of their lives, who have not accepted the narrative written by others. Those whose lives have simply been "written" have no future. But this implies that immortality, for Dostoevsky, is not in fact primarily about reward and punishment, but about the continuance of a meaningful history. If the decay of belief in immortality means, as Dostoevsky clearly thought it did, a decline in moral seriousness, he is not ascribing this just to the disappearance of fears of post-mortem punishment (though he can sometimes write as if this is foremost in his mind, as in his 1878 letter to Ozmidov[15]). In his reflections at his first wife's deathbed, he had already stressed that only immortality could provide a context in which the struggle for an idea moral life could make sense.[16] In his 1876 discussion in *A Writer's Diary* of suicide and immortality,[17] he insists almost feverishly that life without this belief is "unnatural," and adds that love for humanity is impossible unless you believe in the soul's immortality. And in *Karamazov* [book 2, chap. 6], Miusov rehearses what he thinks to be Ivan's argument about immortality—that without it, once again, love is unthinkable, self-interest is unchallengeable, and "every vital force for the continuation of universal life" would be instantly extinguished [94]. Thus, so far from belief in immortality reducing the significance attaching to earthly situations and decisions, it gives them unprecedented value.

Earthly life cannot flourish without the conviction that the narratives of growth, conflict and attention that characterize our life here are not fated to come to an end. As Stepan Verkhovensky puts it at the very end of *Devils*, God will not commit an injustice in extinguishing the love for him that has been learned in the course of a human life [655]. It is almost as though something is owed *aesthetically* to the nature of our life in time. That very lack of closure and indeterminacy about the future which we have seen to be so central equally to Dostoevsky's faith and his fictional writing requires that narrative possibility should not end in death. And if every human agent shares the capacity for living in and through this indeterminacy, there is immortality for all. No one falls out of the picture.

So we can see still more fully the logic of the Inquisitor's attitude to life beyond the grave. If the mass of humanity is never allowed to perform self-defining actions, they have no integral personal narrative to take forward. But if this is the case, it is also true that their earthly fate is not of eternal importance; individuals can always be sacrificed for the good of the social whole. Commentators on the fable often seem to forget that we are introduced to the Inquisitor as the man who has just presided over a spectacular holocaust of dissidents. We should be in no doubt that his universal benevolence is conceived in strictly

general terms. The Inquisitor's sacrificial love for humanity turns out
to be a love that sacrifices rather more than itself, and Dostoevsky evidently means it to illustrate his thesis that without belief in immortality, an *equality* of love for specific human beings, such that the death
or failure of any one of them is equally a tragedy, will be impossible.
The outlook of the Inquisitor is in fact that of the sinister Shigalyov
in *Devils*—a plan for the future that consciously involves the killing of
multitudes in order to establish a despotism of the few for the welfare
of the majority—but dressed in a romantic pathos which would have
been the object of Shigalyov's deepest contempt. We shall be hearing
more of Shigalyov later in this discussion. And of course a remoter relative is Raskolnikov's philosophy in *Crime and Punishment*, which justi-
fies the killing of the superfluous or inferior.[18]

A central element in the diabolical strategy is always going to be
the undermining of belief in immortality, as a way of forcing people
toward the conviction that all value depends on the choice of the will
and no more. And what Dostoevsky wants his readers to understand
is that this will inevitably lead to an essentially *abstract* view of what
counts as human happiness, since it has no ground for affirming the
unique value of each person; the result of this is the mentality that can
contemplate with equanimity the mass slaughter of human beings in
the name of the general good. Once again, the point is being driven
home that the demonic always "de-realizes" or "disincarnates," distracts us from the body and the particular. Thus, if we are to avoid
the politics of the Devil—Shigalyov's schemes—we have to develop a
political imagination that resists abstraction and generality. *Karamazov*
has little to say directly about politics except obliquely in the Inquisitor fable, but Dostoevsky had already had his say on the subject in
Devils, from a number of diverse perspectives. And reference to the
earlier novel reminds us of the tangles into which Dostoevsky could
get himself when trying to be specific about this.

As we have noted, Shatov's political dreams are often close to
the sort of thing Dostoevsky was writing in his own voice. It is easy
to understand why this intense passion for the Russian people and
the Russian soil had attractions—for the simple reason that it is not
abstract. Dostoevsky knew, and in his fiction *allowed* himself to know,
that this vision grated against the daily reality of Russian identity, yet

in his journalism wrote of the unique endowments and unique destiny of Russia with increasing abandon and unrealism.[19] What is more, his passion to affirm the destiny of Russia to direct the moral and spiritual struggles of other nations incorporates a serious self-contradiction: the Russian, observing the failures of other peoples, is on Dostoevsky's own principles bound to have only an abstract knowledge of the problems and how to resolve them. "Dostoevsky is stating in effect that Russians understand the requirements of every other nation better than that nation itself does—an attitude ironically reminiscent of the Grand Inquisitor."[20] The belief that Russia occupies already among the nations a unique place of "reconciliation" implies—if we try to relate it to what the novels are saying, that Russia has no history. Its own spiritual identity has reached such an equilibrium that "events" no longer matter; it can become the author of righteousness and order in other nations. Russia, in fact, is in danger of acquiring a Myshkin-like role in such argument—a position of timeless innocence.

Some of this can be attributed to the growing influence of Solovyov on Dostoevsky;[21] some of it is the legacy of his earliest ventures into political journalism. Scanlan points[22] to the importance of Belinsky's equation of nationality with personality, and this is an important point, since it connects with the concern for the concrete and specific. Just as the uniqueness of the acting person has to be safeguarded at all costs, the same applies to the uniqueness of the nation—though Dostoevsky clearly thought by the end of his career that there was a natural hierarchy among the peoples of the world (this is less evident in his earlier thoughts on national identity),[23] in such a way that the equality of distinctive national identities becomes impossible to argue. But in fairness to him, he wavers noticeably on whether the "Russian idea" is truly capable of being realized in history. If we take chapter 5 of book 2 in *Karamazov* as indicating some of his most developed thinking on these issues—with all the necessary caveats about ascribing the views discussed here to the author without qualification—we can see something of how he could imagine a more nuanced account. The perspective imposed by having to present it first as an abstract argument constructed by Ivan and then as a vision partially but quite substantially endorsed by Zosima gives a vague notion of how something of his intensely nationalistic commitment might find a respectable theological base.

Ivan has written an essay, we are told, on the independence of the Church courts, a significant and contentious question at the time. In this, he has argued that a proper understanding of the Church must mean that any concordat between Church and state is bound to be an unsatisfactory compromise, since the Church presents itself as the ideal future of society. The Church ought to "include" the state, not vice versa. But what this means in practice—as Ivan outlines and Zosima enthusiastically elaborates—is a complete reimagining of the idea of punishment: instead of external violent measures against criminals, the sole sanction is excommunication, so that the criminal may be moved to change. It takes away any appeal by the criminal to Raskolnikov-like sentiments about crime as protest against social injustice. The legitimacy of the social order rests on a principle that is regarded as beyond all challenge, the reality of the Church as the *acknowledged* definer of human value. In such a world, there would be no impersonal punishment; the soul of each offender is infinitely worthwhile and distinctive, and the Church's task is to find the unique therapy that will work for each person [86–90].

Zosima acknowledges that it cannot be predicted when such a system could come into being—perhaps only at the end of time, but perhaps in the near future. Father Paissy is less tentative and offers a confident Dostoevskian prediction that the time is at hand and that the Orthodox Church alone is able to realize such a hope. But what is significant about this curious discussion is that it is free from simply nationalist rhetoric, that it allows a measure of uncertainty as to whether this is actually a practically possible future, and that it depends on an almost unimaginable level of spiritual consensus. It is indeed very close to what Solovyov called "free theocracy."[24] It could be said to be closer to an Islamic model of the role of faith in society than to any classical Christian theory, but it can at least claim a foundation in the biblical conviction that the Church is not primarily an institution amongst others but the promise of a global transformed system of human relationships, which the present institution foreshadows without wholly realizing. It is perhaps the least problematic or offensive face of Dostoevsky's essays in defining an antidiabolical politics.[25]

✠   ✠   ✠

In *Devils*, Dostoevsky had sketched a typology of diabolical victories, encompassing both the personal and the political and suggesting the interdependence of the two. *Karamazov* is in part an attempt to balance the picture, to show what the refusal of the diabolical would look like, again in both personal and political terms, and it is true to say that many dimensions of the later novel are not fully intelligible without the earlier. In *Devils*, we meet six—perhaps seven, if we include Varvara Petrovna Stavrogina—characters representing various stages of diabolical possession—the term is not too strong, given the significance in the novel of the story of the Gadarene swine which is used as one of the epigraphs. There is Stepan Verkhovensky, pathetically self-deluded, living off the half-dramas of a distant youthful radicalism that never really involved him in any serious risk and the remains of a never-consummated relationship with his "patron," Varvara Stavrogina. He has allowed her to shape his existence to an extraordinary degree ("She even designed the clothes he wore all his life herself" [33]), to write him as a character in her world. There are their children, Pyotr Verkhovensky and Nikolai Stavrogin, both of them having spent a long time away from home: Pyotr is a virtual stranger to his father, and Nikolai has grown up under Stepan's tutoring). Pyotr, one of Dostoevsky's supreme creations, is a brilliant and completely ruthless manipulator; it is impossible to know what his true thoughts and feelings are, as his priority, as it appears in the narrative, is always to reinforce his own power over others. Nikolai returns to his home town as the subject of many stories about his strange activities—violent outbreaks, rumors of extreme behavior and secret sins; by the group of local radicals, all in diverse ways marked by his earlier influence, he is looked upon as a sort of messiah. In different ways, he has—like his mother with Stepan—created the personalities and convictions of those around him; but now he is remote and inscrutable and evades all attempts to push him into the various roles scripted for him. And there are the main members of his circle, Shatov, Kirillov and Shigalyov, each with his distinctive philosophical view, derived in different ways from aspects of Stavrogin's past, all in fact inexorably oriented toward death.

Around them are characters who represent an assortment of disorders—the lesser members of the cell, the confused and hysterical Lizaveta Nikolaevna (halfway between Nastasya Filippovna in *The Idiot* and Katerina Ivanovna in *Karamazov*), the insane Marya Timofeevna (who turns out to be Stavrogin's wife), the murderous convict Fedka, the ineffectual governor (von Lembke) and his radical chic wife, and many more. But the basic typology is provided by the immediate cir-cles around Stepan and Stavrogin. No one in the novel emerges as a straightforward embodiment of sense or truthfulness, except the enig-matic Bishop Tikhon in the chapter that was originally suppressed by the censors and was only restored to the text in the twentieth century —a problem in its own right, which we shall look at shortly. As in *The Idiot*, no one is definitively redeemed, though Stepan Trofimovich on his deathbed has made the first tentative steps toward truth, and Shatov experiences a kind of epiphany when his wife gives birth. In short, the focus of the narrative is almost exclusively upon the profiles of the demonic. But this does not mean that all the main characters are "evil"; in an important sense, that is not the point. Stepan and Shatov in particular are essentially decent people, and Kirillov is a generous and sensitive man, but they are far from harmless. Part of Dostoevsky's purpose is to demonstrate that to bring about evil you do not have to have evil intentions. But the more the climate of untruthfulness comes to feel natural to people, the more evil results. The gallery of the "possessed" is thus a gallery of those exemplifying different levels of untruth or refusals of truth.

Shigalyov's ideas have already been touched upon. He is introduced [part 1, chap. 4; 145] as someone who looks as though he is expecting the end of the world, "not at some indefinite time, according to proph-ecies which might never come true, but with absolute definiteness— say, the day after tomorrow, at exactly twenty-five minutes past ten." Despite the faintly comic register (and *Devils*, for all its bleakness, also contains Dostoevsky's most sustained comic writing), this is no casual image: Shigalyov represents the conviction that the future is indeed capable of being planned and controlled. In part 2, chapter 7, he is given the chance to set out his views to the revolutionary cell, and, in a way characteristic of some sorts of radical polemic of the period, he insists that there can be no other logical solution of the social problem than his own [404]. "Starting from unlimited freedom, I arrived at unlim-ited despotism." As we have noted, he anticipates the Inquisitor in the belief that a minority of human beings have to take authority over the rest of humanity, and this will promise "paradise on earth" [406]. It might be preferable in theory to reduce the human race itself to that minority capable of rational relationship and organization, but this might be impracticable. The dictatorship of the enlightened minority at least guarantees the highest achievable level of happiness for the largest number. As emerges in the next chapter, in a conversation between Pyotr and Stavrogin, this will also entail a universal system of spying and informing, and the rooting out of any exceptional excellence in art or science: "A Cicero will have his tongue cut out, Copernicus will have his eyes gouged out, a Shakespeare will be stoned" [418]. Verkhovensky approvingly observes that the human need is not for science but for obedience; and to avoid boredom, there should be, as Shigalyov argues, intermittent violent upheavals—rather like the Inquisitor's toleration of occasional childish rebellion [419].

Shigalyov's thoughts in the meeting prompt others in the group to quote literature they have read urging mass slaughter ("a hundred million heads") as the only sure way of bringing about the promised paradise. But, as one of the local intellectuals observes, the practical obstacles in the way of this mean that the only lasting effect of such rhetoric is to encourage the educated to abandon Russia and look for a peaceful place to emigrate to [408]. As the group seems poised to revert to general aspirations, Pyotr Verkhovensky is able to come in and persuade them that, while the "hundred million heads" may be a metaphor, they have a choice between endless theoretical discussion ("the composition of social novels and the dry, unimaginative planning of the destinies of mankind a thousand years hence" [409]) and short-term, violent action that can deliver drastic change—action that may include "political murder." Pyotr tantalizes his audience with mysterious allusions to a network of cells of five across the country and even perhaps more widely, a network devoted to secrecy and radical action, and he is able to get general agreement that no one would act as an informer in the case of a political assassination. Dostoevsky skillfully displays the way in which the rhetoric of mass murder is toned down as metaphorical, and the same principle of the dispensability of human life in the political struggle is then reintroduced as part of a corporate process of self-dramatization. Shigalyov's proposed scheme for the future—evidently a document of crushing detail and tedium—has been overtaken by a highly focused but skillfully disguised affirmation of the justifiability of immediate and local violence. As Pyotr confides to Stavrogin [419], "What we need is something more immediate, something more thrilling"—not the theory of a controlled society but the experience here and now of controlled killing.

It is not only that Shigalyov's own ideas have a "diabolical" quality in their own right, promising just that termination of history and narrative that we have seen to be characteristic of the demonic; they become a doorway into something much more directly violent. If the idea of a relatively distant end of history is attractive, as it obviously is for the cell, it is hard to refuse the seduction of immediate actions that promise just this release from choice and patience, an end to the confusions of human processes. The fantasy of the returning golden age, paradise on earth—even if Shigalyov's version is notably lacking the romantic glow of other versions sketched in Dostoevsky's fictions by various characters—is revealed as a path to hell. And the narrative of *Devils* moves us rapidly forward to the stage at which decisions about murder are no longer hypothetical.

The only member of the radical group to protest at Verkhovensky's steady nudging toward "necessary murder" (W. H. Auden's phrase in an early poem which he later repudiated)[26] is Shatov, and it is already clear that his protest has marked him down for punishment. Pyotr is able to portray him as an informer and to unite the remaining members of the group in planning his assassination—with the proviso that Kirillov, who has confided his suicidal intentions to Pyotr, will take the blame before he kills himself. Once again, the rhetorical process by which Pyotr persuades an initially rebellious group to follow his lead is skillfully depicted [part 3, chap. 4]. After a chaotic series of events involving local workers rioting, a fire in the town, and two murders (one of the victims being Stavrogin's wife Marya), the would-be revolutionaries suspect that they are being used by Pyotr, possibly to sort out Stavrogin's personal affairs; but Pyotr's "authorial" authority is triumphantly restored as he tells them that one of the murder victims, Marya's brother, was preparing to denounce them to the government and that Shatov is about to do the same. The fiction about Marya's brother paves the way for the case against Shatov, and Pyotr has managed to produce both unanimity and fear in the group, although they distrust him deeply and are still (rightly) convinced that he is "playing with them like pawns" [547–48].

Shatov, impractical, outspoken and lonely, is a natural victim. We have seen earlier in the novel[27] how he has been left by Stavrogin with a muddle of ideas which he cannot himself clarify, but his innate moral courage means at least that he will not be caught up in Pyotr's manic strategies. His Slavophil passion about the "God-bearing nation" has trapped him in the aporia which Stavrogin unmercifully presses on him: that his God is simply the projection of a national identity. There is only one truth [258], so, although every nation must believe that its God is true and great, there can be only one final victor in the historical conflict, only one nation that really holds to the true God.

This is, of course, another version of the end of history. Instead of Shigalyov's universal bureaucracy, the golden age is the triumph of Russia, the time when Russia will direct the destinies of all other nations— "chosen to raise up and save everybody by its own truth" [258]. But Shatov is painfully aware that this feels to him like empty and tired rhetoric; the fact that he cannot truthfully say that he believes in God is a symptom of the fact that he does not really believe in any of his system. He knows he is bound to a lie. His significance in the book is that he is one of the very few who can challenge both Stavrogin and Verkhovensky on the basis of some innate moral obstinacy. Talking with Stavrogin, he recognizes despairingly that Stavrogin will not fill up the void in his system, make it real, make faith in God and the Russian future possible for him, but he challenges his former mentor more fiercely than any other character about his willed indifference to good and evil, and helps us see Stavrogin as—like other Dostoevskian vehicles of destructiveness—essentially discarnate, cut off from the body and the passage of time. Shatov, in other words, is still, at least as much as Ivan Karamazov, caught in the agony of unknowing, longing for commitments that he cannot make; he is not yet "redeemed." But he at least knows what must be denied. Of all the characters in the book, he is the one who most clearly repudiates the Devil.

Shatov and Kirillov both live in Bogoyavlenskaya Street, and, as several critics have pointed out, given that Dostoevsky is never careless about the names he gives to people and places, there is a strong suggestion that both these characters have had some—limited and distorted—share in revelation, epiphany (*bogoyavlenie*).[28] Stavrogin's first visit to Kirillov finds the latter playing with a small child—a mark of both grace and danger in Dostoevsky's world. Kirillov loves children [242], so, says Stavrogin, he must "love life," but for Kirillov, such love is irrelevant to his desire to kill himself. It is irrelevant because moments of love are *timeless*. Kirillov believes in eternal life here and now, and Stavrogin in reply quotes the biblical text we are familiar with from its use in *The Idiot*, about time being no more. Kirillov thus represents, in the first place, the demonic aspect of visionary ecstasy. He is not an epileptic—Shatov, as we have seen, warns him that he may be at risk of developing epilepsy—but his perspective is exactly that of Myshkin, and Shatov's remarks make the connection unmissable. Happiness has no future; when humanity has arrived at happiness, "there will be no more time, for there won't be any need for it," it will no longer be thought of, perhaps being in a sense no longer thinkable [243].

And it is precisely this sense of the overwhelming goodness of this or that moment when life appears so loveable that, for Kirillov, makes everything that exists good. It seems likely that this passage lies behind Ivan Karamazov's reported comments to Lise Khokhlakova about the goodness of everything—though we ought to take Ivan's words as ironic. Kirillov is beyond irony: when Stavrogin asks whether it is good that someone is starving to death or raping a child, Kirillov's response is unequivocal. "And he who blows his brains out for the child, that's good, too. And he who doesn't blow his brains out, that's good too" (a foreshadowing of Ivan's ironic words to Lise Khokhlakova) [243–44]. If people are "bad," it is because they don't know that they are good; once they do, evil will cease [244]. And that will be the end of the world. Stavrogin objects that this was what Jesus taught and it led to his crucifixion; Kirillov counters that Christ will come again in the form of the *chelovekobog*, the "man-God"—a deliberate inversion of the theological term for Christ's dual nature, *bogochelovek*, a term of immense importance to Solovyov, who devoted a series of lectures to the principle of *bogochelovechestvo*, divinized humanity, understood as the new possibility for human nature opened up through its union with divine liberty in the person of Jesus.[29] Meanwhile, Kirillov prays to everything, including the spider crawling on the wall [244]: given the way in which visions of spiders or spider-like creatures work for so many of Dostoevsky's most tormented characters like Svidrigailov or Ippolit (and including Stavrogin himself [696]), this is not encouraging.

But Kirillov's *chelovekobog* is a reality achieved by human decision, not by grace, and the decision is literally suicide, as he explains to Verkhovensky on the eventful night of Shatov's murder [part 3, chap. 6]. The history of humanity is the record of the constant invention and reinvention of God by man, in order to keep on living. Without God, there is no reason for living, yet belief in God is the source of all untruth. God is necessary, but false and impossible. If you hold both these views, says Kirillov, you must kill yourself [611]. But this is not a reaction of despair; it is rather an act of supreme—and saving—*witness*, which will make all the difference for those who come after. Kirillov, the first ever to realize that God is both necessary and impossible, has to show that, if God does not exist, there is no power anywhere superior to the human will. And what shows incontrovertibly the power of the human will? The capacity to destroy itself, the purest possible act of "unreasonable" self-determination. To decide not to be can never be argued or justified; so a decision for suicide, taken specifically to show that the human will is supreme, establishes once and for all that God cannot exist except as the human will. "I am the only man in universal history who for the first time refused to invent God. Let them know it once for all" [613]. Kirillov's suicide is thus a quasi-messianic act: he dies so that others may live because, once it has been established that God is the source of all lies, and that the will is sovereign, human beings may "live in the greatest glory" [614]. This saving suicide is a kind of reversal of the cross of Christ. He, who uniquely provided a reason for life and for valuing everything in the world, "the greatest of all men on earth," died and went into nothingness: he, no less than the stupidest and lowest of human beings, was trapped by a lie. "If the laws of nature didn't spare even him, if they did not spare their own miracle, and made even Him live in the midst of lies and die for a lie . . . the very laws of the planet are a lie, and a farce of the devil" [614]).

Teasing out the argument is not easy, but it seems to run like this. Human beings constantly invent reasons and reasonable patterns for events; behind all these is the supreme invention of God's existence, so that all the untruthfulness in the human spirit can be traced to God.

Jesus was subject to the laws of nature: he died, as all people die. He had not therefore realized—in his acceptance of death and of life after death—that there is nothing beyond the mind and will. He had not entered into the timeless bliss of which Kirillov has spoken earlier in the novel, but remains in thrall to the fiction of time, nature, immortality, and God. To decide for death, instead of allowing natural forces or the decisions of others to kill you, is thus the supreme protest on behalf of freedom from nature, history and God.

Although much of this is a sort of *reductio* of various radical philosophies, particularly Bakunin's anarchism, it is also, as the novel strongly hints, a parodic passion narrative, with the final interview between Kirillov and Verkhovensky a "farewell discourse" like those in St. John's gospel, and, more grotesquely, Kirillov's withdrawal into an inner room to kill himself, leaving Pyotr outside, an echo of the Garden of Gethsemane (where the disciples are told to wait while Jesus goes forward to pray and then to confront his judges and executioners).[30] Of all the figures in the novel, he is perhaps the most heavily surrounded by biblical allusion.[31] Like Shatov, he is the vehicle of what Dostoevsky clearly sees as the demonic, yet he is depicted in unmistakably Christ-like terms. In that regard, he is the most tragically conceived of the whole group. And his presentation as a kind of Antichrist brings into sharper focus the counter-messianism of so much of the narrative, especially in relation to Stavrogin himself. The novel is an exploration not of freedom denied but of freedom perverted, seen as the essence of the diabolical. The Devil, who is, as we shall see quite unambiguously in *Karamazov*, the enemy of any real freedom, is here shown to us as offering a variety of ersatz freedoms, but since he is the spirit of destruction, what we have is a catalogue of freedoms leading to death. For Shigalyov, absolute freedom leads to absolute despotism because the majority of humans are not capable of exercising their freedom rationally. Given the irrationality of so many ordinary human beings (and, as Pyotr reminds us, the irrationality of the gifted and creative as well), there is a natural movement toward the conviction of the dispensability of various kinds of individual). For Kirillov, it is almost exactly the opposite: rationality must be refused as the realm of temporality, law, and natural death, refused in the name of the moment in which epiphany occurs. And the sole, unchallengeable expression of that refusal is suicide, with the killing of others being regarded as "the least important point of my self-will" [613]. And for the doomed Shatov, the freedom to assert the value of the nation as God-bearing collapses under the pressure of the fact that God refuses, so to speak, to be created by the will; Shatov cannot produce a believable God by deciding to do so.

The connections between all these freedoms and the various demonic manifestations in *Karamazov* should be plain. Even without examining the main characters of *Devils*, it is clear that the profile of the diabolical is indeed what the earlier discussion of *Karamazov* indicated. The Devil is out to stop history; he is the enemy of narrative and so of the freedom of persons to shape their identity over time. Being wise as well as terrible, he is able skillfully to propose versions of freedom which in fact subvert themselves and bring about disaster; he is even able to work through a seductive parody of God's love for creation ("God saw that it was good"), by way of the mystical instants of ecstatic acceptance that some experience. He is able to promote the rule of timeless rationality by the appearance of defending the irrational, but the "irrational" without love has no substance, nothing that can sustain desire and movement. As we shall see, the focal significance of Stavrogin in *Devils* has to do with the paralyzing effect of this freedom without decision or commitment.

So far, we have been discussing the ancillary characters ("minor" is hardly the right word, given the energy and depth of their depiction), but it is the central quartet that holds the entire chaotic ensemble together in a single plot. Two parents and two children are presented to us. Stepan Trofimovich and Varvara Petrovna are linked in a sterile pseudo-marriage, and Pyotr and Nikolai are likewise bound in a relationship that is both destructive and inescapable. The atmosphere of sexual frustration and frozenness that surrounds the parents is reproduced in Stavrogin's apparent impotence [part 3, chap. 3], as well as Pyotr's sexless and cynical flirtatiousness (particularly with Mme von Lembke, whom he flatters and confuses until he becomes "as indispensable to her as the air she breathed" [491]). It is not simply that Stepan, as a representative of the liberal generation of the 1840s—and tutor to the young Stavrogin—is being charged with responsibility for the nihilism of the 1860s and 1870s—a journalistic commonplace; there are things that both the young men inherit from their parents which more or less guarantee their diabolical fate. Stepan surrounds himself with manipulative illusions and fantasy dramas and enslaves himself to a myth created by collusion between himself and Varvara; Pyotr uses his inherited capacity for fantasy as a means of power over others. Varvara, as we have seen, invents a persona for Stepan, and her son similarly creates a series of reflections of himself in weaker personalities. But parents and children also complement each other's fates, each helping us see something about the other. Varvara possesses Stepan, and even at the end can barely bring herself to let him die without her detailed direction; Nikolai, in complementary contrast, possesses the souls of those he has been with but can make no decision for them or about them. They die alone. And, again in complementary contrast, the novel ends with two flights—Pyotr stepping on to the train to Petersburg, blithely leaving behind him the chaos and agony he has caused, and Stepan (foreshadowing in an uncanny way the aged Tolstoy three decades later) fleeing from the debacle of the fete, from his public humiliation by his son's generation, from a lifetime of dishonesty. Pyotr will live, Stepan will die—because Stepan has been left with no alternative but the truth about who he is; just as Varvara will live and her son will die, because he has been left with nothing but his own face in the mirror. Parents and children are locked into a closely woven pattern of echoes and legacies.

Stepan Trofimovich makes two discoveries about his life as he is dying. When Varvara catches up with him, he finds that he needs to say to her that he has loved her: *Je vous aimais toute ma vie* [651]. But a few pages later, in a phrase that must be a deliberate echo, he says, after confessing and receiving the sacrament, *J'ai menti toute ma vie* [656]. His love for Varvara has been a steady presence in his selfish and dilettante existence, a love not without some dignity, yet it is bound up with a lifelong falsity and refusal. Faced at the last with the devastatingly simple precepts of the gospel, not through the medium of theology or even liturgy at first, but through the humble and inarticulate Sofya Matveevna, he is—briefly—stripped bare. Briefly; he still compulsively turns to a woolly and self-regarding spiritual rhetoric when he tries to put this into words, yet something has clearly happened, even if it is no more than the recognition of the lie. At the end, he turns away from the diabolical. Early in the novel [51], he has expressed his concept of God in the vague language of a liberal thinking that has digested small quantities of Hegel and Schelling:[32] God is conscious of himself only through the human mind. He identifies with the views expressed in Belinsky's 1847 letter to Gogol—a nice irony, given that it was the semi-public reading of this letter that formed one of the main charges against Dostoevsky when he was arrested in 1849—and he quotes George Sand on the inadequacy of the Christian attitude to women. Dostoevsky's own judgment on Sand was remarkably generous,[33] and the considerable influence on *Karamazov* of her romantic novel *Spiridion* has been spelled out in detail by Joseph Frank.[34] But here she appears simply as one of the usual suspects in a liberal religious pantheon. In contrast, Stepan on his deathbed speaks unequivocally of a God who is "necessary" to him—the direct opposite of what he has said at the start, which assumes that he is necessary to God. Only God can be loved eternally, and this is what guarantees immortality, for God will not cut short the growth of the soul toward endless love. "How is it possible that existence should not be subjected to [love]?" he asks [655], in words that remotely echo the Platonic and Greek patristic axiom that God is "beyond being." And it is now clear that humanity desperately needs to believe that there is something infinitely greater than itself, in which perfect happiness eternally exists; only when we focus on this eternal bliss which belongs to an eternal Other can true happiness for created beings be properly understood and experienced.

As we have noted, this is still cast in the somewhat overblown language of Stepan's intellectual and aesthetic world, but it is nonetheless significant for that. The action of *Devils* is literally framed by the two confession of faith, and it is clear enough that what the novel has to say about conversion is contained in this structural device. The starting point for all the action is something very like an original sin of the liberal mind. It is not atheism pure and simple; in an important and well-known exchange between Stavrogin and Bishop Tikhon [679], "absolute" atheism is commended as the last step before faith. No, the originating problem is the confusion between self and God represented by Stepan's bland observations. The self becomes the "author" of God; without human self-consciousness, there is no divine selfhood. The human intelligence—and, by implication, will—are the sole sources of value. All the diabolical manifestations in the novel come back sooner or later to this basic issue. Freedom from the diabolical must mean freedom, such as Stepan finally reaches, to be glad of the beauty and bliss of what is completely transcendent, and (lest that should turn into another version of the "epileptic" ecstasy that is so plainly judged inadequate) the decision to act so as to bring blessing to others in the name of that excessive and uncontainable reality which is eternal bliss, eternally worthy of love. In other words, only love directed toward the transcendent can generate effective unselfish love within the world. Thus Kirillov's love for children and for the natural world is paralyzed so long as he needs to prove above all that the will is free enough to destroy itself. Shatov's love for the nation is empty and ineffectual so long as the nation is only a large-scale self, giving substance to an otherwise abstract God. Shigalyov's love for the human race dissolves in control and utilitarian calculation because it has no sense of the givenness of human value in each distinct person.

This "original sin," compounded with the dominant will of Varvara Petrovna to control what she loves, is the inheritance of the two central embodiments of the demonic in the novel. They embody two very distinct aspects of the diabolical, which might be called—not entirely accurately—active and passive. Pyotr is the organizing genius of the radical cell, incessantly scheming and maneuvering others into the requirements of his schemes. It remains completely unclear by the end of the book whether he has any larger political purpose, whether there really is any national or international network that he represents, even whether or not he is an *agent provocateur* for the government (as one of the group seems to suspect at the end of part 2, chap. 7; 413, when Pyotr refuses to answer his own question about informing on the cell). As Leatherbarrow notes,[35] he is introduced (in chap. 5 of part 1, a chapter tellingly entitled "The Wise Serpent") as possessing several of the folkloric physical characteristics of a demonic spirit—the thin, close features, and the impression, when he has been speaking for some time, that "he must have a peculiarly shaped tongue in his head, a sort of unusually long and thin one, very red, and with an exceedingly sharp and incessantly and uncontrollably active tip" [188]. But perhaps what is most telling of all is that we are practically never privy to what Pyotr is thinking or feeling (the important exceptions being the extraordinary *Grand Guignol* scene of Kirillov's suicide, which will need longer discussion later on, and to a much less dramatic extent, his conversations with Stavrogin): we cannot deduce what sort of person he is from his actions, since these are all to do with the short-term manipulation of others; we have no insight into his subjectivity. We do not know what his memories are. In a bizarre way, he resembles Myshkin, indeed is almost a negative image of Myshkin.[36] He comes out of a void, out of that convenient all-purpose "Europe" that serves as an almost blank backdrop for Russian fictional characters of the age; he approaches others as the author of their scripts and the one who possesses the key to their fates; he is sexually detached. The only relationship that appears to matter to him emotionally is that with Stavrogin (and he "doubles" Stavrogin in the plot in a way not unlike the doubling of Myshkin and Rogozhin). This is a complex relationship because, as Holquist shrewdly observes, Stavrogin is the only figure who upsets Pyotr's universal authorship. Is Stavrogin a character in Pyotr's narrative, or is Pyotr a character in Stavrogin's?[37]

Part 2, chapter 8, "Ivan the Crown-Prince," is the key passage in understanding this relationship. It is one of the few moments where Verkhovensky appears almost vulnerable, begging Stavrogin to take on the supreme symbolic role in his fantasy. What is this role? It turns out to be virtually that of the Inquisitor: when Shigalyov's leveling bureaucracy has done its work, the tiny elite of rulers will be left at the summit, and at the summit of that is Stavrogin. "Desire and suffering are for us; for the slaves—the Shigalyov system," says Pyotr, anticipating the Inquisitor's pathos and triumph [419]. Recognizable, complex, and historical human feeling is reserved for the rulers, both uniquely guilty and uniquely innocent. Stavrogin must take the place that the Pope would otherwise hold in a global, sanctioned despotism. Pyotr's obsession with Stavrogin is dramatically shown, and it is something far deeper than the homoerotic fixation with which it might be (and sometimes has been) confused. He catalogues, feverishly, all who are really on their side—"the teacher who laughs with the children at their God and at their cradle . . . The barrister who defends an educated murderer by pleading that, being more mentally cultivated than his victims, he couldn't help murdering for money," the officials who are intimidated by the moral and cultural climate (like the pathetic von

Lembke) [421]. The Russian people are sunk in alcoholic stupor and degradation, and all they need is a final push toward cynicism. The plan is panic and chaos, so managed that at last everyone will recognize that they need the hand of a single, absolute ruler, and the hidden heir, Ivan the Tsarevich, will emerge.[38]

Stavrogin dismisses all this as madness, and Pyotr responds furiously: Stavrogin is too much in his debt to say no. "There's no one like you in the whole world! I invented you abroad; I invented it all while looking at you" [424]. And without Stavrogin, he is "Columbus without America": he has no character of his own. Hence Holquist's observation about the symbiosis of the two as author and character to each other. It is worth noting too that Verkhovensky, at the same time as sketching Stavrogin's future glory as world leader, is also trying to persuade him to accord with his plans by promising, obliquely but unmistakably, to arrange the murder of his wife, Marya Timofeevna, so that Stavrogin can marry Lizaveta. His "authorial" ambitions work at several levels, and his sense of frustration at Stavrogin's lack of cooperation is as much to do with this petty local plot as with the global scheme. In fact, he does not wait for Stavrogin's full consent before launching his plan of local disruption, and Stavrogin has already given enough tacit assent to Fedka the convict's offer to kill Marya for this to form part of the bedlam that is unleashed (another trial run for an important *Karamazov* theme, that of complicity in murder without explicit consent). Later he will admit to Lizaveta that he considers himself guilty [522, 529], and Pyotr will try to dismiss the murder as coincidence; he has not, after all, had Stavrogin's express consent, but is still clearly hoping to convince Nikolai that he is indebted to him for the "plot" of his life. Even if he is not now eager to marry Lizaveta, other arrangements can be made ("Let me deal with her, of course" [528]). When Stavrogin still refuses to cooperate, Pyotr threatens to kill him; Nikolai tells him—unsurprisingly—to "go to blazes" [530–31]. In the two chapters that follow, this is precisely what Pyotr does.

Pyotr's demonic profile draws in all sorts of wider themes in the novel, and indeed in other Dostoevsky novels. He is, of course, conventionally heartless and unscrupulous, a manifestly wicked person in a way that Shatov and Kirillov and even Shigalyov are not, but his devilish identity is not constituted by this. He is wholly prodigal of inconvenient human lives, as contemptuous as Raskolnikov of the right of others to exist. Essentially, his only agenda is control, "authorship," and although he is prodigally creative of small plots, there is no wider reconciling narrative in view. His willingness to adjust to the unexpected breach between Nikolai and Lizaveta shows that he is uninterested in psychological continuities: whatever may have happened, an equally satisfactory plot can now be substituted for the failed one. He has no interest therefore in the internal life of any of those around him. They exist simply as material for his work and are not allowed to escape. Typically, the moments where we see him evidently anxious, even vulnerable, are when others—Stavrogin and then Kirillov—threaten to resist his narrative ambitions absolutely. So, in his cavalier treatment of the time of others, their capacity to change and to remember, to be shaped by what has happened to them, in his passionate hostility to signs of freedom and initiative, in his skill at exploiting the errors and disorders of less evil personalities (like Kirillov), he is more clearly "possessed" than any of the lesser figures. And his conversation with Stavrogin about the future he imagines is unquestionably in the same framework as the end-of-history scenarios that we have seen to be most deeply typical of the diabolical mentality.

But he is not self-sufficient, and his relation with Nikolai is crucial. Ivan Karamazov's Devil longs to be incarnate, since there is nothing that can be achieved in history except through human wills. That is why the Devil of Ivan's nightmare is unable to commit himself to any kind of belief, as he has no material and psychological context in which his decision would make a difference, only a solipsistic inner world. We must bear in mind that, while Dostoevsky emphatically believed in the objective reality of the demonic, it is an objective reality that cannot be separated from actual human agents. It is not to be conceived (in Ferapont's terms) as an infestation of identifiable alien creatures. So Verkhovensky *needs* others, supremely Stavrogin, the America to his Columbus. The authorial power he wields is possible only because of various kinds of collusion on the part of others, which allow it to become incarnate. Stavrogin is the keystone of his project partly because Stavrogin is uniquely collusive; not in the sense that he is, like other members of the group, simply weak-willed or confused, but in virtue of something more sinister and, in its own way, equally powerful.

Because he has *ceased to choose*, he is the ideal vehicle for the campaign against self-aware freedom, let alone love. He is *affektlos*; he has arrived at a state which is a sort of diabolical parody of the *apatheia*, the freedom from compulsive emotion, that was the goal of the ascetic life in classical Orthodox spirituality and monastic practice. Thus he is able, again in a parody of the humility of the saint, to take on the pathetic Marya Timofeevna as a wife, and to accept [part 1, chap. 5, 211] a blow on the face from Shatov without retaliation, although he is known to be, says the narrator, the sort of person who would kill without a second thought when insulted in this way.

In the successive interviews between Stavrogin and his disciples, we see something of the history behind his present relationships: he has experimented with a wide variety of philosophies and at each stage has communicated something of them to his associates—who have taken them a little further, to the point where they are destructive and sterile obsessions. Like Verkhovensky, he has "authored" those around, but the difference is that he has lost interest in the process. His creations are cut adrift from him, as if from a deistic Supreme Being who has abandoned his world. He does not love what he makes; to all his circle, he is an object both of longing and of bitter disappointment, a mystery. Just as with Verkhovensky, we are not generally allowed to follow the processes of his inner life in any serious way. The final episodes of what in retrospect might seem an inexorable journey toward suicide are opaque in the narrative, though, in the chilling conclusion, it is made clear that all the circumstances of the suicide were "evidence of premeditation and consciousness to the last minute" [669]. It is as though his death is the only serious choice he has made in the course of the novel.

There is, of course, one exception to the statement about his thought processes, one that brings with it a number of far-reaching questions, and that is the suppressed chapter, "At Tikhon's," which was designed to follow part 2, chapter 8 ("Ivan the Crown Prince"). This relates Nikolai's conversation with Bishop Tikhon, a conversation that seems to take place at the prompting of Shatov [262], and contains the written confession in which Nikolai describes his seduction of a child who subsequently commits suicide. The text was considered too disturbing for publication in the original serialization, but Dostoevsky made no attempt to restore it in the final published version at any time, and it had to wait until 1922 for publication. It has occasioned controversy ever since. Are we to take the confession as true? Stavrogin has specifically denied to Shatov, though "only after a pause that lasted much too long" [260] that he has abused any children, and one of the issues that arises around the confession during his meeting with Tikhon is what the real goal is of the text he shows the Bishop: is it a deliberate self-abasement by pretending to be guilty of something that is clearly believed about him by many, but is in fact untrue? And what exactly is the role of Tikhon meant to be? Does he offer Stavrogin a genuine way out of his wretchedness; does he understand what is being said, or is he somehow deceived, does he fail Stavrogin at the crucial moment (as Boyce Gibson strongly argued)?[39]

Holquist, for whom the silence of Stavrogin throughout the rest of the novel is very important, argues that Dostoevsky's decision not to reinstate the chapter was prompted by sound narrative and aesthetic considerations, not only by the constraints of censorship. Stavrogin never tells us who he is: "he need not tell us who he is because all the others do it for him,"[40] and so his apparent self-revelation in this chapter is inappropriate.[41] But this misses a couple of important points. Even if it were a breach in Stavrogin's silence, there is dramatic precedent for something similar: scholars have long since observed that in St. Mark's gospel Jesus refuses systematically to declare his divine status (the "messianic secret"), and then breaks this silence with a cataclysmic affirmation at his trial, using the divine name "I am" to reply to the High Priest's questioning. Given the messianic resonances that hang around Stavrogin, this may not be an accidental echo. But perhaps more significantly, we have to ask whether Stavrogin really *does* appear to be different in this chapter. His memoir is a written composition, and is treated precisely as such by Tikhon, who is notably cautious about treating it as a straightforward—let alone a sacramental— confession and probes the degree to which it is a true representation of Nikolai's mind; it retains the ambiguity, the constructed character, of a literary document, even if it does relate things that actually happened. It seems, then, that we should not too readily conclude that it is an aberration; indeed, seeing it as an integral part of Dostoevsky's literary strategy casts light on a number of issues.

Stavrogin tells Tikhon that he is hallucinating, that he is visited by "some kind of malignant creature, mocking and 'rational'" [676]; he is experiencing exactly what Ivan will experience in *Karamazov* ("I don't know which of us is real—me or him" [677]), and is caught in the same dilemma of apparently believing in the Devil when he does not believe in God. Is this possible? Perfectly, Tikhon replies—though he warns Nikolai (as Zosima might have done) against assuming too quickly that what he is meeting is the Devil of popular religion. But he also implies that belief in the Devil without belief in God is equivalent to indifference; it is a state in which the only real "spiritual" emotion is intermittent fear. Is that what Stavrogin is claiming? The answer is obviously no; but neither is Stavrogin at the summit of absolute atheism, "the last rung but one before most absolute faith" [679]. Stavrogin must be on the edge of some major act or disclosure that will free him from the reproach of indifference, so Tikhon intuits.

And what follows is the confession, in which Stavrogin relates his seduction of a small girl, his landlady's daughter, and his complicity in her suicide. The detail is as painful in its way as Ivan's catalogue of atrocities against children, and it also echoes the confessions of Svidrigailov in *Crime and Punishment* and the appalling nightmare he experiences just before his suicide, a nightmare in which he witnesses a fourteen-year-old girl's body being recovered from the river after she has drowned herself (because she has been seduced), and a five year old he has "rescued" from a dark corner in the hotel where he is staying begins to exhibit sexually suggestive behavior to him when he has brought her home. In Stavrogin's account, Matryosha, the little girl (Dostoevsky couldn't make up his mind about her age: in the critical text of the standard edition, Matryosha is first described as about fourteen, but has become ten a few pages later; in the text as initially published, which is the basis for Magarshack's translation, she is in her twelfth year),[42] is routinely beaten and bullied. Stavrogin has already been involved in this himself by contriving that she should be blamed for a theft of which she is innocent. He describes his "ecstatic" delight in the sense of self-humiliation through his contemptible behavior in this and other contexts, and does so in unequivocally erotic terms: he will repeatedly check that he is able to stop, to withdraw, "When I was about to explode, I was able to overcome it entirely before it reached its climax" [685], so that the moment of ecstasy is fully *chosen* (it is not difficult to connect this with the later oblique revelation of his impotence with Lizaveta; when he has run out of effective humiliations in memory and fantasy, an act of will alone is unable to produce orgasm, even with a desired partner). When he looks through a crack in the door of the room in which Matryosha has hanged herself, this is presented as just such an orgastic impulse of self-humiliation. Later, when Matryosha's reproachful figure returns in his dreams, it is triggered by the image of a small, red spider which he gazes at as he decides to view Matryosha's body—an image that emerges initially as "a very small spot" in the landscape of a dream of the Golden Age—just the same dream as is associated with Versilov in *The Adolescent* and with *The Dream of a Ridiculous Man*. His marriage with Marya Timofeevna is presented as a response to his sense of humiliation, a further twist to the construction of a contemptible and shameless persona.

Nikolai is proposing to publish this document as an act of self-abasement. But Tikhon's challenges are complex and nuanced. He approaches the document first as a literary critic (we have been told that his cell contains "works of the stage and of fiction and, perhaps, even something much worse" [673]; he is, in other words, a skilled, not a naïve, reader, and this detail is important), and asks whether there might be some changes in style. Is he actually seeking forgiveness? Because the document suggests that he is inviting from others the same disgust and contempt that he feels for himself, this may be, suggests Tikhon, a sign that he is seeking a reason to resent and hate in return (again a partial foreshadowing of *Karamazov*, when Zosima identifies for Fyodor the delights of feeling ill-used). But even putting aside this question, is he ready to cope not only with the pity of the reader but also with the ridicule of the reader? Has he realized that the whole enterprise of public confession and penance of this kind will make him look not only hateful but foolish? Tikhon has read the ambiguity of the document very carefully indeed: it may be a true confession, in the sense of a confession of actual crimes and in the sense of a true mark of repentance. But it is also a skillfully composed piece of writing; it invites an audience to "look," but in the way that the author tells them [699]: it *creates* the first person who narrates it; it does not simply embody or represent a simple subjectivity. In other words, the confession, even if at some level true, is also a fictional narrative, according to the Bishop. And if it is a fictional narrative, any and every reader has the right to attend to its style and to negotiate, as Tikhon is attempting to do, with whatever kind of power the author is bidding for by his style. This confession of moral guilt is not innocent in a literary sense.

Tikhon reminds Stavrogin that his crime may be terrible, but it is not necessarily extraordinary; Stavrogin has at least recognized its hideous character—but the very way in which he has recognized it and abased himself carries the germ of the desire for it to seem something other than squalid and vulgar [702]. Nikolai insists that what he is seeking is to forgive himself, and that is why he is inviting exceptional suffering. Tikhon responds "rapturously" that, if he believes he can indeed forgive himself, he already believes in God; even the intention to suffer and the hope of reconciliation open the way to Christ's forgiveness. And on this note, Stavrogin makes as if to end the conversation, but the Bishop has not finished. Stavrogin must put aside his urge to publish the text as it stands and invite public ridicule and hatred. Instead, he must put himself under stringent spiritual direction—secretly. If he wants to reach reconciliation, Tikhon says, in effect, he must decide to do it without drama. It is clear by now that Stavrogin is retreating both from his intention to publish the confession and from Tikhon himself, and Tikhon, in a last flash of clairvoyance, sees that the young man will want to commit a fresh outrage to avoid publishing. Stavrogin—who has already been prompted by Fedka and Verkhovensky to contemplate the killing of his wife—reacts with outrage—"You damned psychologist!" [704] (echoing his words to Shatov [261], "You're a psychologist," when Shatov has identified the erotic undertow of Stavrogin's acceptance of humiliation). The interview ends.

What has happened? Boyce Gibson reads it alarmingly straightforwardly: Tikhon (who is a spokesman for unorthodox, "Pelagian" theology in that he supposes Stavrogin's self-forgiveness can trigger divine mercy) has brought Stavrogin to the point of genuine repentance and given him excellent practical advice about his future, but at the last moment fails to restrain his prophetic impulse and "lets the devil slip through."[43] This "disastrous outburst of clairvoyance"[44] pushes the plot further toward catastrophe. But, as the summary above should indicate, this is a serious oversimplification of what is going on. For one thing, Tikhon does not say that forgiving oneself is equivalent to divine forgiveness, but that to believe in the possibility of forgiving oneself is tantamount to believing in God—who does not wait until we *have* forgiven ourselves but steps in to complete the work on the basis simply of our desire: the point is that a genuine belief in the possibility of being at one with oneself on the far side of guilt *presupposes* just that utterly independent dimension of reality which the will alone cannot reach or realize, the dimension finally identified by Stepan Trofimovich as the eternally loving and loveable. It is not that he is encouraging Stavrogin in some kind of moral achievement, rather that he assures him of God's presence when he has let go of the dream of moral achievement in genuine self-forgetfulness. But more importantly, Tikhon has throughout the interview been trying to probe the motivation of Stavrogin's text and to deconstruct its apparently simple structure and rhetoric. It is plain that Stavrogin is increasingly eager to avoid this, even before Tikhon's final outburst.

What Tikhon has done is to question whether real repentance can be achieved in writing. The process of composition and self-presentation, the subtle creation of both self and audience through the text, is at odds with the essence of penitence, which is to dismantle the controlling and creating self and become nothing in the presence of an alien, listening mercy, so as to be recreated. That process has to be enacted, and enacted without theatre, in the intimate confidence of conversation with the "elder" that Tikhon recommends. In fact, Tikhon's challenge is, in the light of all that has been said about the demonic, a direct invitation to refuse once and for all the diabolical work of authorship, especially in the form of autobiography. Stavrogin has been compulsively involved in creating (and abandoning) characters; the confession itself shows him doing the same with the wretched Matryosha and her mother. Now in the rhetoric of the text he has written, he invites those who gather around into another piece of theatre, at the end of which his contempt for other human beings will be reinforced. The confession is a diabolical tool. Tikhon, who admits that his "great fault" is an inability to get close to others [701], is obviously struggling between enthusiasm for what is purportedly a great act of humility and a keen literary suspicion of demonic undertones, and up to the last seems unsure of what is really going on in Nikolai. What matters, though, is the nature of his starkly expressed counsel: don't write, don't publish; change.

He is inviting Stavrogin to begin what he is in fact incapable of, a life of self-committing decision, free of drama and contempt for others. So far from his final "prophetic" moment being a failure, it is the confirmation of what he has been suspecting all along: Stavrogin will not change, nor will he even publish his text. His need for humiliation which he controls himself, his distinctive masochism, will not be satisfied either by the uncontrollability of response to his confession (Tikhon has persuaded him that he cannot count on this being as he has fantasized, that his rhetorical control can never promise immunity from just not being taken seriously) or by the secret ascetical reconstruction of his soul that Tikhon wants to see.

But Stavrogin, as was said earlier, has ceased to choose, and so is fatally vulnerable to Pyotr's exploitative scheming. He cannot surrender what is left of his "authorial" liberty, bound as it is to his masochistic passion: he cannot hold back the longing to make others hate him so that he can hate in return. He does not want *any* positive goal any longer, which is what makes him so ideal an ally for Pyotr. His negative detachment and Pyotr's appetite for destruction and power become the twin poles of the catastrophe that envelops the novel's action from this point on. Left to himself, Nikolai would be a figure of tragic self-destruction, whose effect on others would be (though diminishingly as his energy diminishes) to create obsessive and damaging states of mind. In the hands of Pyotr, he becomes the mythical focus for Pyotr's project to end history, and so an engine of far more serious chaos. The face of the demonic in the novel is finally the two figures bound together, active and passive, devilish will incarnate in a body that is empty of the capacity for real willing.

A good deal has been written about the double echo in Stavrogin's name, diabolical and Christological: the name contains a Russian root meaning "horns," which is clear enough,[45] but the *stavro-* element, for anyone familiar with Church Slavonic adaptations of Greek words, would also evoke the cross. Dostoevsky seems to surround Stavrogin's person with a lavish amount of such irony. He is married to a virginal Marya, who takes him for a prince [283]—but then decides he is

an impostor, not the "falcon" of sacred myth. Pyotr says to him that
he is "my sun" [420]. And of course his acceptance of Shatov's slap in
the face shows, "in veiled but unmistakable semblance,"[46] an image
of Christ-like behavior. At the very least, Stavrogin has about him a
strong flavor of parodic Christology, not wholly unlike Myshkin; it is
even possible, George Steiner famously suggested, that he really does
represent a Dostoevskian dallying with the idea of an incarnation of
the "dark side" of God[47]—a figure who paradoxically represents the
absent God whose silence and inaction are the origin of evil. But it
needs to be said that, if there is anything at all in this speculation, its
force is literary rather than metaphysical. The central fact about Stavrogin remains that he is that strangest of literary phenomena, a vastly
powerful cipher. Ultimately he cannot be the author of any other *life*
(though he can drain away energy from lives by creating the obsessional
relationships in which he specializes), because he has lost the freedom
to choose his own personal destiny—to exercise the one proper kind
of creativity given to human beings.

Stavrogin's confession bears out what Dostoevsky was to underline in
Karamazov: certain kinds of narrative lead into silences. The Devil is
the enemy of real narration—that is, narration with an open future,
with the possibility of future choices, further events; and he cannot
himself give the power to narrate. When his servants or allies, like Stavrogin, attempt this, it collapses on itself. Both frightening and potentially ridiculous, it cannot do what proper fictional narration ought to
(what Dostoevsky assumes it should do)—that is, to present a world in
which readers can understand both their freedom and what their freedom is called toward, the humanity that humanity's actual author has
once and for all imagined. Dostoevsky is not the least agnostic—as a
writer of fiction—about the reality of the Devil. But it is clear that he
believes the Devil can never appear in fiction as a character, any more
than Christ can. The reason, though, is completely opposite to that
for Christ's nonrepresentable nature. The life of Christ is a unique set
of events, which has as a matter of fact altered what can be said about
God and human beings; no fictional representation can be contemporary with that alteration, since all subsequent language is dependent

upon it. But the Devil is associated with no such set of events. The Devil's priority is to prevent historical change and to freeze human agency in the timelessness of a "rational" order in which love or reconciliation is impossible. The Devil can only act, as we have seen, by utilizing the vacuum that opens up when human agents surrender to despair or the cessation of desire. He depends on the dissolution of character and can only be shown in fiction by the narrating of this dissolution into untruth or unreality.

But what does this have to say about the opposite process, the growth of truthfulness or indeed of holiness, which is evidently a matter of concern to Dostoevsky? Are we left only with a kind of negative anthropology, mirroring the negative theology that seeks to identify God by saying what God is not? Some of what we have been discussing in this chapter could be seen as such an anthropology; we have at least been given diagnostic tools for grasping where the enemy is at work. But there already hints of a more direct evocation of what Dostoevsky understood to be the perspective of the divine author. In what follows, we shall be attempting to trace those positive lines more clearly, and the starting point is the same conversation between Tikhon and Stavrogin that we have been following in recent pages.

In his classic study of Dostoevsky's poetics, Bakhtin shows how many of the great set-piece confessions and dialogues in the novels are engines of the action to the degree that they appeal for recognition between one speaker and another or between speaker and hearer, even when their surface intention seems to be to defend speaker against hearer, even to deny recognizability.[48] Thus he connects Ippolit's confession in *The Idiot* ("confession with a loophole, just as [Ippolit's] unsuccessful suicide itself was by its very intent a suicide with a loophole"[49]) and Stavrogin's narrative[50] as examples of apparent monologues that in fact carry multiplicities of discourse within them. Although some critics—Bakhtin instances Leonid Grossman—take the style of Stavrogin's confession to be simply a reflection of the deadened and fragmented subjectivity shown in the crimes related, Bakhtin rightly picks up Tikhon's (literary) critical response to the style of the narration. It is "intensely oriented toward another person, without whom the hero could not manage but whom at the same time he despises and whose judgment he does not accept. . . . Without recognition, and affirmation by another person Stavrogin is incapable of accepting himself, but at the same time he does not want to accept the other's judgment of him."[51] Hence the studiedly impersonal tone of the text, the intensifying of an affectation of heartlessness and cynicism, abrupt and harsh. Where it seems as though some more human note might break in, there are carefully crafted breaks or swervings away from the danger area. Stavrogin is setting out "to speak with his back turned to the listener."[52]

In other words, Stavrogin's confession, so far from being a real monologue, is both a struggle to silence other internal voices and a struggle to reach a listener. It exaggerates the pose of cynicism and self-despising as a preemptive strategy to avoid the listener's facile pity or absolution. A facile reaction would be no use; yet, in anticipating and "budgeting" for such a reaction, the writer already dismisses what might be offered, expecting the worst from the reader. Although Stavrogin accuses Tikhon of a "low opinion" of other people [701], the Bishop simply says that he has to judge by what is in his own soul; it is clear that the low opinion is actually Stavrogin's. Bakhtin contrasts this with Ippolit's confession, which is more obviously a desperate plea to be heard and to be loved; its extreme and offensive episodes are a childlike testing of boundaries, not the calculated invitation to despise that we find in Stavrogin.

In the context of Bakhtin's whole argument, Stavrogin's confession acts as something of a touchstone. Confession reaches out to an imagined listener; but it can only bring absolution—that is, some sort of altered relational world—if it is at some level open to its listener, working for recognition. As we have noted, it is characteristic of diabolical speech to move toward silence, not a listening silence but that of incommunicable self-enclosedness, death. To speak as if the other's response were already known and could be dealt with or circumvented in advance, which is what Nikolai wants to do, is to be condemned to death. He longs for Tikhon to offer him forgiveness on the basis of what he has said, because he has realized that the Bishop will not give a facile answer or a sentimental one; *his* absolution is worth having, at any rate, and perhaps that of a small number of others. But he is confused and partly repelled by Tikhon's reply: "On condition that you forgave me also" [700]. Stavrogin thinks at first that this is a monastic cliché, but Tikhon, anticipating Zosima, insists that it is to do with the fact that every sin alienates each of us from every other. What Stavrogin has done is inseparable from what Tikhon has done in the net of mutual betrayal and violence that destroys human life in common. But this means that each sinner has not only to ask for but to offer mercy to anyone who asks. Stavrogin, if he wants to be forgiven, must take responsibility for absolving others—that is, he must let go of the fantasy of being forgiven only by sensitive and understanding souls like Tikhon and treat the Bishop as if he were like the other readers he has already condemned. If he intends to open up the possibility of forgiving himself by his writing, he must "forgive" his readers, accepting in advance all their crass and inappropriate reactions.

As we shall see in later chapters, this cluster of ideas is central to what Dostoevsky opposes to the demonic mind (and it is, of course, what Stavrogin proves unable to absorb and realize). If we want to trace what it is that constitutes resistance to the Devil, we need next to look in greater depth at Bakhtin's analysis of character in Dostoevsky and at what it assumes in terms of reciprocal responsibility for sustaining what is human over against the demonic campaign to reduce and finally abolish the historical and material—and potentially tragic—fluidity of the created self. It is that fluidity that makes fiction possible, and it is the same fluidity that can be drawn into alliance with the demonic. It is Dostoevsky's aim to show his readers what kind of writing it is that both holds this fluidity without artificial and destructive closure and opens the process of storytelling to some kind of healing convergence on an unconditional absolution, and it is the way he handles dialogue that tells us most about how he moves to fulfill this aim.

3

THE LAST WORD?
Dialogue and Recognition

Stavrogin in his confession is trying to shut out the possibility of a free response from his readers: he does not want to be understood. Hence the chilling detachment, the law-court impersonality of much of what he writes, the stress on his "loathing" for his victim and the defiant ellipses at the two most shocking moments—the seduction itself and the suicide. "I nearly got up and went away. . . . When all was over, she looked embarrassed" [687]; in the current critically established text (not used in Magarshack's version), he adds to the first phrase, "I got over this initial feeling of fear and stayed." This is all there is to say about the first moment, and the second is even more marked: he has watched Matryosha going in to the little upstairs room where she will hang herself, and he waits for some twenty minutes; then he goes up the stairs, stands outside the door, and he says, "I looked through the chink a long time, for it was very dark, but not so dark as to prevent me at last from seeing what I wanted. . . . At last I decided to leave" [692]. As Tikhon discerns, Stavrogin is not disclosing any secrets here but refusing disclosure, refusing to be a subject who is vulnerable to both understanding and misunderstanding. Of course, he gives himself away in numerous other respects, but at the crucial moments he determinedly writes as if all that can be said is a description of where he physically was; in both cases, he speaks of "staying" and "leaving" while something happens, as if he is simply witnessing events in which he is not implicated at all. The only discernible emotional coloring is

III

the resolve to overcome any hesitation about knowing what there is to know: but "what there is to know" is a set of facts external to his will.

Two things are going on. The first is the actual strategy in the writing, the alienation that is plainly intended in regard to the potential reader. But the second is the portrayal of a particular model of the self and its acts which is systematically dismantled and rejected throughout Dostoevsky's fiction. Bakhtin notes[1] that he effectively denies an "ideological approach" in which there are "separate thoughts, assertions, propositions that can by themselves be true or untrue, depending on their relationship to the subject and independent of the carrier to whom they belong." There is no "view from nowhere" in his writing; every perception is already "voiced," already associated with "the position of a personality"; hence the style of his journalistic discussions, with their constant invoking of other possible speakers—"I hear someone saying . . . ," "It will be objected . . . ," and so on. He does not write about a unified object-world or a unified system of ideas, but invites the reader to take up this or that position and see what can be seen from there. And in this light, what Stavrogin is doing in his confession is attempting to foreclose any point of view other than that of the inactive observer, himself. These things happened; that is all that can be said about them.[2]

Hence, as Bakhtin goes on to say, the writing itself cannot offer resolutions in an authorial voice; if there is any resolution, it must come through a voice within the narrative leading other voices to some kind of convergence. As Dostoevsky wrote to Pobedonostsev about *Karamazov*, an erroneous world-view cannot be corrected in fiction by argued refutation but only by a "picture"—the picture of a human form around which the conflict and tension of other relationships comes to a point of stability or equilibrium. "The image of the ideal human being or the image of Christ represents for [Dostoevsky] the resolution of ideological quests . . . the image of a human being and his voice, a voice not the author's own."[3] If there is a form of life that can persuade others toward reconciliation with each other and the world, that is what writing in faith has to exhibit. And, as Dostoevsky discovered in the writing of *The Idiot*, this is a far less straightforward exercise than at first might appear—precisely because of the underlying conviction that any human form of life is capable of drawing out diverse response. There is no manifest and unchallengeable last word in the processes of human exchange. But the point remains important. If the demonic is at work, it will not be answered by argument; indeed, to attempt this is to do just what the Devil wants, to conduct the encounter on impersonal grounds. It is only in a specific voice and a personal presence that a reply can be made.

So for Dostoevsky, in Bakhtin's reading, narrative is argument and argument is narrative. The only way in which we are to move toward a sustainable truth, a truth that is more than either a private ideology or a neutral description, is by being immersed in the interaction of personal agents and speakers. We as readers are being engaged by the open-ended narrative of persons in dialogue, invited to continue the dialogue when we have stopped reading, because we are like the characters we have been listening to, we are agents who are formed by the exchange of words. The actual currency of history is language: to speak, as we have done in previous chapters, about the affirmation of history is to speak about the affirmation of language. And if the Devil's aim is silence, God's is speech, the dialogic speech by which we shape each other.

Retracing our steps for a moment, we may recall that the Underground Man's protests against determinism are, among other things, a way of saying that facts do not dictate speech: freedom is exhibited in language itself, and very notably—as we have seen—in the language of narrative fiction. As Stewart Sutherland points out in a seminal essay on the philosophical resonances of self and freedom in Dostoevsky,[4] human agency is distinct because speech makes a difference to it: if a person is told that he is predetermined to act in such and such a way, the act of communication itself makes it possible for him to act otherwise, and serious philosophical dilemmas appear if you try to state a consistent determinist case while giving full weight to this awkward fact. Freedom is inseparably bound up with our nature as linguistic creatures: to say something is potentially to change what another sees as obvious, rational, possible and so on. To speak to someone is to alter his world. And so a narrative about persons is a record of what they say to each other (explicitly and implicitly), how their worlds impinge. Narrative becomes a story of the testing of options and positions by being brought into proximity; in the

presence and under the impact of this position, how does that one survive? What changes and what doesn't in the encounter between this
voice and that? It is this which Bakhtin sees as characteristic of "Menippean" drama in antiquity, incorporating satirical and carnivalesque
elements as it traced the journeys of its characters through complex
plots and extraordinary situations (including dramatically socially varied settings, so that the aristocrat or sage is placed in a low-life context as part of his testing), using extreme states of mind as a tool for
articulating the fragmentation of the characters.[5] Menippean drama
or narrative portrays a hero who is not at one with himself and who
has to be brought to such reconciliation as is possible only by a series
of wildly contingent and often bizarre encounters: Apuleius' *Golden Ass*
is a classic example. In short, the Menippea is an unmistakable statement of dialogue as the medium for the formation of persons and thus
of language itself as the embodiment of freedom.

Central to the genre is what Bakhtin calls "provocation through
discourse or plot situation"[6]; and he notes that the gospels and early
Christian literature represent a triumph for the menippean mode in
their absorption with dreams, extreme situations (martyrdom), meetings of socially diverse characters and testing of positions through
contest and challenge. Underlying all this is the assumption that the
speaking and acting self is not a finished thing; it is not transparent to
itself, let alone anyone else, and its unity and intelligibility has to be
constructed over time. Indeed, as we have seen already, there has to
be a sense in which such unity and intelligibility is never a completed
task, and it is the function of good narrative to make clear that level of
openness. In Dostoevsky's major works, it is *Crime and Punishment* that
most baldly expresses this, with its concluding assurance that the rest
of Raskolnikov's story remains to be told. Contrary to what a superficial reader might think, *Crime and Punishment* does not end with an
unambiguous statement of Raskolnikov's repentance and conversion:
he is still on the threshold of anything like recognizable Christian
faith, and, despite the confidence of Boyce Gibson[7] and some others,
exactly what lies ahead for Raskolnikov and Sonya is not completely
clear. The same uncertainty holds, in a far more obvious way, for Alyosha Karamazov—and to some degree this would have been so even if
Dostoevsky had lived to complete a further stage of the narrative.

There is always more to be said; and this can be, as we have seen it to be in some contexts, something like a diabolical curse, trapping the mind in self-referentiality, or it can be the promise of unimagined futures which could bring renewal. Which it is to be depends upon the degree of genuine openness that exists in the first place—upon the level of risk and trust involved in the exchange which allows real growth to occur. The narrative voice of *Crime and Punishment* begins by creating a self almost impervious to the world of others and the process it traces is not so much that of a simple religious or moral conversion but a movement toward being able to hear and to speak. There is no Dostoevskian hero into whose mind we have such direct insight as Raskolnikov: the book seldom allows us much of a break from the stream of his consciousness—which is also why the reader will remain confused about the exact motive for Raskolnikov's murder of Alyona. There is always more to be said; in this instance, what that means is that Raskolnikov can never himself settle the real nature of his obsessional fantasizing about murder. It is variously presented as an exercise in transcending ethics, appropriate to a superior (Napoleonic) kind of human being, as a practical measure to secure the finances for a future befitting a genius and benefactor of humanity, as an attempt to spare Raskolnikov's family the burden of supporting him, and in the scene where Raskolnikov at last admits his guilt to Sonya, it is a thoroughly muddled appeal to diabolic temptation, even diabolical responsibility for the murder (the person he has killed is himself and "It was the Devil who killed her, not I . . ." [501]). The murder was the result of wanting to know whether he had the "right" to act as if he were not subject to ordinary laws; the question comes from the Devil, who subsequently shows him that he does not have that right "because I am just a louse like everyone else" [500]. The trouble with this is, of course, that it begs the question about whether anyone has such a right. And it leaves Raskolnikov with a very odd sort of penitence indeed which at times seems to amount to regret that he has not shown himself worthy of the great act of ethical transcendence that a truly superior spirit might have performed (presumably by such a murder). He repents a loss of nerve or a failure to rise to the appropriate heights. At least he can now show his strength by voluntarily confessing and bearing the punishment which society has a right to exact.

Right up to the final episodes in the prison camp, he is still in this self-referential prison. As Wasiolek writes, "Raskolnikov can keep alive the conception of himself as 'superior,' as long as he can keep alive an image of society that prevents him from being superior."[8] His longing is for an identity and a significance that do not have to be negotiated or achieved, and—as for some of those we have been considering in the later novels—the naked exercise of will is mistaken for the sign of this identity. As is evident in various references to his sensitivity and generosity, Raskolnikov's "failure" is actually a mark of the many aspects of his character that are profoundly at odds with this fiction about the will. He has not, in fact, committed an *arbitrary* crime, and the killing of Alyona's sister Lizaveta is an act of sheer self-protective panic, in its way more shocking than the murder of Alyona. But it is just this self-protective violence that gives away to the reader something of the root of the problem: to return to Sutherland's discussion mentioned above, the point is that someone who has lost the capacity to hear and speak, to engage humanly with others and to change in response, is already potentially a murderer.[9] The crime comes out of the intensity of an inner dialogue that is practically never interrupted by a real other.

At first sight, this seems to be the opposite of what Bakhtin has to say about Raskolnikov's private world: "His inner speech is constructed like a succession of living and impassioned replies to all the words of others he has heard or has been touched by."[10] But this is to miss the significance of that alchemy by which the words of others are transmuted into an unbroken interior monologue, which is why Bakhtin goes on to note that all the individuals in Raskolnikov's world become symbols or types, in whose specificity he has no interest. All become moments or positions in his interior world: he is, in fact, another example of the "demonic narrator" we have already encountered, for whom there are no true others. And the paradox toward which Dostoevsky points us is that what Raskolnikov sees as an almost unbroken transparency to himself is in fact a systematic flight from reality, his and everyone else's. The boundaries between dream and reality blur, his memory plays bizarre tricks, the actual fabric of the physical world becomes deceptive and fragile. It has been well observed that Dostoevsky does not do landscapes (except with the heavy ironies attached to the landscapes of his "Golden Age" passages); description of the material setting for his scenes is charged with the emotional and spiritual state of his characters.[11] In *Crime and Punishment*, the Petersburg weather and landscape works as a correlative of Raskolnikov's mind, with repeated reference to the summer haze and dust that give the landscape a somewhat dreamlike character; even when the view is clear, it can turn out to be obscurely menacing.[12] The way in which the "outside" world is spoken of becomes part of the process by which the great project of self-affirmation is uncovered as an unconscious amputation of self from world: transparency to yourself is not to be attained by introspection if what is "inside" is so hazy and unreal.

This brings us to a major theme in Dostoevsky's understanding of human maturation and its opposite, which can be summed up briefly as the supreme importance of *visibility* for human flourishing. All those characters in his major work who are crippled by antihuman forces inside and outside them are imperfectly visible, and those who are on the path to some sort of healing are those who take the risks of being seen. In all the major novels, we are presented at significant points with characters revealing or trying to reveal or importantly failing to reveal who they are, with confessions, monologues, and autobiographies of varying success and intelligibility. Raskolnikov's final confession of his guilt is only an outward manifestation of the failed exercise in self-knowledge that makes up the greater part of the book as we are admitted again and again to his obsessed consciousness; but we also have the lesser self-revelations of Sonya and of Svidrigailov. In *The Idiot*, Myshkin describes quite lengthy episodes in the past (the Swiss idyll with Marie and the children) and Ippolit attempts a monumental, rambling self-justification prior to his threatened suicide. Stavrogin's confession has already been examined in depth, but it is not quite alone in the novel: as we have seen, Shatov and Kirillov are given extensive "confessional" opportunities. And in *Karamazov*, the Inquisitor fable is only part of a lengthy and complex apologia on Ivan's part—balanced (or so Dostoevsky intended) by the recollections of Father Zosima. All are seeking to manage the business of becoming recognizable to others; they bring their self-descriptions into dialogue—or, in Stavrogin's case, offer a self-description calculated to forestall dialogue. And this alerts us to the various ways in which the pathologies of the novels' characters can be traced to an inability or unwillingness to become visible.

We can see this at work in the very early novella, *The Double*, an exercise rather in the manner of Gogol which Dostoevsky did not repeat but from which he learned a good deal. The foolish and apparently self-satisfied government clerk, Golyadkin, somehow "generates" a double, a "Golyadkin junior," who resembles him exactly and increasingly threatens his personal and professional life until he is finally committed to a mental institution. The entire story is told as through Golyadkin's eyes; we have no way of "knowing" whether what is being narrated is a fantastic Gogolian fable or an oblique account of a mental breakdown. Nor does it matter. The story is about the fear of losing control of how one is seen. At various points [e.g., 212, 230] Golyadkin panics about what will happen if his double does something disgraceful that will be attributed to himself, and this is clearly an anxiety quite fundamental to the story. Since he is constantly talking to himself— that is how most of the story is told—the appearance of the Double is at one level not surprising. Golyadkin manages his anxiety by a stream of would-be reassuring discourse addressed to his shrinking and fearful self; but the strategy is not working. The anxiety escapes and takes physical shape. It becomes a literally uncontrollable other, out in the world. The splitting process has something to do with an experience of more than usually painful humiliation after which "The inner conflict is dramatized"[13] and the Double appears—first, it seems, as another unstable and anxious voice, then increasingly and frighteningly as the one who possesses all the confidence that Golyadkin senior lacks, patronizing and undermining him.

Golyadkin's anxiety about making himself visible, about emerging as a vulnerable speaker on the stage of ordinary human interaction, is the source of the "doubling," comic and tragically pathological at once, that finally takes him offstage for good. He cannot find a voice that is actually his own; his rapid, inconsequential inner conversations reflect a desperate effort to find assurance that he is "all right" [132]. "This question is always answered from the possible and presumed point of view of another person. . . . It is in the reaction of the other person . . . that the whole matter lies."[14] But Golyadkin cannot produce by his inner pseudo-dialogues a genuinely *other* voice that can give him what he needs; ultimately he can only produce a solidified form of his anxiety. And the implication of this is that to find a voice of one's own there have to be truly other voices allowed in. This is why Golyadkin's small-scale obsessions and anxieties pave the way for Raskolnikov, who is similarly presented to us in terms of his restless, nonstop inner to-ings and fro-ings, and can only assert and assure himself in an act that decisively cuts him off from ordinary human discourse, as decisively as Golyadkin's madness. As Sutherland says, murder such as Raskolnikov commits is "*prima facie* evidence for mental illness. To set at naught *all* respect for human life is to set oneself apart from fellow human beings in the most radical way possible."[15] And Raskolnikov's move toward the relative sanity of admitting his guilt is very significantly pushed forward by Sonya's presentation to him of the supremely "other" voice, that of God, as she reads the story of the raising of Lazarus from the dead. Raskolnikov's state is effectively death; and the significance of Christ's command to Lazarus, "Come *forth*!" is obvious.

Between Golyadkin and Raskolnikov comes the Underground Man, determined not to "come forth," to become visible, but equally not quite trapped in the way the others are. He has moments of Goly-adkin-like absurdity and anxiety (the episode with his friends), but his self-examinations are also somehow unsparingly truthful. He is able to see himself as the mirror of a wider human reality, to recognize both that he will appear absurd and unlikable *and* that these responses are in fact responses to what others find disturbing and unacceptable in themselves. His misanthropic savagery and malice—he genuinely *is* an unpleasant person—arise from the consciousness that he is articulat-ing honestly what others will not own. He may be "invisible," but he is there to remind his readers or listeners that he is making visible the aspects which they (deliberately or not) are concealing. Like so many others in Dostoevsky's fictions, he is a displaced novelist, an author who makes up characters. As he says—and as he literally demonstrates in his constant inner dialogues—he has made up the responses of his readers: we are his characters [44]. He knows us because he has made us, in a parody of God's loving providence. We cannot escape him, as he gleefully reminds us more than once [e.g., 25, 42–43]; he has seen through us because he is us. What we think we can deny he knows we can't. In other words, unlike Golyadkin and Raskolnikov, who have retreated into the doomed enterprise of a self-sufficient inner world, he is making a very serious bid indeed for recognition by others in what he says. He is not looking for assurance, but for the acknowledgment that he is speaking the language we (really and internally) speak but are ashamed of.

The second part of *Notes from the Underground* is something like an enacted parable of the condition we share with the Underground Man, as he savagely reminds us at the end of the anecdote (he has only done openly and exaggeratedly what we are all involved in). If our state is truly as he has depicted it, a constant exercise in denial of our feebleness, vanity and confusion, as well as a constant evasion of our real freedom, how could we ever sincerely love or accept love? His sadistic mockery of the prostitute Liza, his hatred and fury toward her because he has let her see something of his vulnerability and his despair of being "good" or loving, and his refusal of the acceptance she tentatively offers him [112–20] are once again defiant challenges to the reader; can we deny that we know what he is talking about? (It is, incidentally, not an accident that Alyosha Karamazov, talking both with Ivan and with Lise Khokhlakova, admits that he recognizes and shares their negative or blasphemous impulses; if he were confronted with the Underground Man, he would accept the latter's implied challenge to confess and acknowledge his solidarity in shame.) The Underground Man is not—as he is sometimes taken to be by critics—simply a representation of moral distortion, even of linguistic pathology. On the contrary, he is a figure whose purpose is to reveal the nature of our language and our investment in language and our moral constitution in language. As we have seen, he lets us know that what we say is not the inevitable effect of what we perceive as given in the world around us, even in science and mathematics; we are free to be perverse. He lets us know that what we say to or of ourselves is constantly liable to turn into self-protective fiction. He lets us know that if we do not speak and listen openly to one another, we have no intelligible life, no authentic presence to ourselves—no way out, that is, from the self-imprisonment of a Golyadkin or a Raskolnikov. His own admitted failures, the minor and not-so-minor atrocities he is guilty of in his social encounters, are presented without mercy to make the point that we are addicted to self-constructed images of who we are to such a degree that we cripple ourselves in the actual business of encounter with material, intelligent others.

The Underground Man "knows all the possible refractions of his image" in the mirror of his reader's consciousness,[16] and he knows that he can always *say more.* He remains free to reply, privately or publicly, to any address that claims to define and so to silence him. "His consciousness of self lives by its unfinalizability."[17] But the further point that Bakhtin does not quite make here is that the liberty of the Underground Man to say more is his liberty to invite, even compel the reader to do the same, and to recognize that there are elements of self-recognition that have not yet been drawn out in the reader's own discourse. It is not only the saints in Dostoevsky who prompt self-revelation. Here it is a highly self-conscious sinner. What sets him apart from the demonic voices of later figures is simply that he has no interest at all in ending history or silencing others; he is still speaking, and, if he (like Stavrogin) anticipates hostile and condemnatory responses, he is ready (unlike Stavrogin) with a human reply.

So these earlier Dostoevskian texts have a good deal to say about why Stavrogin's confession works to show us what "diabolical" or "possessed" communication can be. There are those whose speech is in fact incapable of "saying more." When others respond, that response is instantly factored into what is already there. Thus Golyadkin and Raskolnikov repeatedly and as it were automatically de-realize the others in their environment—dramatically so in the case of Raskolnikov's crimes. But they are neither of them setting out to isolate themselves; both are brought to realize in different ways that they have been trapped, lured into monumental error and self-deceit. For both, a kind of insanity is the effect of this, but neither is presented as a damned soul. However, if their isolation had been willed and conscious, if the de-realizing of others had been fully recognized and consented to, this would alter the picture. Stavrogin stands at the point where he can either take the risk of accepting the uncontrollable reaction of others, including both absolution and mockery from those he does not respect, or retreat into the refusal of discourse and change that his rhetoric already threatens. In choosing the latter, he establishes his fate: his history is ended, and his suicide is virtually inevitable. Perhaps, like the Underground Man, he needs to be more pettily and humanly angry before he can be reconciled to the alarming freedoms exhibited in the speech of real human others.

☗   ☗   ☗

In the "Revolutionary Catechism" of Nechaev, the opportunist radical who was part of Dostoevsky's inspiration for the character of Pyotr in *Devils*, we are told that the true revolutionary "has no name."[18] And it is a central element in Dostoevsky's portrait of the diabolical character that such a person avoids being identified, bound to a history or a project or a set of relationships. Pyotr is in this sense a character in flight from visibility. We have already noted the very overt diabolical elements in the description of him on his first appearance; and Leatherbarrow, in his discussion of this episode,[19] draws attention to one particular feature of the description which not every translation captures. There is an abundance of "sort of" and "as it were" elements, signaled by the Russian *kak*; it is as though his very physical presence is ambiguous and deceptive, not quite there, in keeping with his rapid but not particularly purposive movement: "He walked and moved about very hurriedly, but he was in no hurry to go anywhere" [189–90]. From the beginning, in other words, we are warned that he is someone avoiding and frustrating the observation of others. When he is galvanizing the comically dysfunctional radical group in the direction of violence, he at the same time slips away from personal engagement, emotion, unguarded reaction. It is completely in character that he (like Stavrogin) simply ignores the question about whether he will himself promise not to inform against the group after he has extracted commitments from everyone else [413]. He meets suspicion or resistance with aggressive counterattack, and when questions arise he will evade them by opening up new avenues of anxiety that weld the group together under his direction [part 3, chap. 4]. As he disappears from the novel, ensconced in a first-class railway carriage, he leaves his faithful and naïve lieutenant, Erkel, bemused and depressed at what seems to be yet another incomprehensible stratagem [624].

He "has no name"; despite his roots in the town where the action takes place, he has spent practically all his life somewhere else, without proper parenting or education. He belongs nowhere, and the constant illusion he creates around him, the atmosphere of conspiracy and hidden significance, is one way of hiding, suggesting that, wherever he is, his "real" life is elsewhere.[20] On one of the rare occasions when we hear him speaking with something like a human voice, his conversation with Stavrogin in part 2 chapter 8, he declares his love for "beauty," even in the form of idols [420]. Beauty is for him, it seems, simply a matter of compelling surface attraction: Stavrogin is "beautiful" to him because of the fascinating mysteriousness of a man who cares nothing for his life or anyone else's. Beauty, we might say, is redefined as glamour, in its old sense of a dangerous magical aura. It is not something which calls or interrupts or requires self-disclosure and self-scrutiny. Those who rather glibly quote Dostoevsky as believing that "beauty will save the world" (as in the notebooks for *The Idiot*, the phrase being then ascribed—tellingly—to Myshkin himself [613]) have not always taken on board passages like this one in which he provides the case for the prosecution, showing how useless such a slogan is in the abstract. It is possible to have, like Pyotr, a concept of beauty which amounts to nothing more than what fascinates and serves particular needs. An aesthetic like this is another mechanism for evasion and absence.

But there is one other moment where we come, fleetingly, somewhere near a human response in Pyotr, and this is the chilling episode of Kirillov's suicide. After their final, heavily charged conversation and Kirillov's savagely sardonic drafting of his suicide note, Pyotr is left alone while Kirillov goes into the next room with his gun. His anxiety mounts as there is no sound of a shot, and eventually he too goes in to the neighboring room. What follows is one of Dostoevsky's most memorably "filmic" scenes, a Gothic nightmare. Kirillov is pressed tightly against the wall, motionless and silent; Pyotr brings his candle up to Kirillov's face, and Kirillov suddenly knocks it to the floor, seizes Pyotr's hand and bites his little finger. Then, after bellowing *seichas, seichas* ("now, now!") ten times, he shoots himself [620].

Even Pyotr takes a while to recover his normal equilibrium after this. Why the assault and the bite? Somewhere in the background is the folkloric motif that invisible creatures can be made visible if you succeed in grasping hold of them. And more directly, it is as though Kirillov is forcing Pyotr into connection with his own body by inflicting acute pain. Bitten and wounded fingers, as we have seen, occur in *Karamazov* with a rather similar meaning; whether we should think in terms of some kind of sexual significance is no more clear than in Alyosha's case, but it is not impossible. For a moment, Pyotr is indeed painfully incarnate (perhaps given a sexual identity through the assault on a symbolic and otherwise invisible penis), as he is not anywhere else in the novel. And with this unwelcome incarnation come ordinary emotions of physical anguish and fear. Pyotr has been fleetingly but effectively nailed down to a time and place, to a body. Of course, he recovers with astonishing speed, and no one (except the implausibly omniscient local narrator of the novel) will ever know that his mask slipped; in the final scene of his farewell, his "bad finger" is "elegantly bound in black silk" [622], a reminder that he is not invulnerable. But he is about to vanish again, and there is not the least indication that what has happened has drawn out a lasting response.

So Stavrogin and Pyotr alike, though in dramatically different ways, are seeking invisibility, seeking to be beyond the scope of any other's gaze. It is a mark of their inhumanity. But as we have noted, there are other sorts of inhumanity: if Myshkin—whom we have already seen to be comparable in various ways with the two "demons" of the later novel—is also not quite human, can we see in him too the same flight from visibility? Certainly, he is not consciously in search of a strategy for concealment, let alone invulnerability; at first sight, he is apparently a deeply vulnerable person. When he is slapped in the face by Ganya, there is no fear that he will react as everyone expects Stavrogin to react when struck by Shatov: his first thought is how deeply humiliating *Ganya* will find the memory of this act. Yet there is evidently something amiss. We do not witness his mental processes except in the important episode when he returns to Petersburg and to Nastasya after promising Rogozhin that he will not do this [part 2, chap. 5]: here he is presented to us as the prisoner of an obsessive state, like Raskolnikov, and the parallel is not an idle one. He cannot own any desire in the public realm of speech and negotiation. What he has said to Rogozhin and what effect his return may have are overtaken by a compulsion which he has no words or resources to examine, no way of opening up to language. And throughout the novel, the utter opacity of his motivation continues to confuse and frustrate. What began as a charming and rather comically naïve clumsiness in picking up the "feel" of those around him—as in the rambling anecdotes with which he entertains the Yepanchins in the early scenes—gradually mutates into a passivity or indeterminacy that seems like a mirror of Stavrogin's—not deliberate, not consciously malign or even indifferent, simply unconscious, but with the same effect of drawing others into a void and thus pushing their destinies out of shape, often lethally so.

The hint—mentioned earlier—of an assimilation of Myshkin to the Holbein image of the dead Christ may be borne out by this. Remember that the Christ figure is in profile: so too Myshkin never seems to turn full-face to his interlocutors, despite the appearance of utter transparency. It is no accident, in this connection, that Aglaya and her sisters assimilate him to the "Poor Knight" of Pushkin's poem, whose face is hidden by his visor; there can be no portrait of him [289–95]. In his heart he carries an image of his beloved, which will always be unaffected by any real change in the lady—"it was enough that he chose her and believed in her 'pure beauty'" [291]. Myshkin is teasingly discussed by Kolya and the young ladies as a possible model for a drawing of the knight; it is a very revealing paradox, the idea that he is an appropriate model for someone whose face cannot be seen (not to mention the sidelong reference to a love that is indifferent to what actually happens to its object, or, more accurately, which prefers the image of the beloved to the reality). To be visible, you need a history, a set of differentiated memories defining a position within human affairs. Myshkin is described[21] as not wanting to confront what is going on in his mind and feelings, and it is hard to avoid the conclusion that he has no equipment for making that kind of sense, and so for presenting himself in relation to the conversation of others. If Stavrogin ends in deadly isolation because of his determination to control his self-presentation so tightly as to foreclose human response to what he says, Myshkin ends in the same condition because he has *no* control over his self-presentation. And the very paradoxical outcome is that this, which one might think ought to leave him "exposed," leaves him in fact unrecognizable—invisible in the sense of not being there to be made sense of by and with others.

This, incidentally, is why it is important not to misunderstand Evdokimov's remark about the holy figures in the novels as "faces on the wall," like icons in the Orthodox church or household. An icon comes with a narrative—literally a history of the prescribed disciplines that have gone into the process of its painting, more broadly a history of the person or feast depicted. It invites an engagement with both the spiritual practice and the event or individual shown. And Dostoevsky's "iconic" figures, particularly the two monastic elders, Tikhon and Zosima, insist on being "seen"; they may not be major agents in the plot as we should normally understand it,[22] but they both choose strategies of vulnerability in their communication—Tikhon by his admission of weakness and insensitivity and his request for Stavrogin's forgiveness, Zosima by his prostration to Dmitri Karamazov and his autobiographical reflections. Holding an iconic role in this context—and Evdokimov has pinpointed a significant theme—does not mean passivity.

Thus it is possible to read *Karamazov* as narrating the processes by which each of the brothers emerges into "visibility"; each puts at risk his own control over how he is seen and responded to, so as to be remade. This is clearest in the case of Alyosha as he comes out from the monastery and quite literally becomes visible in a new mode. Lise, who has made fun of his monastic cassock when they meet at Zosima's, tells him what he should wear when he leaves the community [255], and when we meet him in part 4, chapter 4, sure enough, he has "greatly changed since the time we left him" [681], having assumed ordinary lay dress, indeed, rather fashionable lay dress if we are to believe Mrs Khokhlakova [732]. It is a small touch in the portrait, but not an unimportant one. The cassock to some extent prescribes what can be said about him and how people will react to him; now he is open to what others say without this automatic defense. Just as Lise tries to create a new character for him by prescribing a new wardrobe (an unsettling echo of Varvara and Stepan Trofimovich), so others will now be more free to say what they please about him, to make of him what they want. He has relinquished one kind of power and taken a further step into the open exchange of human discourse.

Ivan's story is more complex and less resolved. We meet him first as someone who—a little like Stavrogin—speaks obliquely through the variety of positions which he argues almost for the sake of arguing, although each of them represents a real insight to which he is wedded. His article on the church courts which is discussed at the monastery is not simply an abstract exercise: Ivan is following through an understanding of what the Church genuinely is which is far from trivial. If the Church is what it claims to be, then, for Ivan, this is what it should be arguing; otherwise it becomes another political group struggling for ordinary political power (the Western Catholic error as Ivan—and

Myshkin, and Dostoevsky—saw it). Likewise, we cannot quite tell what the nature of Ivan's commitment is in the Inquisitor fable. Alyosha is right to suspect that it is in praise of Jesus at least as much as otherwise [339], and Ivan hastens to deny that he is somehow supporting the Inquisitor: "Why are you taking it so seriously?" [342] In short, Ivan seems to be someone who wants to slip away from owning the words he speaks, so as to remain hidden, free from what he has said. "For the moment that is what you are doing: amusing yourself with your despair—in articles for journals and in worldly disputations, yourself not believing in your own dialectics and with pain in your heart smiling skeptically at them to yourself," says Zosima to him [95]. And in the series of extraordinarily crafted conversations with Smerdyakov (beginning with book 5, chaps. 6 and 7 and culminating in the three encounters in book 11), this obliqueness becomes as destructive as it is in *Devils*. Smerdyakov hears what Ivan has said and wants to know, straightforwardly, if he means it, if he really is saying that "everything is permitted." He imitates Ivan's indirect speech, so that he is able to signal clearly (or so he thinks) to Ivan that Fyodor's murder is planned and to believe that Ivan has given him the nod by agreeing to go to Chermashnya (so as to have an alibi but not be too far away when the catastrophe happens). The three final conversations between Ivan and Smerdyakov show an increasingly horrified and confused Ivan realizing that Smerdyakov is not speaking only about Ivan's silent complicity (about which Ivan is himself agonizingly uncertain) but about Ivan as the inspirer of the act itself. "I was only your minion . . . and fulfilled that task in compliance with your instructions" [796].

Vladimir Kantor, in an important article on the relation between Ivan and Smerdyakov,[23] insists, rightly, that the reader should not accept Smerdyakov's version of events. The servant, like others in the novel, fails to hear what Kantor calls the "subjunctiveness" of Ivan's utterances, the "one *might* say" register of so much of Ivan's discourse. "It is this absence of self-definition in Ivan that leads to the tragedy."[24] This is completely correct as far as it goes, but what needs to be added is that the lack of self-definition in Ivan is inseparable from his desire to preserve a degree of hiddenness to his persona. He fails to enter the dialogical world; his nightmare meetings with the Devil show that he is moving, inexorably it would seem, toward the position of Golyadkin and Raskolnikov. He can no longer sustain the tension of an inner fugue of utterance and response, a dialogue that can never break out of the individual mind, position and counter-position, and so has set out on the process of "splitting" that leads to collapse, as we have seen with Golyadkin.

But Ivan is a far more serious and mature figure in every way than Golyadkin (or Raskolnikov), and the confrontation with the unintended effects of his oblique and self-isolating rhetoric shocks him into his decision to give evidence at his brother's trial, evidence that will expose him to opprobrium and perhaps legal charges. Although he then breaks down dramatically in court after saying that Smerdyakov murdered Fyodor, "and I put him up to it" [807], so that his evidence is not taken seriously, he has in fact exposed his soul—and those of others. "Who does not desire the death of his father?" [807]. Like the Underground Man, he has entered the human conversation to expose what *others* want to keep hidden, and what he says cannot be heard. But it is, at last, and in a deeply challenging way, what I have called a bid for recognition. His admission of responsibility for what he has said, his ownership of his own speech in the public context, is a movement away from the diabolical that has virtually captured him. Appropriately enough, we do not learn his final fate.

And to mention responsibility here—a theme to which we shall be returning—is to understand also what is happening to Mitya Karamazov in the dénouement of the novel. Mitya has not been presented as an evasive character or as one preoccupied with defending an image of himself. On the contrary, he is to all appearances self-indulgent and unreflective; he acts from unexamined passion and acquisitiveness. When he talks to Alyosha [book 3, chap. 3] about his love for the earth (commentators have made much of the echo of the earth goddess's name, Demeter, in Mitya's name, and have noted the references to Ceres, the same goddess's Latin name, in the poem he quotes in this chapter), he offers a statement of faith that is curiously parallel to what we have encountered in other contexts as the ecstatic and timeless vision of the epileptic: at the moment of self-abandonment in debauchery, there is also a "fall" into the depths of nature itself that is, Mitya implies (with a sidelong reference to Goethe), something akin to kissing the earth—that recurrent Dostoevskian symbol. "I may be cursed,

I may be base and vile, but I too shall kiss the hem of the robe in which my God enwraps Himself" [144]. He senses in such moments the joy that is the hidden pulse of the world. Yet at the same time he is keenly aware that the beauty that draws him, especially in erotic encounters, is ambiguous, "a terrifying and a horrible thing" [144], capable of attracting people equally to "the ideal of the Madonna and . . . the ideal of Sodom" [145]. The human heart, battlefield for God and Satan, is "too broad" for comfort. In other words, Dmitri is as reluctant as Ivan to "stake" himself in an act through which he becomes answerable: his strategy for meaningful action is an amoral ecstasy, trusting to find God at the end of any self-abandoning response to beauty.

But in prison a major change occurs. Prompted in part by the dream immediately after his arrest in which he sees a landscape of burned houses, homeless peasants and a crying baby [648–50], he has become aware of a world of utterly pointless suffering, and, he says, "a new man has been resurrected within me" [756]. What his own undeserved arrest has made possible for him is the recognition of an identity hitherto hidden: "He was imprisoned within me, but he would never have appeared, had it not been for this lightning bolt" [756]. And this new man—whose face, Dmitry insists, can be uncovered in the most debased criminal—is fundamentally one who will willingly assume responsibility "for all" ("I shall go for all, for it is necessary that someone shall go for them" [756]). In the "underground" environment of prison, God is needed more than ever, and his praise will sound: it is enough to know that God is. Without this, there is no one to be thanked and loved, no possibility of loving humanity [757–58]; the themes are those touched on by Ivan much earlier—not to mention the brief echo of Stepan Trofimovich's discovery of God as that which can be eternally loved. Once again, as with Ivan, exactly what will happen is left open. Can Dmitry bear the weight of vicarious suffering he has accepted? Alyosha himself is unconvinced [969–70], and Katerina is contemptuous of the whole notion [964–65]. But Alyosha also insists that Mitya should not forget the "new man"; he even goes so far as to say that not accepting his unjust sentence (i.e., planning to escape) might be preferable to the risks of rebellion and resentment in the wake of a rash decision. "The fact that you have not accepted that great torment of the Cross will merely help you to be aware within

yourself of an even greater duty and debt, and by this awareness hence-
forth, all your life, you will perhaps assist your own regeneration more
than if you had gone there" [969].

What matters is that Mitya has discovered something that cannot
be ignored; a dimension of his identity has become visible to him and
he is determined that it should be visible to others. If Alyosha gently
dissuades him from making it visible in the most dramatic and costly
of ways, it is nonetheless real and lasting for that. So Zosima's prostration before Mitya in book 2, chapter 6 [101] is indeed, as the elder
tells Alyosha [369] a true recognition of his destiny to suffer—but not
necessarily to suffer as he might impulsively choose. Zosima, like Tikhon with Stavrogin, seems to sense the possibility of Mitya making a
violent and sinful decision, and begs Alyosha to do what he can to avert
it; but it is clear that he is also aware of the pain by which Mitya will
purge his guilt, whatever that guilt may be, in a way very different from
Tikhon's clairvoyance about Stavrogin. Zosima does not see the future,
but he sees the human face and its potential, and sees that Mitya is
somehow inviting suffering. The question will be whether it is only
punitive suffering or whether it will be generously embraced. Thus,
Mitya has *already* become visible to the elder, unwittingly. Zosima's gift
is to see what others are reluctant to face in themselves, and by that
act of recognition to enable them to bring it out, of their own accord,
into the world of shared speech. What Mitya finally brings to light by
embracing his sentence is the possibility of a creative freedom which
Zosima has seen as the reverse side of his propensity to arbitrary violence and passion.

For all three brothers, the emergence into visibility, the new owning of themselves and their words and acts that is prompted by the
action of the novel, represents a movement into vulnerability. They
can be, as never before, the material of the narratives told by others—
something particularly marked with Mitya, as he listens to the vastly
complex and distorted stories told about him by both the prosecution
and the defense in his trial. In a way, Alyosha's dissuasive to Mitya
against simply accepting his imprisonment is a warning against a new
form of trying to avoid being caught in the speech of others: the silent
suffering of the unjustly condemned prisoner might turn out to be all
too attractive as an unanswerable "last word" in Mitya's life. But if

mature humanity as it is sketched in the novels means accepting that there is no last word that any one of us can possess, perhaps it is better for Mitya to settle for the more ambiguous future, the insecure human project of constructing a life (a tough and demanding life in exile, but essentially an "ordinary" life) with Grushenka; it is more open to the continuing labor of bringing itself into speech and finding what can be said not only to others but "after" others, in the light of what is said to and about it.

Thus *Karamazov* sketches different ways in which subjects or speakers may seek to protect themselves or have a last word—the sacred and socially fixed identity of a professed monk, the detached play of ideas in the inner life of the intellectual, the passionate immersion in the moment of the sensualist. It is not just that the brothers "represent" different human temperaments (a critical commonplace of the last generation), or successive stages in understanding the human good:[25] more specifically, they dramatize refusals of dialogue. Obviously, Dostoevsky did not believe that monasticism as such or the intellectual life as such or even the sensual life as such was necessarily an embodiment of such refusal (he had a good bit of sympathy and understanding for all of them); but he is showing in his narrative how each has the capacity to *subvert* the kind of narrative he writes. There is a sense in which you could not write a novel *just* about a monk, nor just about a wholly detached intellectual, nor a sensual and instinct-bound man. To the extent that each of them in themselves is in retreat from a dialogical world, in which they not only have to undergo but have to "negotiate" the perception and misperception of others without claiming privilege, they resist that cooperative discovery of the truth of the self that is at the heart of Dostoevsky's method.

⟨⟩   ⟨⟩   ⟨⟩

If Dostoevsky, then, is implicitly defining for us what resisting the Devil involves, it is clear that central to such an enterprise is—to put it provocatively—the importance of possible error and even lying. There is a great deal in the novels that turns on gossip, malicious rumor and invention and similar familiar accompaniments of human life in common. We are frequently told of what "the town" believed about this or that event or personality; we have repeated secondhand reports of happenings, whose base in fact remains unclear. There are episodes of outrageous slander—the incident of "Pavlishchev's son" in *The Idiot*, Fyodor Karamazov's freewheeling scurrilities about Zosima. And there are characters of varying degrees of wickedness who specialize in unreliable narration, from the pathetic General Ivolgin to the murderous Pyotr Verkhovensky. The trial in *Karamazov* is a protracted exercise in unreliable story-telling by witnesses and lawyers alike. All these instances are there to remind us that what the Underground Man tells us about language is true in a variety of ways. If what we say is not unarguably dictated by a set of plain facts, our capacity for slander is a metaphysically significant thing. What is more, if we speak what we believe to be truth—especially truth about ourselves—we must not be surprised if it is misheard or consciously distorted. To enter into conversation is always to be in this sense at risk. And when faced with such response, we have the options of simply repeating our words or of looking for others: in both cases we acknowledge that recognition has not properly taken place, but in the former we do no more than return to where we started. In the latter case, in contrast, we take responsibility for the misrecognition and explore what we have *not* said—both the options for expressing ourselves that we did not take, and, more importantly, the unnoticed element in ourselves that we have ignored. The words of others, even, or especially, when they represent misunderstanding and misrecognition, open to us areas in ourselves that have been hidden or alien or simply not worked through.

The enterprise of growth and so the life of narrative thus always involves a venturing into that uncontrolled territory where dialogue and interaction bring to light, not to say bring into being, hidden dimensions in a speaker. To engage in this venture is to accept at the outset that no speaker has the last word, and that the position taken up in an initial exchange is going to be tested and shifted and renegotiated in the process. It is to accept that at the outset no one possesses the simple truth about their own identity or interest, and to treat with the deepest skepticism any appeal to the sacredness of an inner life that is transparent to the speaker. Mitya may refer to the hidden man who has been made to "appear" by his experience; but it is clear that this new man is (as Alyosha's remarks later on imply) not a full-fledged spiritual identity but a set of capacities for feeling and perceiving that have been dormant in Mitya's unreflective life so far. And the implication of this is that the identity of any agent at all is dependent for its definition and its realization on dialogue extended in time. To quote Bakhtin once more: "Dialogue . . . is not a means for revealing, for bringing to the surface the already ready-made character of a person; no, in dialogue a person not only shows himself outwardly, but he becomes for the first time that which he is—and, we repeat, not only for others but for himself as well."[26] To show the inner life in writing is always to show an engagement—indeed, Bakhtin's translator uses the loaded word "communion"—with others.

So one of the most serious mistakes we could possibly make in reading Dostoevsky is to suppose that his fundamental position is individualistic, simply because of his passionate opposition to determinism. Freedom is *formally* the capacity of the will to locate and define itself, and, as we have repeatedly seen, it can be used arbitrarily, reactively, self-defensively and oppressively. But what all these uses have in common is that they lead to one or another kind of death. They all forget the basic insight that freedom is most clearly seen in *language*, in the capacity of human agents to go beyond either mere reaction to or reproduction of the world of material stimuli; and if this is the case, freedom is inevitably bound to time and exchange, since language is unthinkable without these. So in stressing equally the central human significance of both freedom and dialogue, Dostoevsky's fiction steadily pushes back against a view of freedom which considers the arbitrary as the essential—and also against a view of dialogue which sees it as an adjunct to the dramatic encounters of fixed characters. The other—the speaking other—becomes the condition of any freedom that is more than an exercise of the will for its own sake. That kind of exercise, Dostoevsky implies, is fatal to freedom itself in the long run, as it confines freedom to a self-limited world which ultimately collapses upon itself. Freedom as detachment or freedom as self-assertion will equally lead away from language, toward the silence of nonrecognition.

There is more to say about the intrinsic connection of freedom thus understood with the sacred, but we shall return to this at more length in the final chapter. However, it should be clear from what has been said so far that such a connection is, in Dostoevsky's world, inescapable. The "unfinalizable" character of dialogue, for Dostoevsky, projects the idea of a continuation of growth and self-definition beyond death. And, as we have seen, the affirmation of a realm that is "outside" the ensemble of impersonal or mechanical systems, outside of mathematics and physics, by way of the affirmation of human liberty posits a space for an "excess of being." What seems at first sight to be a very improvisatory account of how identity is constructed, an account that might lead us to think in terms of voluntaristic models, is actually set against a background of depth and surplus in reality itself which holds and makes sense of all these dialogical processes. The absolute necessity for *recognition* in the exchanges of dialogue means that, while we can indeed at one level say what we please (that two and two are not four), the construction of a life requires that we discover how we can speak in a way that does not just repeat or reproduce what is given, yet is at the same time occupying the same world of thought and perception that others in their speech inhabit. Speech may be free but it needs to be *hearable*—otherwise it fails finally to be language at all. And I as speaker need to acquire the skills to listen or my response will be no response.

But because recognition is complex, because the learning and exercise of these skills takes time, we need to be cautious about supposing that we have once and for all heard what is said to us. We do not have the last word about ourselves, but neither do we have the last word about what we hear. This seems to be what lies behind the quarrel in Florence between Dostoevsky and his future (not very reliable) biographer Strakhov in 1862, described in Frank's biography,[27] a quarrel which casts some interesting light on *Notes from the Underground*. Strakhov had been insisting that everyone should be held responsible for the logical consequences of their positions: logic is logic and "really, it is impossible that 2 plus 2 do not equal 4."[28] Dostoevsky's reply was that, while no one would seriously dispute that two and two are four, if there is a logical incoherence in what someone is saying, you have to ask what, beneath the surface of the words, is going on. Apparent nonsense suggests that someone is trying to say something other than what you have heard in the mere words; there is interpretative work to be done. Strakhov's impatient dismissal of this is evidently related to his conviction, as reported in his recollections of this conversation, that human beings are fundamentally "rotten"; so, we must deduce, if they are saying nonsensical things, we have no metaphysical or theological ground for giving them the benefit of any doubt there may be going.[29] Dostoevsky's repudiation of this rests, in contrast, on the belief that there must be something in the nonsense of another speaker that *can* be recognized, that has a human claim of some kind, and his view, no less than Strakhov's rests upon a theological base.

The two men were arguing about Russian radicals. Dostoevsky had just had a meeting in London with the doyen of émigré Russian radicals, Alexander Herzen (a somewhat risky matter for a person with Dostoevsky's record), and his appreciation of Herzen's sensitivity and brilliance was considerable, despite the disagreements, and never entirely disappeared. Strakhov, an uncompromising conservative, had no time at all for any attempt to "understand" the radicals or to look for common ground, and this seems to have been the occasion for the quarrel—quite a serious one, which goes far to explain the later animosity of Strakhov to the novelist, as Frank observes. It is an exchange that throws light also on some of what is going on in both *Devils* and *Karamazov*. There are characters in both who have uttered things which set in motion trains of disastrous events, but the sense in which they are fully responsible for these is a matter which Dostoevsky handles with great subtlety. Stepan Trofimovich is at the root of many of the problems of *Devils*, yet he is treated with charity by his creator, and allowed to make a (fairly) good end. Even more markedly, Ivan Karamazov has, in his various musings and arguings, planted the seed for Smerdyakov's crime—or at the very least, has nourished the growth of Smerdyakov's amoralism. Yet, as we have argued, he is not treated by Dostoevsky as materially guilty, and, especially in his protracted conversation with Alyosha in book 5, reveals his own inner inconsistencies freely—very much in the way Dostoevsky seems to have in mind in his defense against Strakhov. Dialogue goes on because of a trust that recognition will be possible. And acknowledging that misrecognition happens is part of the fuel of continuing the process; acknowledging that I misspeak myself prompts me to allow time for the probing of another's misspeaking. To assume that the words I am confronted with represent systematic coherence is to treat the words of another as if they were indeed the mathematical formulae of the world outside of which freedom and discourse stand.

So if the novel is the record of dialogue, it is also the record of mistakes, of the comic and tragic mishearings of what is said and the false starts and self-deceptions of the speaker trying to say who he or she is. Inconsistency is the energy of the novel, not because of any supposed exaltation of the arbitrary, that persistent misunderstanding of Dostoevsky as a proto-Sartre, but because it is this which animates the process of dialogue. If I am hidden from myself, it is not because there is a buried identity which sustained introspection and careful self-observation can exhume, but because my identity is in the future, unfolding itself as it is formed in speech, and thus in encounter. This of course applies not only to what characters say, but to their emotional self-representation. It is a commonplace in reading Dostoevsky to note the rapid emotional swings that can take place within a few pages—or indeed paragraphs. The word "suddenly" (*vdrug*) is as regular a feature of Dostoevsky's narrative as of St Mark's, and it frequently signals a dramatic emotional shift. This is, among other things, a way of underlining two points. The first is that what a character is saying during an episode is always vulnerable to interruption from the level of the unsaid, destabilized from within the speaker, who realizes some of the extent of his or her "misspeaking." The second, though, is that this should not lead us to suppose that emotion can substitute for language or that language is most truthful when it is most transparent to emotion, since it too is simply a moment in the process of the construction of the self in encounter. And we are left with the question which Dostoevsky evidently believed to be the one that a good novel ought to awaken in the reader: what is it that "true" narration narrates?

In the four major novels, Dostoevsky experiments freely with his style of narration. *Crime and Punishment* is told by an omniscient third-party narrator, but a great deal of its substance is in fact first-person, as we follow Raskolnikov's feverish thought processes. *The Idiot* is told in a conventional third-person style, though one which Dostoevsky intends to read awkwardly (as the introduction to McDuff's translation points out); and it constantly bewilders by alluding to encounters off-stage, inviting the reader to fill an enormous and pretty arbitrary six-month gap in the middle of the story, during which, quite clearly, a great deal of major significance for the main characters has occurred. The narrator shamelessly disappoints any expectations of omniscience.

Both *Devils* and *Karamazov* use the device of a (rather pompous and not always very bright) first-person local narrator, but seem almost willfully to strain our credulity by ascribing to them knowledge of completely private scenes; they also incorporate into the text substantial narratives from characters—Stavrogin's confession, the memoir of Zosima—whose status and accuracy are left in some degree open. It is significant that at Mitya's trial we learn that the deplorable Rakitin has published a life of Zosima [853], as if to remind us that there will always be an alternative story to be told. Numerous small details in these last two novels underline the limited perspective of the narrator, yet others invite us to believe him when he tells us about what he cannot possibly know. The effect of all this, in all these texts, is to take some of our attention away from the narrator, certainly to lead us to regard the narrator as sharing at least something of the same questioning and incomplete perspective that we have. Like the narrator, we are *witnesses* to a process that is presented as irreducibly mysterious, the mutual discovery of the speakers. Subtly, Dostoevsky has told us that not even the novelist has a "last word."

The question of whether there is in any sense a last word that belongs neither to characters nor to the author is one that has attracted some attention in the literature. Bakhtin in the late notes appended to the English translation of his book on Dostoevsky's poetics gestures toward this question, and Diane Oenning Thompson, in an important essay in 2001, directly addresses the issue of the role of the divine Word in Dostoevsky.[30] Bakhtin underlines the distinctive newness of Dostoevsky's handling of authorial relationship to characters, pointing out the fact that the author in Dostoevsky is in some senses *alongside* his characters,[31] but he also argues that this does not mean that we are to think of the author as somehow passive. The author's activity is "a questioning, provoking, answering, agreeing, objecting activity"; it may interrupt, observe, nudge the reader with varying degrees of shamelessness, but it does not drown out the otherness of the character or offer to "finish" the character in terms of the authorial consciousness. In allowing this time for the speech of characters to unfold, the novelist is in a relation to the persons of the narrative comparable to God's relation with humanity, "a relation allowing man to reveal himself utterly (in his immanent development), to judge himself, to refute himself."[32] The Dostoevskian writer's stance is in fact a glimpse, an analogical hint, about the nature of such final truth as we can imagine—a patient presence, in dialogue with which the maximum range of material is brought out from the depths of the speaking agent and developed and evaluated. This is the clear implication of Bakhtin's phrasing here, and it cannot be stripped of its theological resonances.[33] A "last word" in this connection could only be what is heard in an eternal exposure to the "questioning, provoking" (and so on) voice of the ultimate author. If fiction shows character in the light of this relation of creator to creation, do we then—if we want to think of ourselves as intelligent and free—have to think of ourselves in relation to an eternal witness? If we did not do so, would we not be locked in unfreedom in one or other of its forms—entrapment by a world of impersonal process or by self-referential isolation?

Although debate continues about Bakhtin's religious agenda,[34] it is beyond doubt that he at the very least makes lavish use of theological models and idioms to clarify what he wants to say about the novelist's work. And it is a subtle comparison, which allows the theologically minded reader to see the kind of otherness that exists between author and character in the Dostoevskian world as giving a clue to the otherness of God and the human creation. It is an "alongside" relation that is at the same time very different from a mere occupying of the same space. The author does not *contend* with his or her characters, and so does not appear as *a* character in any simple sense. In whatever it is that moves the interaction and discourse of the characters toward life and definition rather than death, we can see the authorial energy that makes a narrative of the whole rather than an assemblage of disconnected reporting. But that energy, as Bakhtin sees it, cannot be coercive, must act only through the provision of the time in which response can be made and exchanged. In a word, the author takes responsibility for the time in which the narrative unfolds, setting out the landscape in which each is given the possibility of speaking and hearing. The moment of response in the continuing dialogue is itself the gift of a future; that is the mode in which the authorial initiative is present within the text itself. And as we have noted above,

Bakhtin understands Dostoevsky's vision of Christ to be that of a presence within the historical narrative that perfectly and unconditionally gives time and space to others in the way the creator does, so that there is the possibility for every character to find his identity in relation specifically to him. He is the "last word," not as the force which provides the final episode in a sequence or closes down the otherness of other characters, but as the presence with whom ultimately every speaker may discover an exchange that is steadily and unfailingly life-giving and free of anxiety. Christ is, within history, the possibility for us of a future without fear of the other, an assurance that within other and more conflicted dialogues there is still the potential for life. So, if there is an authorial last word to be discerned in the novels, it must be in the form of presences who through their discourse move others to some extent away from fear. The "Christ-like" function of Tikhon or Zosima or Alyosha is to speak words that open the possibility of absolution and reconciliation (and Myshkin is only *partially* a Christ-bearer in that his words of acceptance or compassion do not connect fully with the real otherness of his interlocutors; as he has no "history," he cannot relate to the historical nature of others).[35]

This is to go rather beyond Bakhtin, of course, though it is little more than an unpacking of the hints he gives and entirely congruent with the ways in which he generally uses theological analogy. Thompson is more direct, chiefly because her focus is upon the way in which the *biblical* Word functions in the narratives, understanding by this "any saying, image, symbol or thought whose source can be traced to the Bible."[36] Because Dostoevsky cannot—as a bare cultural fact about the modern age—simply reproduce an "innocent" invocation of this Word, taking for granted its transparency to transcendent authority, he has to find ways of embodying this Word within the ambiguity and "sideways glance" (Bakhtin's phrase) of his modern fictional discourse, so that it may "hold its own and emerge with its semantic authority intact."[37] This is a percipient account of the challenge that faces Dostoevsky, but Thompson's discussion never completely makes it clear whether the transcendent Word is *limited* to those instances where there is a fairly direct positive allusion to biblical text or even doctrinal idiom. Her account is framed in relation to events where some theme from the Christian tradition is brought in as a catalyst for the action, so that we can think in terms of a Word that offers transformation and renewal. As Malcolm Jones notes,[38] the results of an inquiry in those terms are actually rather thin. What might give it a bit more body would be, first, more consideration of those many places where characters are engaged in *parodic* and ironic representations of scriptural or traditional situations, and second, a tracing of how the transforming and renewing Word is heard and in some measure recognized simply within the process of dialogue itself.

Thompson very reasonably expresses caution about irony. The biblical Word can be "ironised to the annihilation of its essence"[39]; yet the ironic use of biblical, doctrinal, or liturgical allusion is one of the most powerful ways of testing the "semantic integrity" of the material. Thompson grants this in her discussion[40] of Marmeladov's rhapsody on the Day of Judgment in *Crime and Punishment* (though it is difficult to agree with her comparison of this to the *sermo humilis*, the "humble style," as defined in mediaeval rhetoric and homiletics; Marmeladov's is an extravagant and bombastic composition whose comic grotesqueries would have strained any traditional homiletic categories); but the point can be extended. The "biblical Word" may be audible in, say, the Gethsemane echoes in the murder and suicide scenes in *Devils*, the various blows or slaps in the face administered to significant characters like Myshkin and Stavrogin to illustrate the ambivalences of biblical non-resistance, the skeptical re-creation of the scene of Christ's ascension into heaven by Ivan's Devil and so on. The titles of chapters 3, 4, and 5 of book 9 of *Karamazov*, representing Mitya's ordeals after arrest as *mytarstvy*, the word used for post-mortem purgatorial trials in Orthodox devotional literature, reflects the same kind of echo. Awareness of this more pervasive reference to Scripture and liturgy—the sort of awareness more fully worked out in Salvestroni's work on Dostoevsky's readings not only of the Bible but of some of the spiritual teachers of the Eastern Christian tradition[41]—allows us to gain a better sense of how the word of biblical and doctrinal allusion is rooted in the overall sense which Bakhtin intimates, that the very continuance of the narrative in the possibility of recognition and even reconciliation is itself a word of grace. "The biblical word can never be finalized by an ironic word," says Thompson,[42] yet *even* the explicit biblical word—as in the examples she mentions, not least in the story of Stepan Trofimovich's last days—is not immune from irony; its work is decisive, yet not coercive, and therefore unfinished. And if it is unfinished, it can always be "answered," well or badly, by human speakers, it can be misheard and misappropriated, it can be ironized or functionalized. The role of the explicit biblical Word in Dostoevsky's narratives is less that of a decisive intervention of the transcendent, cutting through irony and obliqueness, more that of a reminder of the depth behind all the exchanges of discourse, a depth offering not a simple last word but an assurance of some foundational energy that keeps human narrative open to absolution, whatever occurs. Thompson says that "only the Logos offered Dostoevsky an unassailably serious word from which one can at critical moments 'cast off irony.'"[43] In a very important sense this is undoubtedly true, but the casting off of irony cannot in Dostoevsky's world simply be the introduction of a moment in discourse that cannot be answered or continued.

If we take the two best examples of an explicit biblical irruption into the narrative, the point may be clearer. Stepan Trofimovich's last days are depicted with a poignant sympathy that still does not deny itself the comic and the satirical. Stepan is genuinely moved and changed by hearing Sofya Matveevna reading the Bible, and he recognizes the fundamental dishonesty of his life. But—as he knows—the only words he has for this recognition itself are dishonest and inadequate ("I'm lying even now" [645])—the pretentious waffling of a would-be intellectual, larded with his trademark French phrases. The pathos of these pages is in the tension between a genuine repentance and a continuing confusion and proneness to self-serving fantasy. Stepan is surrounded by huge ironies: "Deliverance only came on the third day" says the narrator [648] about Sofya's vigil by Stepan's bedside—but that "deliverance" is also the comic denouement of Varvara Petrovna's arrival, a third day which is not just a third day of resurrection but a third day like that on which the marriage at Cana is said to have occurred. It is as though the long-deferred and feared consummation of the relation between Stepan and Varvara is being announced. And Stepan notices for the first time the lake outside his window, recalling the lake into which the devils of the gospel story drove the herd of pigs [648] (Thompson rightly notes the significance of the third day and the lake). The biblical word, you might say, is prodding his consciousness and ours from every side, but it is nonetheless ambiguous and even potentially parodic. Finally, when Stepan has confessed and received Communion, he falls back into his usual idiom, wittering about the "respect" he feels for the ceremony and preparing a polite and patronizing dismissal of the priest's unadorned homily. Varvara protests animatedly at his "yes, but": "There's no *mais* about it, no *mais* at all!" [655] She knows that Stepan is the man he always was; given time, he will absorb even the wonders of his discovery of the grace of Christ into his private world of delicate spiritual sensibility. And yet he *has* changed, and he movingly tries to say what this means; perhaps the most "transparent" moment is when he repeats—in French!—his acknowledgement that he has lied all his life [656]. He rambles on, again movingly combining a passion to share what he has been given with the vague generalities of his philosophy. He dies peacefully, and Dostoevsky clearly means us to see it as a good death and as near a Christian death as Stepan is likely to have. But the point is that, while Stepan has heard the transforming Word, still, as long as he lives, it will be vulnerable to *what more* can be said in the human world where all words can be followed and answered. Of all the characters in the book, he is the one who is most obviously "saved" from the demonic; but we cannot just celebrate that salvation as a triumphant intervention which removes all uncertainty and ambiguity.

No more can we do this with Alyosha Karamazov. Once again, we have an apparently unambiguous biblical interruption, the reading of the story of the marriage at Cana, after which Alyosha has his vision of Zosima. It is, on any showing, one of Dostoevsky's most strikingly intense pieces of writing, and would certainly have to be classed as unironic in itself. However, it is very definitely not the end of the story, not even of Alyosha's story. His role in the remainder of the novel is, as has often been noted, unexpectedly muted, and the rest of his story, as envisaged by Dostoevsky,[44] does not suggest a steady advance in uncomplicated or conventional virtue (he was, on one plan, to have become a revolutionary activist). In other words, granted the exceptional force of the Cana passage, we are still left with an incomplete human history that has to be worked out in whatever conditions, internal and external, arise. The Word has truly come to him, and been received, but the receiving is still to be lived and spoken in the speaking and hearing of a life subject to the unending exchange of other words.

So "last words" are not to be identified straightforwardly with this or that moment in the narrative. This does not mean, though, that there is, for Dostoevsky, no point of reference beyond the dialogic flow, no Word behind the words. From time to time, there is an encounter that "penetrates," to use Bakhtin's language, in such a way that unexpected futures open and the diabolical threat of self-imprisonment and exile from history is turned away. Such encounters are not without shadows and ironies, and like every other encounter they exist with the possibility of rejection, capture or misunderstanding. They are epiphanic of the Word not simply because they reflect the language of orthodox revelation—though this is nonetheless of cardinal significance for Dostoevsky—or because they decisively alter character or plot (they may or may not do this), but because they evoke what Gary Saul Morson has called[45] an "assumption of plenitude" in the background of the narrative, a hinterland to which the entire process of conversation and formation of character relates. It is not so much that there is something in the dialogic flow that permanently escapes or is safe from irony; rather that there are moments, interventions, which are not *dissolved* by irony, not by even the most acute expression of it. Certain moves in the dialogue, certain advances into the "hinterland," while still open to contrary voices, represent an irreversible step—like Stepan's repeated conviction that he has been lying. He cannot now, whatever else happens, simply ignore the new level of self-perception attained. It has become public, something he and others can talk about, part of the process, casting a new light. It is worth remembering that Dostoevsky could expose his own most passionate feeling to the acidity of his own irony. As we saw, he could put into the mouth of Ivan's Devil his own words about hosannas emerging from a crucible of doubt, and make them sound like a cliché. What would make the words more than a cliché would be not that they command such veneration or carry such manifest authority that they are incapable of being ironized. It would be that when subjected to this disrespectful treatment they do not disappear, they do not become contemptible or ineffectual. And Dostoevsky can only find out whether this is so by subjecting them to the harsh light of irony. Truthfulness does not carry a certificate in its face, in other words; it has to show that it can sustain itself against assault and still give promise of "abundance," in Morson's words.

"The ironisers of the highest truth themselves become ironised by the irresistible claims of that truth."[46] This is well said; the only qualification is that such a process of being out-ironized by the depth of some word, some "penetrative" encounter, can only be narratively established by allowing the process to test the word or encounter to destruction. Recalling Bakhtin's recognition of the carnival element in the mediaeval mystery plays, we can see something of this at work in, for example, the parodic shadowing of the Nativity story by the broad comedy of the sheep-stealing drama in the Second Shepherds' Play of the Wakefield Cycle, or, more darkly, by the unrebuked ribald brutality of the torturers gathered around a wholly silent Christ in the York Play of the mockery of Jesus. It is perhaps visually paralleled in Bosch's paintings of the tormenting of Christ; and in modern literature it is related to Flannery O'Connor's strategy as a self-consciously Catholic novelist in approaching major themes such as baptism or absolution, by way of grotesque parody and distortion (see above, p. 6). Certain things are—to pick up Thompson's phrase—"unassailably serious." But we shall discover this *in narrative form* only by letting them be assailed as relentlessly as can be.

This is how the dialogical principle works. And just as it insists that we see the identity of each speaker or agent as inseparable from how they continue their exchange with the contingent complex of words and circumstances thrown at them, it also insists that any insight, any visionary determination of how it is with human beings and their world, has to be mapped on to the territory of the fiction by a process in which it is systematically tangled with its opposite. This is the root of that feature of Dostoevsky's work that caused so much distress to Freud and has been the occasion of many other misunderstandings. Freud's complaint that Dostoevsky essentially trivializes the moral life by implying that we must go "through" sin to true moral maturity, and invoking a self-inflicted suffering as the satisfaction offered to the murdered paternal authority[47] rests on a widespread and multilayered misreading: Dostoevsky is not a writer who romanticizes sin as an exercise of will to be countered by a corresponding exercise of the will in self-humiliation. Popular as such an interpretation has been among inattentive readers who have somehow associated Dostoevsky with something like a "decadent" sensibility, it entirely misses that ambivalence about will that we have already traced in these chapters. There is no ambiguity at all about the destructive character of evildoing—we have only to think of Stavrogin, and while Bishop Tikhon intuits in Stavrogin a buried passion and seriousness that set him apart from the indifferent majority, he is clear that the child abuse of which Stavrogin is guilty is a squalid and disgusting wickedness with nothing about it of "Byronic" glamour. More importantly, the cliché about "holy sinners" in Dostoevsky's fiction obscures the central distinction between the dialogical definition of goodness and some sort of mystical convergence of good and evil. That Dostoevsky should have projected a novel on *The Life of a Great Sinner*, using, as has often been noted, the rather technical *zhitie* for "life," as in the titles of the lives of the saints, is certainly significant for understanding the agenda of *Devils* and *Karamazov*, but it is nothing to do with a substantive fusion of the sinner as such with the saint, let alone with the idea scouted by Steiner[48] of a "hint that evil and the violation of human values are inseparable from the universality of God."

But it is undeniable that for Dostoevsky good is neither knowable nor effective if it is not engaged historically and specifically with its opposite. Evdokimov notes that freedom has to confront its own possibilities of denial if it is really to be self-determining.[49] As we have seen, Myshkin's "undialectical" or unfallen goodness is destructive. Not growing out of an adult sense of choice, it cannot think in terms of actions that make a difference. Yet to imagine actions that make a difference is also to imagine a diversity of action, to imagine what is not chosen as well as what is. If—like the Underground Man—we want to reject a world in which there is nothing to learn, we have to reject any ideas of goodness that are insulated from the awareness of their opposite. And it is sometimes the case (here is the difficult and controversial point Dostoevsky is making) that it is only the working-out in imagination of the range of destructive possibilities that clarifies what is the good. Because this involves telling the stories of those who work that out not only in imagination but in act, it is tempting to conclude that sin is properly or routinely a stage on the way to sanctity, but this is not what Dostoevsky's fictions are arguing. Indeed, it is the very *fictional* nature of the exploration of sin that is central here. Fictional narrative (*The Life of a Great Sinner*) is the medium in which choices and their effects are rightly explored; to say that only by *narrating* evil can we understand good is crucially different from saying that only by doing evil do we become holy. Those who have suspected Dostoevsky of a covert "beyond-good-and-evil" philosophy have failed to see how the actual writing of fiction works for him as a way of focusing on moments of indeterminacy in which multiple possibilities have to be imagined if the decision actually (narratively) taken is to be properly represented and understood as a *human* decision—that is, as one that is part of a narrative of learning.

Gary Saul Morson, in a fine essay on reading Dostoevsky,[50] has observed that in most fiction "a first reading often becomes an anticipated rereading, as we try to place details into a structure whose outlines we will know but which we now must limn"[51]—whereas Dostoevsky's fiction insists that we attend to its moment-by-moment openness. Morson takes *The Idiot* as the most obvious instance: we know a good deal about the chaos of its planning and the lack of direction in the author's mind as he began the writing, but "At some point in his writing, Dostoevskii evidently realised that time and process were in fact his central themes. The book, he discovered, was about the implications of how it was written."[52] Dostoevskian fiction assumes a poetics of development or process,[53] refusing to let the reader reduce incident or character to elements in a structure. How much better do we understand any specific element in the narrative of a Dostoevskian novel when we have reached the end of the book? We go back, not to see how it relates to an overall plan but to read it again in its own inconclusive terms: what more is there that could be said?

And that is why these considerations properly belong with what we have been considering in this chapter in terms of dialogue and the ethics of recognition. The persons of the narrative arrive at such definition as they have by their exposure to the process of dialogue, exchange; when they are closed off from this, they die and are the cause of death in others. But this also means that the person whose trajectory in the narrative is at least in some degree toward life rather than death has inevitably to accept a kind of solidarity with the isolated and death-bound. They recognize in themselves the same freedom that can turn itself inwards. The death-bound may not act so as to make themselves recognizable, may seek hiddenness, but one of the marks of those who are still growing or learning in the process that is being narrated is that they have some skill in recognizing them nonetheless. They acknowledge themselves to be in the same position of indeterminacy; they do not take their lives or their "life-bound" characters for granted. They know their capacity for death; which is also why a "sinner" aroused to an awareness of his death-bound habit is potentially redeemable. And even a slight manifestation of human vulnerability, if acknowledged without shame, can leave this open (Pyotr Verkhovensky, remember, on his last appearance, has hidden the evidence of his wound). This is the truth behind the bromides about holy sinners in Dostoevsky. But because this means that every moment of self-awareness is a moment of knowing one's manifold and deeply shadowed capacity, then, as Morson says, the nature of this fiction is to draw attention to its own process, to its unresolved character: what happens does not *have* to happen— and so, in trying to reconstruct the past, there is no such thing as what *must* have happened. Consequently, Dostoevsky can exploit, skillfully and even mischievously, the uncertainty implicit in the voices of some of his narrators. Morson points[54] to the incident—or nonincident—in part 2, chapter 5 of *Devils* (a chapter which will be further discussed in our final chapter) where Lizaveta makes as though to strike Stavrogin in the face when they are briefly brought together by the jostling of the crowd. Does she or doesn't she mean to hit him? Our narrator sees nothing, but others assure him that Lizaveta's hand was raised. Yet this is, the narrator says, his main reason for relating the preceding events, in a chapter remarkably full of hints and symbols. How can a whole chapter rest, apparently, on an incident about which the narrator is unsure? It is a cardinal instance of a narrative technique which drives us to reread, not in order to grasp structural clues we have missed, but to attend to the "something more that could be said" which surrounds every moment of the narrative, a sort of aura of uncertainty.

Morson suggest, intriguingly, that all this entails a sort of theological underpinning significantly at odds with orthodox (not to mention Orthodox) thinking. "The God who foreknows all—God the Father—has little, and grudging, place in Dostoevskii's Christianity. Rather, he stresses the Son, who participated in history and suffered with us, and, in *The Brothers Karamazov*, the Holy Spirit, which does indeed intervene in the world."[55] But if our earlier reading of Ivan's nightmare and what the Devil there has to say about God's purposes has any merit, this conclusion about the theology of the novels has to be queried. Quite apart from the doubtfulness of associating the Holy Spirit especially with *Karamazov*, for which the textual evidence is thin at best, and the oddity of ascribing foreknowledge only to God the Father (theologically it is a property of all three persons of the Trinity), it assumes that timeless divine omniscience is necessarily something exercised at a succession of temporally located moments—that is, at point t2, God knows what is going to happen at point t3, as surely as he knows what *has* happened at point t1. But if timelessness is taken seriously, we should have to say that what happens at all points is equally and in some sense simultaneously known to a God who is fully aware of every factor that has contributed to events at each moment—including the fact that this or that act was freely chosen. Morson dismisses rather too readily the response of both theologians and secular determinists, the redefinition of freedom in terms of "absence of external compulsion."[56] Surely the point is that freedom for a human agent is, concretely, the sense of possible choice; and the arguments summarized by Sutherland about the distinctive role in human action played by language and its capacity to affect choice would bear this out. There is no outright contradiction between Dostoevsky's narrative method and a belief in divine omniscience, even in the ultimate purpose of reconciliation about which Ivan's Devil speaks. It is not a covert determinism, since we have seen that, as far as even the best-informed willing subject is concerned (the Devil is in a good position to *see* what is going on in the heavenly world, or so he tells us), no response is ever coerced. But, in relation to God, neither is it allowed to be final. And how—if at all—this fits into a theology concerned to hold to a determinate date for the end of all things and the Last Judgment is not an issue on which Dostoevsky spends any time. If there is a tension with traditional theological categories, it is here rather than in any supposed separation of Father, Son and Spirit.

And if we recall Bakhtin's complex efforts to develop a satisfactory analogy between God's relation with creation and the author's with his or her work, we should be aware that—as Morson himself seems to acknowledge ("Raskolnikov kills the old lady every time"[57])—however much we say about authorial indeterminacy, we are still reading a work that has been written; to say that Dostoevsky's narrative focuses on the indeterminacy of each moment is not to say that the work as written does not tell a specific story. To recognize that this author's way of telling obliges us to see that there is no "must have" about the happening of the events is not to claim that the fiction does not put before us a world in which continuous action occurs and in which there are connections between diverse acts and happenings. The author creates; the particular authorial skill which Dostoevsky displays so outstandingly lays out for us that creation so that we do not sense authorial coercion or interruption, but are wholly drawn in to the felt openness of each moment, the "many possible novels"[58] that surround the text. As was said earlier, the authorial "providence" is in the provision of the time for change or for learning, the background plenitude which continues to resource the narration and thus to give to the characters an excess of reality over and above the sum total of their past or their present circumstances.

Part of what distinguishes Dostoevsky from an existentialist concern with the *acte gratuite* and also from an ethic that is only interested in crisis is of course the sheer fact of narrative continuity. The focus on the indeterminate moment is not a way of saying that the only important decisions are those in which everything is thought to be at stake; rather it says simply that as a matter of fact each moment is a moment in which something else *could* be happening (abstractly). Nor does it mean that a good act is solely one in which our will is exercised against instinct or nature, in a Kantian way. What is decided naturally opens or closes other possibilities; the ordinary self-discipline of attention to the perceived need and the specific reality of the other (back to Shatov's wife in childbirth) makes possible more of the same matter-of-fact attentiveness. Obsession with the moment at the expense of this is precisely what Dostoevsky's fiction does *not* hold up as the key to the moral imagination. For all the often bizarre and apparently contradictory swerves of intention and emotion—think of Mitya's struggle over whether he will indeed kill his father—we are expected to understand that a decision when it is made becomes part of a personal narrative: it does not leave us in a continuing trackless waste of motiveless assertion of the will. What Dostoevsky is charting, again and again, is the state of extreme irresolution over extreme decisions, but he does so partly to emphasize that these states are the places where we are able to see the truth behind all our acts and policies—that we are not compelled to say or do anything. And since love is the crucial instance of freedom, as we have seen, love that is able to give sustained attention to the other and to hold open a door for change in them, while "free" actions that are not so grounded and directed become further steps in the chain of self-enslavement.

The *shape* that love takes in this context is, as indicated already, the assuming of responsibility—owning one's words and acts, being answerable. That means, of course, accepting that what is said and done is not the "property" of the agent or the speaker: what I say and do and thus who I am is inseparable from how it is received and answered in the reality of others; at its highest, it is a manifestation of that "communion" which Bakhtin understands as the key to such solid identity as can be grasped in the Dostoevskian character. But this responsibility takes further definition—as commended by Father Zosima and aspired to by Mitya Karamazov—in the form of accepting responsibility for the other, and ultimately "for all." How is this compatible with the rather different process of developing a (particular) identity in the processes of actual exchange and converse? On the face of it, taking responsibility for all sounds like another distancing or depersonalizing, de-realizing strategy, as well as having uncomfortable echoes of some of what Dostoevsky wrote at his first wife's deathbed: surely to take responsibility for the other, especially for the crime or sin of the other, is close to that absolute refusal of the self that he seems to endorse in those notes? If there is indeed some consistency to Dostoevsky's anthropology, we need a way of untangling this urging of universal responsibility that does not lead to a dissolution of real speech and encounter, another form of that resolution beyond language and history that the novels depict as demonic.

4

EXCHANGING CROSSES
Responsibility for All

Twice in the major novels we come upon an incident that throws some light on the notion of taking responsibility for the other, and before looking in greater detail at the prescriptions attributed to Zosima in book 6 of *Karamazov*, it will be helpful to spend some time on these incidents. Orthodox Christians wear a crucifix around their necks; and the exchanging of crosses is in popular Orthodox practice a sign of committed friendship. The two occasions in the novels when this is described are both of substantial significance in marking the moral geography of the narrative. After Raskolnikov has confessed his guilt for the murder to Sonya, and has begun to form his intention of confessing to the crime, Sonya asks ("suddenly, . . . as though she had just remembered something") if he is wearing a cross. He is not, and she offers hers to him. But, as she explains, she has already exchanged crosses with Lizaveta, the second of Raskolnikov's victims: she is giving Raskolnikov her (presumably second-best) cypress wood cross and keeping Lizaveta's copper one. For Sonya, this is a sign that "we shall bear our crosses together" [503–4]. But Raskolnikov is not ready for this; only when he has finally decided to go to the police does he return to Sonya; "I've come for your crosses" [622].

As he recalls, after the murder of the old pawnbroker Alyona, he had pulled off her body the cord around her neck on which she kept her purse—and also two crosses, one of cypress, one of copper with a small icon inlaid in it [96]. These are the crosses he ought to be wearing, he tells Sonya [623]. He accepts her wooden cross "as befits a member of the common people," and while this is said in a mocking tone, it expresses what Raskolnikov is very slowly trying to assimilate for himself—that he is not an exceptional soul but an ordinary criminal, neither a Satanic nor a Napoleonic giant but a plain sinner. But the crossed lines of the exchanged crosses may be, Dostoevsky hints, still more complex. Sonya has given her cross to Lizaveta, a cross with an inlaid icon like the one Raskolnikov pulls off Alyona's body and throws down. Had Lizaveta given Sonya's cross to her sister? And the other cross worn by Alyona is described originally as of cypress wood, though Raskolnikov remembers it as silver; rather as if he, now wearing Sonya's cypress cross, is reluctant to identify with Alyona, his victim, whom he has so consistently thought of in dehumanizing terms (a "louse" is what he repeatedly calls her, even after he has decided to confess; see, for example 617, where he is talking to his sister and reverts for a moment to the claim that he is only confessing his "mediocrity," his inability to carry through a great design of moral protest, yet a little later, he is again admitting that he is a "villain" and that the sin is real). If the cross with the icon is indeed Sonya's, Sonya becomes very plainly the conduit between all three characters in the crime: she has taken on Lizaveta's cross, identifying with her simplicity and vulnerability. Lizaveta, willingly or not, has shared her cross, the sign of Sonya's compassion, with her sister, and it is her cross, a cross like Alyona's, that Raskolnikov now wears as he faces his suffering, again the mark of a compassion that will not leave him abandoned. Sonya is the unifying factor, the point through which the lines pass. Granted all the reservations we need to keep in mind when tempted to talk about Christ figures, Sonya does very obviously function in the plot as—at least—what could be called a *Platzhalter* for Christ, someone who takes the place that belongs to the Savior within the human transactions of the narrative. And this makes it also appropriate that, faced with Raskolnikov's initial mockery of her faith—how can she know that God will save her little sister from the same fate of being forced into prostitution? what does God *do* for her? [382, 385]—she has no clear answer except to say that God does "everything" [386]. That is, like Jesus in Gethsemane, because she has to take the place of God in what we called the moral geography of the story, there is, as it were, no

God who can help her from outside; there is only the reality of God sustaining her entire identity.

Sonya is characterized throughout by her radical selflessness—not, it should be noted, without a capacity for confrontation; she is not in the least passive in relation to Raskolnikov. Indeed, it could rightly be said that she takes responsibility not just for sharing his suffering but for getting him to take responsibility as a criminal and act accordingly. Rather too much is made of her in some commentary as a helpless figure whose only concern is to suffer; she is stubbornly resolved to make Raskolnikov reenter common humanity, and she is there [626] to check that he does what she has told him to do. And in the Epilogue, while she patiently puts up with Raskolnikov's resentful harshness, she also manages to organize a reasonably successful small business and to manage an efficient system of welfare for his fellow convicts [646, 651]; she is not a cipher or a doormat. This suggests that the taking of responsibility for the other that emerges already in this novel as a major theme involves the responsibility for making responsibility possible for the other, not merely a resigned acceptance of the other's load. If we think of Tikhon and Stavrogin, of Alyosha and Mitya, and also of Zosima's story of his encounter with the Mysterious Visitor in his reminiscences (to which we shall be coming back shortly), it is obvious that this is a recurring motif, which will need further exploration. Taking up the cross with and for another is not a removal of responsibility from the other; rather the contrary.

One last pattern in this picture is worth noting. Not only has Lizaveta exchanged crosses with Sonya; it is she who has given Sonya the New Testament out of which she reads to Raskolnikov the story of the raising of Lazarus [386]: "here was another piece of news: there had been some sort of mysterious get-togethers with Lizaveta—holy fools, the two of them" [387]. The divine word addressed to Raskolnikov actually comes indirectly from his victim. But his immediate response is at best deeply ambiguous, at worst diabolically perverse: he wants to see Sonya as someone who is like him, who has "stepped across" a moral boundary and is "special," the member of an accursed elite for whom ordinary morality is surpassed. Taking on suffering means not Sonya's useless lamenting over the horrors of proletarian oppression in Russia but acting to "break what has to be broken . . . and to take the suffering upon oneself"—a revolutionary sacrificial heroism in which suffering is the key to *power* [392]. Raskolnikov cannot hear the divine word until he has stopped imagining suffering in this heroic mode and understood his solidarity with Lizaveta, his victim: he will hear what she has to say on God's behalf only when he literally puts her cross around his neck— not only taking responsibility for the guilt of her murder but accepting that he and she are part of an indivisible moral world in which there is no one for whom I am not answerable.[1]

The other instance of a significant exchange of crosses occurs in *The Idiot*, once again in a context where the apparently simple act is charged with the memory and meaning of other exchanges. In part 2, chapter 4, Myshkin visits Rogozhin in his home, and first encounters the Holbein reproduction on the wall. Rogozhin questions the Prince about his faith, and Myshkin, having originally evaded the question, answers eventually with a series of odd and apparently disconnected anecdotes. One of these is about how he allows himself to be cheated by a drunken soldier offering him a "silver" cross for twenty copecks—in fact a cheap tin cross on a dirty ribbon. Selling your cross is a serious matter, tantamount, Myshkin thinks, to selling your Savior [258]. But the Prince has no ground for condemnation; what in going on in a heart so degraded as to sell the sign of his baptism is impenetrable and is yet one more sign of that mysteriousness that surrounds religious belief and makes it so exasperatingly elusive for the unbeliever. A few minutes later, Rogozhin asks if Myshkin still has the cross, and pro- poses to exchange it for his own gold one; Myshkin agrees, delighted that they are now "brothers," and Rogozhin proceeds to introduce the Prince to his aged mother for her blessing.

The "doubling" of the characters of Myshkin and Rogozhin is an aspect of the novel we have already noted, and the exchange of crosses reinforces it strongly: these two are to carry each other's destiny in various ways. Certainly each of them bears the consequence of what the other does or, rather, what the other is, and they cannot survive without each other. But the narrative says more than just this. The exchange of crosses happens in the wake of their discussion of faith, which itself is stimulated by the Holbein picture. Myshkin's response to Rogozhin's questioning about his religious belief is centered upon the conviction that when atheists talk about religion, they are always taking about something different from what believers actually mean; his anecdotes are an almost Wittgensteinian catalogue of diverse uses of the language and gestures of faith, designed as much as anything to show that an answer to the plain question, "Do you believe in God?" is going to tell you almost nothing of the meaning of faith. Faith even includes, as Myshkin indicates in the most grotesque of his anecdotes, the peasant crossing himself before he murders his friend for the sake of a watch. But this suggests that Rogozhin, in accepting Myshkin's cross, accepts with it this radically fluid and even centerless account of belief. The cross, coming as it does from the soldier who wants to be rid of it for money he can drink, is a tool capable of many uses, material and psychological. It may stand—as Myshkin clearly wants it to —for the parental love of his last anecdote, the woman crossing herself at the sight of her baby's smile, so reflecting God's parental delight in humanity. But it may also be an amulet representing nothing but the desperate and "agonizing" prayer of the murderer, praying for forgiveness as he cuts his neighbor's throat.

Rogozhin's sardonic smile as he accepts the cross from Myshkin tells us that this version of religion's ambivalence is not unwelcome to the person he knows himself to be. Nor is it alien to the overwhelming and depressing atmosphere of Rogozhin's house, which has been inhabited in the past by members of the *skoptsy* sect, the castrates [242]; Myshkin asks about the interest of Rogozhin's father in sectarian religion, not only the *skoptsy* but the more mainstream Old Believers [243], and teases Rogozhin that, left to himself, he would grow into a man like his father, fascinated by the old customs, isolated by his wealth [250]. Against this background, Rogozhin's morbid fascination (again apparently reflecting his father's feelings) with the Holbein Deposition is somehow understandable: he is drawn to the images and memories of a religious belief that is enclosed and sterile, to the pseudo-icon of the dead Christ. Of this standing before the corpse of faith, the cheap tin cross fraudulently sold—the mark of a dead faith exchanged for drink—is an apt symbol, indeed a symbol of the social degeneration Dostoevsky laments elsewhere and which Zosima has things to say about. Myshkin may enthuse about the mother and her child and speak as if this kind of faith could be stirred up by sustained missionary work among the Russian people, in whom these beauties of religious understanding are inseparably mixed with the corruptions he has related: the woman may have been the wife of the drunken soldier selling the cross. But Rogozhin's response, the request to have this cross for his own, suggests that Myshkin is, not for the first or last time, being sentimentally unreal. The tin cross is a sign of responsibility renounced. Myshkin's purchase of the cross implies that, despite his insight in seeing that atheists are not talking about what religious people actually say, do, or think, his own responsibility is still in question. He has not, after all, answered Rogozhin's question about his own commitment, and how can we know that the mother's smile is "essential" in Christian faith rather than the murderous peasant's prayer?

In other words, and in marked contrast with Sonya Marmeladova, the cross he offers is not his own acceptance of a path of risk and cost so as to open a way for others. God's delight in his human creation is undoubtedly a central element in Christian faith, but it is not the program for a campaign of popular education among the Russian people ("There are things to be done in our Russian world!": this might be a bright and naive student radical of the Russian sixties [258]). Likewise it is crucially true that we cannot pass judgment on the heart of another; but Myshkin's response of loving equanimity leaves open the question of what *responsibility* he takes for the drunken soldier. Significantly, he does not seem to have a cross to give him in return. And what he receives from Rogozhin is a gold cross, suggestive of Rogozhin's wealth, that wealth which gives him his freedom for chaotic indulgence and his power over the weak and confused crowd of inadequates who shadow his steps. Myshkin himself, with his new wealth, acquires a power he does not know how to use; it is as though he has indeed taken on Rogozhin's burden, but cannot bear it in a way that changes things or that makes responsibility possible.

This is admittedly a "hard" reading of the exchange of crosses, but its location in the narrative strongly supports taking it in this way. Not only does it follow the tour of Rogozhin's house and the discussion of religion; it precedes the complex and in some respects pivotal episode of Myshkin's return to visit Nastasya Filippovna, the visit which provokes Rogozhin's attempt to kill him and which is aborted by his epileptic seizure [chap. 5]. If the critics are right who have seen this as Myshkin's half-conscious pushing of Rogozhin toward violence by giving him proof of his continuing love for Nastasya, it is an appropriate continuation of the exchange of crosses: the inner indeterminacy of these nonidentical spiritual twins is proving to be a vortex in which each draws the other further down into confusion. As we have seen, they take on each other's destiny; but the symbiosis is increasingly damaging, as neither knows how to be or to act *for* the other.

So these two episodes in which crosses are exchanged give us some hints of what we must bear in mind as we read Zosima's repeated injunction to make yourself "responsible for all." For Sonya, the exchange of crosses is an outward sign of where her energy is constantly directed: she is committed to self-sacrifice, to the acceptance of suffering, but this is neither suffering as a path to power (which Raskolnikov initially finds attractive) nor suffering as pure passivity. It is the acceptance of the painful cost of action that will alter the world for others—not action that "breaks what must be broken" in Raskolnikov's terms, but the actions dictated by assuming that one is answerable for the life and the good of others. She thus acts as a connecting figure between killer and victim: she stands before Raskolnikov on behalf of Lizaveta and Alyona, voicing their claim to be regarded as human. She demands of Raskolnikov the acknowledgement of his humanity, in the form of confession and visible repentance. And in thus offering a common ground for killer and victim to be seen as human, she defines the space in which their stories may become part of one narrative; she becomes, it is tempting to say, a Dostoevskian author, providing time and space for unforced human growth (a process still significantly unresolved in the actual narrative of *Crime and Punishment*).

In contrast, the exchange in *The Idiot* tells us that, while our "implication" in each others' lives is inescapable, it may work for mutual subversion or damage as well as healing. The cross may be a resented burden or a superstitious defense; if it is not a free assumption of the *specific* cost of another's need or suffering, the exchange of symbols becomes a reinforcement of what is static or destructive in the other and tightens the spiral of unfreedom in both. The cross for the soldier who sells it has become an empty signifier—or, better, a signifier of emptiness, like the picture of the dead Christ. Myshkin's unquestioning and unjudging acceptance of it is meant as an act of generosity, but in the context it raises the constant question that *The Idiot* puts before us about the nature of his human "density" and fleshliness, his capacity for any kind of self-commitment. Sonya is a "site" where others meet; the openness, the apparent emptiness of pride or aggression in the innocent Myshkin, seems to promise something similar; but the reality is darker and more tragic.

⟡   ⟡   ⟡

It is time to turn to the most sustained discussion of "taking responsibility" in Dostoevsky's fiction: the sixth book of *Karamazov*, "The Russian Monk." It continues to attract a measure of critical bafflement as well as some theological unease (more of that in the final chapter), given that Dostoevsky clearly meant it to have a pivotal place in the whole novel. Leatherbarrow, in his study of the demonic in Dostoevsky's work, reads it as a mark of the inability of the realistic novel to deal with grace (a point rather like Holquist's—above, p. 48—about the impossibility of portraying Christ in fiction): when speaking about grace, the novel can only revert to a "monological" idiom which is alien to the overall mode of this fiction. Despite all Dostoevsky's ingenious intertextualities, the parallels in "The Russian Monk" with situations elsewhere in the novel, murders, false accusations, dramatic confrontations and prostrations and so on, it can only read as an exercise in novelistic sleight of hand—using the "demonic" form of the novel (demonic as challenging God's sole power of creation) in the service of a foreclosed theological resolution.[2]

There is certainly a prima facie case for all this. At times the style of Zosima's reported utterance is, on a first reading, flaccid and pious, and the rather rambling material on reading the Bible [376–83] sits uncomfortably with much else in the section. If this is meant as a riposte to Ivan Karamazov, generations of readers have been disappointed or have felt their suspicions confirmed that Dostoevsky was incapable, when it came to it, of expressing positive faith. But first impressions should be challenged. We should beware, for a start, of assuming that the Zosima dossier is an undifferentiated unit, simply broke up into sections. As we shall see, there is internal dialogue even here. And with every "insertion" in Dostoevsky's fiction—the Inquisitor, Stavrogin's confession, Ippolit's manuscript—we have to be wary of supposing that it is a wholly innocent "quotation." Style tells you something, context tells you something.[3] Zosima is an old monk, who naturally uses an idiom pervaded by liturgical resonances and by what reads to us as a rather artificial piety and fervor (compare it with the letters or discourses of the historical eighteenth- and nineteenth-century Russian saints and spiritual fathers); he is also seriously ill and so can be expected not to be concentrating with full energy. What is more, the whole section is presented as written up from Alyosha's notes of Zosima's last evening alive, and the narrator begs leave to wonder whether these notes in fact represent jottings from other sessions as well [371–72, 419], given that other things were discussed that evening, and Zosima was not the only one to speak. In short, Dostoevsky has performed his familiar trick of leaving the reader just enough room for critical suspicion or at least a degree of alienation: this too is a *story*, the story of what Zosima said, and it is as much a part of the whole narrative labor of the novel as anything else, as much open to the "more-to-be-said" dimension which allows every utterance to be questioned. Even if Dostoevsky had *meant* these pages to stand as being beyond possible irony, he has inserted them in a novel where everything is vulnerable to this.

This is not to say that we should read "The Russian Monk" as anything other than a reflection, for the most part, of some of Dostoevsky's most passionately held beliefs. But if we recall that he can put into the mouth of Ivan's Devil one of his own most distinctive phrases and treat it as a weary cliché, we should not be surprised if "The Russian Monk" allows us a similar distance. This is what Alyosha heard or remembered: and naturally certain things come into focus—the relations of brothers; murder; servants and masters (several have noted that Smerdyakov, as both brother and servant, has never received the respect that Zosima commends); the corruption or exploitation of children. So the least we can say is that this is Zosima mediated through Alyosha, who is an "unfinished" character, and so, if this section is read or heard as "voiced" by Alyosha, we need to attend to how what is said is acted on or responded to in the rest of the narrative. And, to make the most obvious point in this connection, we have already observed how the sweeping generality of "making oneself responsible for all" is both embodied and qualified in Mitya's experience.

With those caveats in mind, we shall be looking at the various levels at which the idea of taking responsibility operates in Zosima's reflections and reminiscences. It is fairly clear that there is a certain cumulative quality to what is presented, beginning with the recollections of Zosima's brother and finding fullest expression in the very direct and uncompromising teachings of the last two sections [415–19]. The account of the sickness and death of Zosima's brother [372–76] is obviously prompted by Zosima's admission that Alyosha reminds him of this long-dead brother, and it is in some ways the most puzzling part of the Zosima dossier. The narrative itself is conventional in a way we tend to think of as Victorian; touching consumptive deaths are so much a staple in sentimental fiction of the era.[4] But this is all the stranger given that Dostoevsky elsewhere is unsparing and unsentimental about consumptives (Katerina Ivanovna in *Crime and Punishment*, Ippolit in *The Idiot*). And the spiritual transformation that overtakes the dying Markel is simply presented as a sudden miracle: we have no context in which to put it. In one way, this is arguably realistic. The young Zinovy, the future Zosima, is observing as a child something happening to a brother eight years older, and thus inevitably observing from a distance of experience and understanding. But the effect is of a conversion seen wholly from the outside; we have no sense of how Markel learns what he so passionately and confidently asserts. And because Dostoevsky sets such store by locating spiritual growth in the context of a process, a growth over time, we are left both challenged and frustrated.

To this extent, a reading like Leatherbarrow's is intelligible: this is not quite the stuff of Dostoevskian fiction. But it is of course itself only the beginning of a story. Zosima is *not* Dostoevsky, and he is, we could say, learning how to relate the narrative of learning. What we read is Zosima trying, failing, and trying again to communicate. So Markel's language at this point *ought* to sound odd and even unconvincing. When he says to his mother, "each of us is guilty before the other for everything, and I more than any" [374], his mother cannot understand, any more than we can: is Markel really "worse" than the robbers and murderers of whom the world (especially the Dostoevskian world) is so full? When he speaks about being in paradise and when he begs the birds to forgive him, it is not surprising that the doctor and others conclude that his mind is weakening.[5] He dies in the confidence that, although he does not know how to love the creation, the creation knows how to forgive him—simply, it is implied, by being what it is, the manifestation of God's glory [375]. But he also confides to his younger brother the task of "living for him" [376], and this sets the scene for what follows, as Zinovy/Zosima reenacts Markel's conversion but narrates it from the inside.

"Live for me" says Markel to Zinovy. The younger brother is to become "answerable" for the older one's insight and experience, he is to be responsible for living on his brother's behalf and so expounding his insight over time in a way that is impossible for the dying youth. In other words, Zosima's narration accepts and enacts the gulf between knowing from a distance the vision of reconciliation and knowing it directly as a moral atmosphere—and thus knowing what to do about it, how to inhabit it freely. There are clear echoes of those broader themes about the distance between world and language, fact and response, which we touched upon in the first chapter. The second section of Zosima's recollections [376–83] is in a sense a long gloss on the theme of stories that create a spiritual and moral landscape which remains dormant in the soul even if it is not fully inhabited; the stories of Scripture work in this way, and we are evidently meant in this section to hear not only Zosima's practical advice to parish clergy and his concern about biblical illiteracy, but also his laying of foundations for the story of his own conversion. Quite literally, Zinovy keeps the Bible with him but never opens it [383] in the years of his youthful apostasy. And what finally triggers shame and penitence is the moment when he becomes aware of the humanity of his servant after he has beaten him savagely. He is watching the sun rise and listening to the birds singing—a very direct echo of the language of his dying brother about the glory of God all around and the disfigurement of the human heart; he senses shame and recognizes that it is to do with how he has treated Afanasy [385–86]. In a way that ought to remind us of the beginning of Raskolnikov's slow transformation, he is spoken to by his victim, whose helplessness somehow gives voice to the glory of God.

From this follows his behavior at the duel which his rashness and vanity have provoked, and here, like his brother, he insists that "life is paradise," and that only human pride and sin shut us out from the present enjoyment of this glorious state [388]. He makes himself ridiculous; though the ridicule subsides when he lets it be known that he is going to be a monk. Monks are allowed to be ridiculous, and are relatively harmless from the world's point of view. And this is why the story of the Mysterious Visitor has to follow. Thus far, just as the first episode of these reminiscences risked getting stuck in a sentimental Victorian deathbed piety, so the story of a conversion leading to a monastic vocation has risked getting stuck in another conventional pattern. The underlying theme about responsibility, the recognition of involvement with every human being's fate, is slowly being tested in increasingly complex narratives, with the "happy ending" of each being promptly challenged. This begins to look more like a Dostoevskian narration after all.

And just as Zinovy's conversion echoes Markel's, so in the story of the Mysterious Visitor there is a partial recapitulation of the themes of the preceding section: Zinovy provokes the duel out of an unrequited love (which is in fact to do more with his sense of status, of what is due to him and from him, than anything else), finding that he is ready to kill rather than admit either the loss of the beloved or the unreality of the emotion ("I later perceived . . . that it was possible I had loved her with such passion not at all" [384]). As he tells the story, the Visitor has been, unlike Zinovy, obsessively in love, which is why his violence is directed not against an imagined rival but against the woman herself, whom he murders, casting the responsibility on a servant. It is rather as though the elements in Zinovy's experience have been dismantled and reassembled in more tragic and serious form, and the penitence involved is likewise going to be a more serious matter—so much so that the Visitor comes to the point of planning to kill Zinovy as the recipient of his confession [401–4]. When he makes his public confession— with echoes of both Raskolnikov and Stavrogin in the background for readers of the earlier novels—it is simply not believed: it is assumed that he has gone mad (as was assumed in the case of Markel). There is no escape into a monastery for the Visitor, only into unexpected (and slightly artificial) terminal illness. And for the once popular Zinovy, the object of admiring fascination as a potential monastic recruit, there is a markedly hostile reaction: his first essay in taking responsibility in relation to another has produced a very mixed result, and he is obscurely held to be to blame for the Visitor's decline into insanity.

In the context of the whole of Zosima's narrative, a pattern, even a process, begins to emerge. The unspecific taking of responsibility for all which Markel celebrates is gradually being acted out by Zinovy, first by his recognition of the humanity of his servant and his opponent in the duel, then by his involvement with the Mysterious Visitor and his Sonya-like determination that this man should publicly take up the burden of his guilt. And while Markel dies in the odor of sanctity, and Zinovy's initial conversion brings mild celebrity, the actual and concrete business of taking responsibility for someone else is revealed to be risky. The ridicule and unpopularity which Zinovy at first avoids falls to his lot after the Visitor's public confession. Living "for" Markel has turned into living in some measure "for" the Mysterious Visitor, taking on some small part of the public opprobrium he himself is spared. The Visitor has to accept in advance a kind of death, the death of reputation, of the love of his family, of self-respect; so Zinovy insists, quoting to him the biblical text (John 12:24) that serves as the epigraph of the novel itself about the grain of wheat falling into the ground and dying so as to bring forth fruit, as well as Hebrews 10:31, "It is a fearful thing to fall into the hands of the living God." Having accepted this, he is mercifully spared the full effect of his confession, but Zinovy undergoes a smaller, but still real, death in reputation and trust. In other words, Zosima's narrative is not a simple series of vignettes illustrating a single point; it builds gradually to a recognition that Markel's paradisal vision is attainable only by a willingness to embrace actions that carry serious risk, and that will not by any means guarantee a "paradisal" outcome in any obvious sense. From the initial generalizing and sentimental vision, we are moving inexorably toward a genuinely novelistic one. Frank's observation[6] that the three stories Zosima tells are a *mise en abîme*, a sort of miniaturization of the main themes of the novel in somewhat altered form, is accurate so far as it goes, but it seems that the relation between these stories themselves has something of the same character.

And in this light we can also see that the continuation of the main novel's narrative can be expected to continue the trajectory of Zosima's recollections. We have been watching a narrative pattern building, and, in the concluding sections of the Zosima dossier, there is a certain amount of summary and generalization from the stories (we shall shortly be looking at what is said there). But although Zosima's stories are over, and his life in the novel is almost over, the entire corpus of the dossier is a stage in the advance of the whole novel which, like any other moment in Dostoevskian narrative, invites more to be said. When we come to read Mitya's passionate and rather confused thoughts about how he is going to take responsibility for all, we should be reading it as a further twist in the steadily developing "problematizing" of the theme that has been going on in Zosima's stories. From the unsullied intentions of Markel, to the costly but ultimately conventional and acceptable conversion of Zinovy, to the more costly and less acceptable conversion of the Visitor and the necessity for Zinovy to accept hostility and suspicion. We must see Mitya's struggles as the next stage: the spiritual renewal of someone who knows himself to be an unsaintly man and yet called to what all human beings are called to—universal responsibility. As his self-knowledge grows, he becomes more realistic about what he can bear at this moment, and Alyosha reassures him that the renewal is real even if he has not found the resource to realize it in the most radical way possible. As with the Visitor, it is as if the radical intention, the acceptance in advance of what is involved in embracing suffering for the sake of honoring this universal responsibility, is taken for the deed, and Mitya is to be spared the full consequence of his willingness to suffer. It is not that the whole sequence beginning with Markel represents a weakening of the original vision; it is more a case of the vision being gradually "incarnated" in more and more complex circumstances—being tested in the dialogue, the more-to-be-said, of the novel's process. Thus, so far from being a completely alien intrusion into the novel, Zosima's dossier is actually a text that reinforces the direction of the novel overall, allowing a major theological and moral theme to be narratively introduced, tested and refined and "fed back" into the mainstream of the story.

It is time now to look more closely at the theme itself and how it is developed by Zosima. There are several meanings given to "taking responsibility for all." Markel appears to begin from a sense of his unworthiness to be served by others: for him to be "responsible" is for him to accept that whatever is "owed" to him he owes to others, but more so ("I more than any" [374]). And this spills over into his prayer for forgiveness from the birds and the rest of the natural world: he has offended them by ignoring their revelatory character. In this light, he can say finally that he has offended against all and thus must take responsibility for all, knowing that there will be mercy. This is reinforced by what Zosima himself says to the young peasant he meets in the second section of reminiscence: the Word of God is addressed to and reflected in all things, and everything except humanity is naturally turned in yearning toward God (interestingly, he refers to a saint taming a bear, which suggests that he may have known at least some of the traditions around Serafim of Sarov, of whom this story is told). Responsibility is at least the acknowledgement of a fractured relation between humanity—specifically each person's human soul—and the rest of creation, a fracture for which human beings have to take the blame. They cannot discern the Word in the natural order, but once that discernment has begun, absolution comes simply in the acknowledgement of failure and the discovery that it can be otherwise—the paradisal consciousness Markel speaks of and which Zinovy describes to his colleagues at the aborted duel ("all that we have to do is to want to understand, and at once it will begin in all its beauty" [388]).

But we are already talking of different kinds of responsibility. Markel speaks of taking responsibility for sins and crimes as well, not only one's own generic failure to see but the specific outrages of human sinners. This is where the conversation with the Mysterious Visitor leads [392]: paradise is here and accessible, if we only want it, but wanting it entails "each person being guilty for all creatures and for all things, as well as his own sins." How far the speaker understands what he is talking about at this juncture remains questionable, since the Visitor's rhetoric is still about how this will certainly come to pass according to its own kind of "law"—a rhetoric which Dostoevsky had used in his notes at his wife's deathbed but is not found in later works, except here. We need a little caution before assuming that the Visitor has understood it any more completely than Markel has: the process is still unfolding. The Visitor is holding back in regard to the one thing that in fact prevents reconciliation from happening in a law-like fashion—the fear of unconditional identification, involving not just a generalized sacrifice but the cost of one's security and reputation, becoming ridiculous, the surrender of dignity and control that so paralyzes Stavrogin. So long as this is engrained in humanity, it must be idle to talk about inevitable processes of healing or spiritual maturation. The Visitor talks about the enormous perils of isolation, but at this point he remains isolated himself. He has not accepted the expiatory suffering of being publicly condemned. And although Zinovy does not consciously accept this on behalf of the other, the effect of his advice and understanding is to put him in a place where some amount of that condemnation becomes his. So when he returns to the theme in his thoughts on judgment and perseverance [415–17], he is far more concrete: the sinner whom you are invited to judge is someone for whose condition you have to share the blame.

The horrendous perils of isolation are spelled out by Zosima in the fifth section of the dossier [405–7]. With a rather alarming prescience, Zosima observes that, while we are constantly told that the world is getting smaller because of better communications, the fact is that isolation is intensifying, not least because what is communicated is a universal set of consumer desires and a fundamentally individualistic concept of rights. Freedom has been redefined as the ability to create fresh demands and satisfy them, and the effect is that the wealthy are lonely and depressed and the poor resentful and vengeful ("while they have been given rights, they have not yet been afforded the means with which to satisfy their needs" [406]). Expectations are raised and disappointment is correspondingly intense. And slavery to what is consumed, addiction, makes nonsense of any claim to be fighting for a better humanity. A person who is self-enslaved can only live an isolated life, with a steady decrease in joy [407]. The monk, who lives in solitude so as to break himself of the slavery of acquiring and consuming, is the least isolated of humans; perhaps monks because of this will once again become "leaders of the people," as in Russia's great days. And Zosima ends the section with an affirmation of the God-bearing destiny of Russia that reflects his creator's views all too straightforwardly. The relation of master and servant—an issue very visible in the narrative overall—is presented as a sort of test case for Zosima's ideals. Reconciliation will come, he says, when the rich man is ashamed of his wealth and the poor man is moved with compunction at the humility of the rich [409]. Once again, Russia is confidently presented as the place where real mutuality between master and servant, rich and poor, can be realized—will certainly be realized, because Zosima may not use the language of the inevitability of laws but has no less confidence than the Visitor that change *will* come.[7]

By this stage in Zosima's exposition, the reader may be pardoned for feeling some confusion. The specificity of taking responsibility for all seems to have mutated imperceptibly into a more sweeping set of social concerns and possible solutions. But Zosima has not quite lost the thread, and in the sections that follow, we are back with the original insight. We are to pray for sinners and to love them in their sin, mindful of the fact that they bear the indestructible divine image, with the highest potential among earthly creatures for reflecting God's love; but since all things manifest God's love, all things demand the same intensity of respect (including the animal creation; it is worth recalling here Raskolnikov's traumatic dream [*Crime and Punishment*, 67–73] about the tormenting of a horse by a drunken peasant). And (an important step in the developing vision) this has to be acquired and nourished, it cannot be left to chance—anyone may love casually, by accident, but the mature believer sets out to work at it [413–14]. Once you have recognized your complicity in the world's evil, once you have grasped that an angry or contemptuous face will pass on its own lesson to any child you pass in the street, you know that you must ask for the universal forgiveness of which Markel spoke. Eccentric it may well be, but to approach creation with a prayer for mercy makes the entire life of creation, human and nonhuman that little bit easier [414]. Taking responsibility is the opposite of "foisting your own laziness and helplessness on to other people" [414], which is to follow Satan in his journey into isolation. And we should note as well that the heavy stress here on choosing a new life, choosing to humble oneself, means that the paradisal vision here in view is something rather different from the timeless ecstasy of Myshkin and Kirillov; it is bound up with a policy for action, only realizable when certain choices are made.

And this then returns us to the theme of taking responsibility for the actual sin of the person you might be tempted to judge: "were I myself righteous, it is possible that there would be no criminal standing before me" [415]. Leave the sinner to condemn himself, and if he will not or rejects your solidarity, never mind because someone somewhere will have a new path opened up by what you have done and find it possible to judge themselves and shoulder their burden. Even the judge in court—who has to pass sentence—should act in this spirit, presumably by leaving the offender the appropriate dignity in what he must now suffer. When opposition and malice meet you, ask forgiveness from those who are being difficult or at least make yourself their servant. If you are rejected by all, "bow down to the earth and kiss her." Face the truth that even if you have been righteous, your virtue has not enlightened others [416–17]; even if your deeds have shown some of the divine radiance and it has made no difference, the light abides. "You . . . must work for sake of the whole" [416–17]; as you "moisten the earth with the tears of your joy," be confident that your actions are anchored in God's future, nothing less and nothing else.

The final reported discourse, on hell, stresses the self-chosen nature of punishment: the possibility of forgiveness is always present and the righteous in heaven are always ready to receive the damned, but those in hell know that they can no longer love—though Zosima wonders whether their grief at not being able to love opens them up to an unselfish gratitude for the love of the blessed in heaven, which in itself is a *sort* of love. For others, there is no alleviation: "they are already willing martyrs" [381]. They are in revolt against reality itself, demanding that there should be no God; they long not to exist. They represent, in fact, the final stage in that affirmation of freedom as the purely arbitrary assertion of self that we have seen as a mark of the diabolical elsewhere—the condition in which the absolute liberty of the willing self becomes more important than reality, the state of mind of the Underground Man frozen for eternity in its misunderstanding of the nature of liberty. This is the ultimate fruit of the refusal of responsibility in all the senses the word has acquired in Zosima's musings and stories.

The fact that he repeats so frequently—and more or less word for word—the formula about "being guilty for all" (not the most helpful of translations) "taking responsibility for all" or "everyone being responsible, or liable, for every other" does suggest a degree of uncertainty about what is being said, and as we have seen, the phrase, with other related expressions, covers a broad range of meanings. And in its various occurrences, it is associated with ideas that are not necessarily intrinsic to it or that are at least a little ambiguous in Dostoevsky's own novelistic mind. Zosima does not provide a systematic statement about the essence of Christian ethics. But he does provide an orientation for understanding some of the criteria in *Karamazov* and elsewhere for recognizing good and evil, and the repeated trope of kissing the earth and soaking it with tears is here given slightly more substance. It is clear that the unmistakable sign and effect of evil is isolation and, conversely, that good is always associated with a surrender of the aspiration to define oneself solely by and for oneself. It is also clear that isolation from the material order of creation is as significant as isolation from other human beings—confirming what we have seen earlier in this discussion about the dangers of trying to be removed from the temporal milieu and the material body. The extra dimension added by the language of responsibility, though, is the conviction that there is no circumstance in which it is either impossible or useless to seek whatever action or involvement one can that will give space or time to the other for his, her, or its flourishing before God. As has been hinted already, as we have seen in the case of Sonya, taking responsibility in this sense of allowing space and time is itself a "novelistic" virtue. The person who takes responsibility assumes the burden and the freedom of a sort of *authorship*. Responsibility is an invitation for others to be freely what they are. This will sound like a paradoxical definition, given that "taking responsibility" for another is usually and naturally heard as meaning some degree of taking responsibility *from* them. But in the way Dostoevsky sets it out, both narratively—as with Sonya and Mitya—and theoretically—in Zosima's discourses—the salient point is that what is other to the deciding mind is given the free capacity to do what is in accord with God's purpose, just as in the ideal form of Dostoevskian authorship.

Thus taking responsibility for the earth and the material environment, and asking forgiveness from them, watering the earth with tears, does not mean, as it is often and unhelpfully taken to mean by religious commentators, simply a Russian mystique of the sacredness of *mat' syra zemlya*, "moist mother earth."[8] The rhapsodies of Marya Timofeevna in *Devils* part 1, chapter 4 about the moist earth as the true "Mother of God" [154] have been taken too hastily for an expression of Dostoevsky's own spirituality. As so often, we have to recognize that these words contain both central Dostoevskian themes—no one could deny the almost obsessive importance to him of the image of watering the earth with tears—and the extraneous "otherness" of the character who is speaking. And in this instance, Marya's long monologue about her life in the convent is shot through with ironic reference to the wider plot as well as clear and poignant evidence of her mental confusion (she fantasizes that she has had a child whom she has drowned, pointing us to the theme of *ersatz* and spiritually murderous parenting that pervades the book,[9] to the murder of Shatov—to whom she is speaking and whose body will be dumped in a pond—and to the drowning of the demon-possessed Gadarene swine in the lake). She is in some sense a prophetic presence, but we are warned to read her words with care, alert to these broader references. To the extent that she proclaims that "God and nature are one and the same thing" [154], she is echoing the confusions of others who have turned their backs on a transcendent reality, including both Shatov and Kirillov. In the novel, it is not the moist earth which is "the hope of the human race," as Marya says, but the eternal love which Stepan Trofimovich affirms at the end—as necessary to humanity, he says, as the earth we live on. Yet the watering of the earth in tears *is* significant: when Shatov tells Stavrogin to go and do it [261], it is as a sign of reconnecting with a reality Stavrogin has been fleeing from, reconnecting with what is outside his head or his will. Watering the earth and asking forgiveness from the natural order shows that the isolated self has acknowledged its given limits, its *locatedness* and materiality, and so the inescapably other character of what it encounters. The person weeping over the earth is repenting of the compulsion to abandon the present actuality of the earth, and this compulsion is, in this novel especially, a distinctive mark of evil. In the light of this, Marya is right to the extent that reconciliation with God and with nature are inseparable.

When Alyosha falls on the earth in tears after his dream or vision of Zosima [469], his reconciliation with the earth and his awareness of being caught up in a cosmic exchange of forgiveness and penitence are bound inextricably together. What sets this apart from the "pantheism" some have detected[10] is precisely the emphasis on forgiveness; what is happening is not a natural process, an absorption in cosmic harmony, but one that involves decisions, awareness, attention, just that attention to the prosaic and specific that we have repeatedly seen to be in the novels a sign of grace. The network of repentant seeking for mercy and the free bestowal of mercy is a network of moral agents; we have already seen in the narrative of *Karamazov* by this point something of the nature of the obstacles to grace, and we cannot therefore treat this passage as commending any kind of shortcut to reconciliation. Kissing and watering the soil demonstrates simply that the hellish isolation of the self offends not only other human agents but a larger order: to ignore the fact that the nonhuman creation is manifesting God's beauty is deeply dangerous (partly but not entirely because it licenses the cruelty to animals that Dostoevsky touches on as, once again, a mark of evil). It fails to let creation be itself; it is a failure in Dostoevskian authorship—seeking for a meaning that can be imposed irrespective of what is actually there.

In relation to other humans, the point is still more obvious. To take responsibility is so to act and speak that the options of others are clarified, not controlled. And this can happen only when there is an imaginative penetration into what is other: I become responsible when I can indeed "answer" for what is not myself, when I can voice the needs or hopes of someone other without collapsing them into my own. And to become responsible "for all" must then mean that I set no limits in advance to those for whom I am obliged to speak: this is why taking responsibility is assimilated in Dostoevsky to the acknowledging of the dignity of every other. Returning for a moment to Raskolnikov, we can see why the taking of Lizaveta's cross signifies a first step in ethical change, a recognition that she bears a significance in her own right. As we noted earlier, Sonya's role as the narrative point where the moral substance of murderer and victim meet implies that she is already aware of these significances and is acting in an "authorial" capacity in brokering the possibility of a different set of relations from those of violence and killing. As for Mitya, his discovery of responsibility comes with the dream [part 3, chap. 8] in which he is faced with the vast, anonymous suffering of strangers; when he wakes up, he finds that someone has placed a pillow beneath his head: *he* has experienced the kindness of strangers. He is both challenged to see anonymous sufferers as real subjects and shown himself as an anonymous sufferer, and he grasps the all-important truth that in the context of that equality, any act of hatred against another is a betrayal of all and any act of generosity to another is an affirmation of all. He is ready to admit

[652] that he has sinned in intent. He has been ready to kill his father, even if he is actually innocent of the crime; he has reduced his father to something less than human (as he has also ignored the humanity of old Grigory whom he has attacked and seriously injured; he has already [623–24] confessed to this and expressed his shame) and now has somehow to restore the loss that represents. As the police take him away, he asks forgiveness from the peasants standing around— who, Tikhon-like, respond by asking his forgiveness too [653]. It is not that Mitya gets to the point where he can fully articulate the voice of his victim, Grigory, or his intended victim, his father; he is still feeling his way. But he has acknowledged that there is a voice to be heard that is not his own.

Giving room to the voice that is not your own is, we have argued, near the heart of Dostoevsky's fictional method. Ruth Coates, in her important monograph on the theological themes in Bakhtin, discusses Bakhtin's growing interest in authorial "silence" as it is hinted at in the Christ-like figures in Dostoevsky's novels—those who, in the terms of the present discussion, offer time and space to others. "Here we see," she writes,[11] "the continuation of the kenotic motif of active self-renunciation, as responsible authors/others facilitate the self-disclosure of their partners in dialogue rather than impose a definition from without." Responsibility is a bracketing and quieting of the self's agenda for the sake of another voice, and to the extent that a novelist silences his or her first-person intervention, the novelist is assuming responsibility for the characters in the "Zosiman" sense. We have seen (above, p. 138) how in Bakhtin's reading of Dostoevsky the author's absence as author mirrors God's relation with creation, and we have seen how Dostoevsky's own authorial strategies experiment with various ways of securing the absence of an authorial last word or even a dependable authorial perspective. What is emerging with greater clarity is how this mode of authorship is to be understood as a modeling of the ethical vision contained within the novels.

Another admirable recent work on Bakhtin, by Alexandar Mihailovic, has a chapter on "Answerability and Ethics: Toward a Philosophy of Activism," which explores Bakhtin's extremely complex and rather fluid reflections on the nature of ethical action, but what is plain from this discussion is the significance in his thinking of an "incarnational" impetus—or what Mihailovic vividly calls, the "non-alibi" principle. Ethical action is never retreat into the self; it is rather the "fixing" of the self in a specific place, owning words and actions as having a center in the acting person.[12] But this is not an assertive or exclusive strategy. One becomes actively answerable only by self-renunciation; indeed the very act of refusing the option of retreat into the self and staking an identity in the historical world is a form of self-surrender.[13] By emerging into a world that is other and engaging with discourses that are not one's own, the speaking self resigns the fantasy of self-definition. And where the "ethics of authorship" are concerned (the title of Mihailovic's last chapter), what is entailed for an ethically defensible authorship is the willingness to define the authorial voice only by the creation of a complex drama of other voices, in which the writer's own perspective is not marked. We are back with the late Bakhtinian reflection on the author as character, and the pretty overt association of this with the actual narrative of divine incarnation in Christ.[14]

It should be clear that we are here at some distance from the younger Dostoevsky's musings in 1864 about the cancellation of the ego so as to attain the true condition of God-like or Christ-like love, although the roots of the later conception are certainly traceable here. The earlier language lends itself too easily to the simple interpretation of a self-denial or self-withdrawal, a final negation of the "I"; the developed understanding of responsibility insists on the taking of a position in order to create space for the other. It is no part of Dostoevsky's ethic to commend anything like an invitation to the other to take one's place, a passive acceptance of annihilating injustice. Admittedly, Dostoevsky's language courts misinterpretation. But if freely accepted suffering is the medium in which, like Mitya, we atone for our sins, and if this may entail the accepting of false or limiting pictures of oneself, this is balanced by the stress on what has to be a profoundly *self-confident* as well as self-conscious exercise of liberty in order to achieve such acceptance. We have seen that Zosima emphasizes the need for labor and ascetical effort in learning to take responsibility, and Alyosha's final advice to Mitya not to attempt a level of sacrifice for which he is temperamentally unprepared is a working-out of this caution about grand gestures of renunciation. Certainly, the path commended is one in which the ego as defined solely by itself does indeed die. But that death is a process in which—as Mitya intuits—another kind of subjectivity dawns, not the simple triumph of a drastic self-alienation. If another Hegelian allusion is not inappropriate, what we are speaking about is a dialectical negation whose point is the *recognition* of self in the other and in the ensemble of otherness that is the world's process.[15] In the simplest terms, it means that the self remains a locus of feeling and thought, and specifically of love. The American critic Alan Jacobs, writing on "Bakhtin and the Hermeneutics of Love," observes how Bakhtin moves away from identifying the biblical *kenosis*, self-emptying, with a "self-evacuation" that leaves subjectivity alienated or contentless.[16]

So the question with which we began this discussion, at the end of the last chapter, finds some answers in this context. Developing an identity in the processes of converse and exchange is not a different thing from taking responsibility for all. What happens in the apparently radical assault on the ego at certain levels that is implied in the latter strategy is, it seems, inseparably bound up with the linguistic task of hearing and articulating, voicing, the other; it is about letting one's own voice be molded by that encounter, silenced in its own uncritical or precritical confidence, so that the exchange is real—a matter neither of treating the other as the peg on which to hang preprepared ideas and ego-centered concerns, nor of abandoning one's own voice in abjection before the other, but of discovering what the other can say in one's own voice, and what one can say in the other's voice. In that mutual displacement, something new enters the moral situation, and both speakers are given more room to be who they are, to learn or grow by means of this discovery of "themselves outside themselves." It is another and an older sense of "ecstasy," and one that has strong theological roots, especially in Eastern Christianity: God's action toward the world, supremely in the incarnation of the Word, is an act of "ecstasy." God determines to be God in the medium of the other, in the medium of finite and material life, but of course does not cease to be God, and the fact of God's living in the medium of human existence drastically alters what is possible for human nature. While one cannot say with any theological probity that this works the other way around in the same way (given the traditional commitment to the strict unchangeability of God's nature), it could nonetheless be said that at least what is possible for God to communicate of the divine is also altered in the incarnational encounter.[17]

Finding an identity in dialogue and finding an identity in taking responsibility converge because finding an identity that is resistant to the demonic and is therefore "life-bound" is always in the Dostoevskian world finding an identity in freely creating time and space for the other and voicing their perspective and interest. This also helps us see why the issue of true and false parenthood is of such concern to Dostoevsky in his fiction; this is an obviously focal instance and metaphor for the process of giving time and space to otherness, and we have noted how the diabolical takes root where this relationship is distorted or perverted. It is vaguely in the background in *Crime and Punishment*, where it is not unimportant that Raskolnikov has no father and that his mother is possessive, confused, and unconsciously manipulative. It figures in *The Idiot* only indirectly: Myshkin is an orphan, part of his rootless or depthless persona, and he inherits the wealth that complicates his life still further from a distant figure, with whose putative son he has to negotiate. It is foregrounded in dramatic fashion in *The Adolescent*, in which Versilov as the failed and absent father is set against the saintly Makar, and in which also sexual rivalry between the generations plays a crucial part. Versilov anticipates Fyodor Karamazov, though he is a far less gross creation, as well as echoing Stepan Trofimovich, and Makar, who talks, like Markel and Zosima, about birds and stars as manifesting God's glory, looks forward very plainly to Zosima. But in *Devils* and *Karamazov* it is a theme that has become inescapable. In the former, the two young antiheroes of the novel are who they are in part because of absent fathers or false fathers: Pyotr has been sent away from his father as soon as possible, and the fatherless Nikolai has been tutored by Stepan Trofimovich in a way that leaves him with a void in the center of the spirit. In *Karamazov*, Fyodor's brutality and irresponsibility as a father is central to the plot. The fact that (echoing the plot of *The Adolescent*, only painted in more primary colors) he is a rival to his son for the affections of Grushenka is a powerful sign of his transgression of the father's proper role, and his cynical indifference [133–34] as to whether Smerdyakov is his son or not (he in any case refuses to treat him as such) reflects in another way the same refusal to accept what is involved in fatherhood. Alone of the three legitimate sons, Alyosha discovers another kind of fathering in the love of Zosima—Zosima who instead of pressing him to reproduce his own style of life and vocation, urges him precisely to become "other," to go out into the nonmonastic world. And alone of the three, Alyosha finds ways of relating to his biological father that are not hostile or contemptuous partly, we must suppose, through this experience of spiritual fathering.

Parenting (both fathering and mothering, though the latter does not have quite the same profile in the novels) is the most literal instance of bestowing space and time on a human other; when it becomes a relation in which that otherness is denied and in which liberty is stifled or rivalry nurtured, it is a channel for the diabolical. By refusing to someone the consciousness of being rooted in time and place (the psychological dimension of that *pochvennichestvo* that mattered so much to Dostoevsky), it disables the process of growing into responsibility. When Ivan Karamazov makes his startling comment to Lise Khokhlakova and then at the trial about how everyone wants to kill their father, he is reflecting not only his own tormented state of mind but a cultural milieu in which fatherhood is not understood and so is savagely resented and rejected (the anticipation of Freud is of course a much-discussed matter which the modern reader cannot ignore, but we need also to read this strictly within the framework of the novel, where it is not primarily about the byways of the subconscious). Much of Dostoevsky's world is a place where the "natural" relation of parenthood is virtually in abeyance—which means that the potential for irresponsible relations in other contexts is far greater, and the need more urgent for the spiritual parenting represented by Zosima. And if we connect the very beginning of Zosima's reported discourses with this theme, we can see that (oddly, at first sight) parenting is compatible with fraternity: Zosima's love for Alyosha is not only that of father for son but that of brother for brother, since Alyosha reminds him of Markel. This seems to suggest that parenting in its most constructive manifestation may always have in it the inescapable element of dependence, but equally generates the shared space of brotherhood or sisterhood, of common humanity and interdependence. Whether or not we should think of Dostoevsky as consciously connecting this, as some would want to argue,[18] with the notion of fatherhood in the context of the doctrine of the Trinity, where dependence and equality are fully compatible, the analogy is a useful one for making sense of the pattern he is advancing.

In any event, the model of parental responsibility envisaged is very clearly one that has to exclude rivalry. Girard's discussions of Dostoevsky[19] have understandably been challenged as being rather short on analysis of the actual texts in any depth, but he is surely right in seeing the problematic of parent and child in the novels as bound up to some extent with this issue of rivalry: the father is the source from which the son learns but therefore also the paradigmatic rival for the objects the son learns from him to desire. The bad father in the novels—Fyodor Karamazov above all, but also Stepan Verkhovensky in a different mode, as the constructor and maintainer of a world without transcendence in which all relationships are "laterally" negotiated without the critical mediation of that which is beyond mere desire and possession—is one who allows no way out from the rivalrous relationship and no means of naming and thus exploding the dysfunction that arises from this rivalry. The bad father thus creates a prototype of the threatening other who must be resisted by withdrawal and ultimately violence.

So a world in which responsibility for all can be learned and nurtured must be a world in which we critically reexamine our grasp of the parent-child relationship. Dostoevsky again seems uncannily prescient in expressing anxieties about "feral" children or children without clear moral landscapes and location, and he gives to Fetyukovich, Mitya's defending counsel, an eloquent statement of how parental failure produces an "animal" character [876]. But we are not to suppose that he simply endorses Fetyukovich's conclusion—that respect for fathers has to be earned and has no meaning where there is no love, and that Mitya should be acquitted because of his unhappy background.[20] This is manifestly a liberal sentimentality from which the protagonists in the novel would shrink; it ignores the two cardinal points in Dostoevsky's ethic of responsibility. We are free to choose, whatever our history, and we have to relate to what is actually the case in the world (including the biological fact of fatherhood). Nonetheless, the scenery of *Karamazov* is haunted by children whose viciousness is very near the surface—the boys whose bullying of Ilyusha Snegiryov is so starkly described in book

10. Many readers have voiced a sense of anticlimax about the fact that the novel ends with Alyosha's address to the schoolboys after Ilyusha's funeral, but, whatever the artistic success or failure of this, it should not be read as a distraction. Alyosha is seeking to recreate in some degree that relationship combining fatherhood and fraternity which he has experienced with Zosima, in a world where the alternatives for the rootless child seem to be resentful dependence or feral autonomy. He is taking responsibility—not just as a Boy Scout troop leader, to quote one dismissive commentator (Czeslaw Milosz), but as a Dostoevskian author, both the giver of time and space for maturity and a *sharer* of that time and space in a dialogue that nourishes genuine freedom.

As Susanne Fusso notes in her study of the family in Dostoevsky,[21] discussion of parenting cannot be isolated from discussion of sexuality. If we are thinking about how we manage otherness, what is to be said about that further instance of irreducible otherness that is sexual differentiation? Given that sexual difference is from one point of view the cardinal case of difference without competition, yet also the cardinal case of the desire of an other that we can never fathom and which is therefore always exposing the incompleteness of my own desire, there ought to be some fruitful lines of inquiry to be followed in relation to the issues we have just been discussing. But this turns out to be an elusive theme in Dostoevsky. By way of preliminary, remember the significance of sexual confusion and frustration in *The Idiot*, and that in *Devils* the diabolical is implicitly characterized by sexual sterility—the relationship of Stepan and Varvara, Stavrogin's (probable) impotence. It is quite true that Dostoevsky practically never portrays happy couples (Dunya and Razumikhin in *Crime and Punishment* are probably the nearest we get), and that he constantly upsets the conventional novelistic expectations of his era by refusing us marital happy endings. The complexity of his understanding of the role of women in general in his fiction deserves more attention than can be given here; enough to say that there is little sign of a salvific mystique around woman as such. Evdokimov goes so far as to argue[22] that Dostoevsky's conception of love more or less excludes any idea of eros as a "sublimating power" drawing together the resources of male and female in a healing balance or fusion; and he claims that in the novels "woman has no autonomous or independent existence; she is only the destiny of man."[23] Yet if the demonic is characterized by a denial or frustration of sexual union or balance, we should expect something positive to emerge about it.

On the whole this is another case of Dostoevsky's "negative theology": the significance of eros is defined largely by the tracing of its absence or perversion. Perhaps the nearest thing to a positive account comes in relation to the initially ambivalent figure of Grushenka in *Karamazov*. Some of her story echoes that of Nastasya Filippovna, but she has evidently emerged with more fundamental self-reliance. She is a focus of erotic unsettlement for the whole Karamazov family, but the most important episode in this respect is book 7, chapter 3, her long encounter with Alyosha. Rakitin, a malign "authorial" presence if ever there was one, wants to see Alyosha seduced by Grushenka, as a kind of correlative to the loss of his spiritual or theological virginity that has occurred after Zosima's death, but he has reckoned without the basic generosity of Grushenka, who draws back from her erotic play with Alyosha on learning of the elder's death. She will not offer herself either as consolation or as the material for symbolic rebellion; she gives him room for his mourning and thus also gives herself room to be something other than a character in Rakitin's plot. Alyosha recognizes her as a "sister"; later on they will be able to collaborate effectively for Mitya's sake in intelligent friendship [book 11, chap. 1]. And it is no accident that Alyosha's engagement to Lise Khokhlakova fades out of the narrative. A fantasy relationship has been overtaken by a real one, Alyosha is free to relate to women as fellow adults and Grushenka is, finally, free for lifelong partnership with Mitya, who knows that he cannot bear his suffering without her [book 11, chap. 4].

Grushenka at any rate is not simply a passive female whose "destiny" is man; not only does she appear—like Nastasya Filippovna—as that dangerous phenomenon, an economically independent woman, she also appears as a woman who is not constrained by the pressures of the marriage market. Despite—or because of—her status as a woman outside ordinary respectable society, she is to a notable degree in control of her sexual destiny, which means that she is able to see herself in some contexts as not just a desirable sexual object. As Leonard Stanton puts it in an interesting discussion of her role in *Karamazov*,[24] she both arouses and diverts Alyosha's latent erotic desire; she is able to relate to him as something other than a lover. She is capable of being a sister and a friend.

Here we have to guess rather at what Dostoevsky might be sketching, but it is not unreasonable to see the Grushenka episodes as suggesting that "responsible" relationships between man and woman depend on the capacity to understand the erotic relation as coming to proper maturity only when it is seen in a wider context. Man and woman are not simply bound together in symbiotic complementarity; they can experience their otherness in other ways, in sibling relation, in friendship. The sexual other is not just there to complete my erotic fulfillment; sexual otherness is more than that, and we become responsible sexual agents only when we have discovered that we can relate to the sexual other in more than merely erotic ways. There are hints of this in the relationship of Sonya and Raskolnikov, though this is a much cloudier matter for all sorts of reasons, not least Dostoevsky's narrative reticence. But *Karamazov* at least hints in the direction of a reading of sexual relation that goes beyond both rivalry and mutual possession. If this is correct, we can, retrospectively, see the frustrated or sterile relations of the earlier novels as exemplifying the impossibility of erotic responsibility for those who have already in various ways shown themselves unable to deal with real otherness.

The foregoing discussion of responsibility as a theme in Dostoevsky's ethics is in part meant to help us grasp that, when he talks about the need for love as the foundation of a renewed human community, he has something more specific in mind than a generalized lyrical and benevolent sensibility. The fierce critique directed against Dostoevsky (especially *Karamazov* and the Pushkin speech) by Konstantin Leontiev made much of the many senses that could be given to the word "love" and the risks of a cosmopolitan rhetoric of benevolence[25]; Leontiev (of whom there will be more to say in the next chapter) argued that Dostoevsky had betrayed both his own convictions about the particularity of the Russian vocation and the specificity of Orthodox Christian teaching about love, which began firmly with the duty of love toward and within the visible Body of Christ, the Church. He accused the novelist (accurately enough in this case) of echoing some of the ideas of George Sand,[26] and of purveying a psychological rather than spiritual account of Christian love (*psikhichnost'*), tainted with a humanistic and tragic pathos:[27] what he famously called "rosy" Christianity. But what we have been examining in this chapter so far does not easily support such an indictment. Whatever the precise relation of Dostoevsky's vision to traditional Orthodoxy, it is hard to dismiss it as no more than the sort of sentimental goodwill Leontiev castigates. And, although Dostoevsky does not directly quote the biblical injunction to "carry each other's burdens" (Gal 6:2), his concept of responsibility is almost unimaginable without the theological underpinning of a model of corporate life in which the basic image was to do with the sharing and exchange of suffering—"coinherence," to use the word beloved of the Anglican poet and theologian Charles Williams.[28]

Most importantly, Dostoevsky believes love is *difficult*; for all the passages that suggest (like Markel's apostrophes or Mitya's claims for "a tragic hymn to God, with whom is joy" out of the depths of humiliation and captivity [757]) that the love of God and neighbor is so natural that, with the removal of a few evil habits, it will surge up of itself, it is clear that the novels overall present a picture of effective, unsentimental and potentially transforming love as something painfully learned. Ivan's admission that he cannot understand how one can love one's neighbors [309] and the general suspicion with which we are invited to approach rhetoric about universal love tell strongly against any facile humanist cosmopolitanism. Dostoevsky's human beings are not innocent or naturally loveable. Versilov believes it is impossible to love the neighbor without despising him, and that love for humanity can only be love for your own ideal—that is, for yourself [*The Adolescent*, 213–14]; his love for the beings of the Golden Age about whom he dreams so poignantly is just such a love for his own private ideal. And even the children whom Ivan professes to love are shown in *Karamazov* to be capable of sadistic cruelty to animals and to each other (Ivan does not have much to do with any actual children; Alyosha, of course, does): Dostoevsky's notes[29] show that he wanted to avoid unreality and sentimentalism in his depictions of children. Ivan's declaration that he can only love a man who is hidden from him for "the moment he shows his face—love disappears" [309] is a powerful challenge to the central theme we have explored in the novels of *visibility* as the mark of emergence from isolation and death.

The Orthodox theologian Georges Florovsky, discussing Dostoevsky in his magisterial history of Russian religious thought,[30] suggests that what Dostoevsky is saying is that proper Christian love is "love for the freedom of one's neighbour" [31]: "It is impossible to love man simply as man—to do so would mean to love man in his arbitrarily given condition, not in his freedom. But to love man in his ideal image is still more dangerous."[32] You may quarrel a bit with the wording of this—Zosima's injunction to love man even in his sin suggests that loving humanity must include some sort of love toward the concrete human condition, arbitrary or not, granted that such love does not mean uncritical passivity, but the basic point is a crucial one. What love is directed to is not a present condition as the final and definitive state of humanity—a passive acceptance of what happens to be the case. That would be to reduce love to the level of automatic response to the given which the Underground Man and his progeny so furiously reject. But neither is it the love of a Shigalyov or even a Kirillov for a humanity that does not yet exist, so that the present obstinate solidity of things and persons can be swept away in a passion of destruction, for the sake of a dreamed future. And of course it is not the love of an Inquisitor, determined to create an environment in which a reduced and enslaved humanity will be spared as much suffering as possible. Love is directed toward an actual and material present, toward specific and not always naturally loveable persons as possible bearers not only of individual freedom but of liberating powers for each other. It is love that recognizes a universal dimension in its exercise, not out of a generalizing goodwill for all but out of a recognition that each deserves the same attention as a potential agent and liberator.

Florovsky goes on to underline the risk of imprisonment by dreams—by the "ideal image" which blocks out the actuality of human existence—and he acknowledges that Dostoevsky himself is capable of this enslavement, never fully surmounting the temptation to "organic" resolutions of the question of Russia's future, the rhetoric of Russia's destiny and the inevitability of its realization.[33] But Dostoevsky's "dream" does not simply coincide with his "vision"; he "dreamed about

'Russian socialism' but he envisioned the 'Russian monk.'"[34] And the Russian monk, the person who has digested Zosima's teaching, is not a hero who constructs abstract social harmony but someone who works slowly on the recalcitrant material of human feeling and will, on the "flesh" of humanity, not looking for results in the world historical process. As Florovsky says, Dostoevsky never loses focus on the Word made *flesh*, and if we look at the notebooks for *Devils*, we find in the notes and drafts for Stavrogin's conversation with Tikhon[35] the contrast drawn between trying to "make a leap," changing the world by some dramatic gesture or policy, and the process that will "regenerate the image of man in oneself." The notion that renewal can be brought about by anything other than the labor of self-restoration is illusory. Here Dostoevsky anticipates a debate that was to surface at the beginning of the twentieth century among Russian intellectuals. The Marxist economist turned Orthodox philosopher, Sergei Bulgakov, was to write in 1909 a very influential essay on "Heroism and the Spiritual Struggle"[36] in which he contrasted the revolutionary maximalism which was continuously in search of the dramatic "leap" that would precipitate a new order, even if this entailed a total denial of existing relations and conventions of human behavior, with the *podvig*, the spiritual discipline, of the person prepared to begin with the transformation of the will itself and so to attend to the smallest of local duties and demands. Only the latter, Bulgakov argued, could deliver us from the disastrous prospect of a revolutionary politics which boiled down to an unceasing trial of will, a constant testing and transgressing of limits in the name of autonomy.

Love for the freedom of the neighbor is inevitably love that looks critically at its own definition of freedom. The neighbor's freedom cannot be loved if one's own is exalted over all other priorities; so to love freedom in others, actual or potential freedom, is to embark on a process of decentring the self (a better phrase than "emptying" or "denying" the self, given our earlier discussion). But the ultimate source of this remains the divine authorship to which all agents equally relate. Each is given scope, given time and space by the foundational act of "love for the freedom of the other" that is creation itself, and the conversion of the individual to self-renewal occurs when something of that divine decentring breaks through. As we observed in the first chapter, the Inquisitor fable in its full narrative context depicts a divine act on the part of Christ, a word of mercy from elsewhere, which spurs Alyosha to his imitative kiss for Ivan. And the combination of the gift of Lizaveta's cross and the reading from Lizaveta's Bible in *Crime and Punishment* has the effect of beginning to introduce Raskolnikov into a different moral and spiritual world. The identification of God with the helpless and forgotten victim, with the "accidentally" murdered Lizaveta—and the exploited and disgraced Sonya as she reads—or with the many anonymous and silenced victims of the Inquisitor amongst whom Christ stands, echoes the creation "out of nothing" on which the universe rests: it is not a case of humanity somehow rising to identification with God through spiritual excellence and moral achievement, but of the divine gratuitously taking the form of those most deeply humiliated and stripped of status and pride, in order to affirm their human dignity and eternal significance to their persecutors. The presence of God with the humiliated is not a matter of God literally overturning the direction of history to exalt the humiliated so that they now have the same power as their oppressors have had; it is a "voicing" of their reality by manifesting that their lives are rooted in his. And the human imitator of divine love is one who has first recognized his or her dependence on the grace and glory that is secretly all around, ready to absolve, and then has taken on the same task of "voicing" the reality of the other, especially the silenced and despised other.

The theme sketched by Florovsky is echoed by Evdokimov when he says that Christian love of self is love for "God's view of the self," God's vision of the created self as a reflection of divine liberty[37]; because the divine liberty is always exercised in mutual love and creative self-bestowal, the image of God in us can never be identified with mere self-identity—hence the importance of the dialogical construction of selfhood for us. Kirillov, in this connection, perfectly exhibits the mistake of fallen humanity in reducing the image to autonomy and thus to the arbitrary exercise of will, a freedom in no sense anchored in a good that is more than the will's self-approval.[38] So to love the freedom of the other is also to love oneself appropriately—as an agent of God's giving of liberty to the neighbor, as a God-like "author" of their identity; that is, not as a dictator of their fate but as a guarantor of their open future.

We began this chapter with an examination of the two incidents where crosses are exchanged between characters, noting the sharp differences between the two stories and their significance. The incidents have some bearing on the wider theme of "doubling" in the novels, and it may be that in the light of this chapter as a whole there are some considerations on this question to be looked at before moving on. It is a commonplace of commentators that characters in Dostoevsky are often paired or doubled, as if to indicate that there is a connection or that one is inconceivable without the other. The concept is loose in meaning, as will be obvious when we look at its supposed instances, but there is no doubt that Dostoevsky, by presenting so many pairs of characters in close association with each other, is using a tactic for underlining that interdependence of identities which we have been exploring as a general theme in the fiction, the incompleteness of individuals simply as individuals. But in the context of our examination of the theme of responsibility, we can distinguish between pairings that actively build identity and those that represent a mutual dissolution of real identity. Thus in *Crime and Punishment*, Raskolnikov is paired both with Sonya and with Svidrigailov, who "voices" the most anarchic and amoral elements in Raskolnikov's confused store of philosophies.[39] The second half of the novel can be read as a sustained struggle between Svidrigailov and Sonya for Raskolnikov's imagination; it is only by the combined force of Sonya and Raskolnikov's sister Dunya that Svidrigailov is defeated and left to the terrifying squalor of his internal spiritual landscape ("try supposing that all there will be is one little room, something akin to a bath-house, with soot on the walls and spiders in every corner, and there's your eternity for you" [345]). His suicide is as logical as Stavrogin's; it is significant that at one stage in the book's drafting, Dostoevsky planned suicide for both Svidrigailov and Raskolnikov. The question is whether Raskolnikov will accept some—any—kind of answerability to what is beyond himself, even if it is only the bare act of bowing and kissing the ground in public, or whether he opts for Svidrigailov's self-regulated world. The pairing that gives life is the one where the two characters are not simply reflecting to each other their own interiority. Raskolnikov is tempted and fascinated by Svidrigailov, but it is finally Sonya's capacity to offer a larger moral space that triumphs.[40]

Thus doubling or pairing works as a way of distinguishing in the narrative between relations that, by simply mirroring, imprison both characters and relations that offer mutual change because they open a horizon of real difference—in this case, by way of Sonya's unself-conscious ability to locate herself, despite her "sinful" status, in relation to the continuing mercy of God. If we turn again to *The Idiot*, where we find the most systematic patterns of doubling in any of the novels, we find a comparable problem but for a different reason. It is not that Myshkin and Rogozhin mirror each other directly or reinforce each other's perspectives, as Raskolnikov and Svidrigailov threaten to do, but that their complementarity is too symmetrical and too bound up with their role in each other's fantasies and the consequent rivalry over Nastasya. Neither *escapes* from the other—as the harrowing final scene after Nastasya's murder shows. And the pairing of Nastasya and Aglaya likewise collapses into the imprisonment of mutual fantasy; in a way that reflects the relation of Myshkin and Rogozhin, they can see each other only as competitors for the Prince. In this as in other ways, *The Idiot* offers the least positive pattern of all the novels; there is no liberating, "responsible" pairing here.

On the doublings in *Devils*, we have already looked at some of how this works. Stavrogin and Pyotr are, as we have seen, locked into the contest about which is "character" to the other's "author," and the absence in both of them of any center of desire or energy that is directed to an other means that their symbiotic relation is what we have been calling "death-bound." The pseudo-exchanges that the two of them set up or collude with—Fedka taking responsibility for the murder of Marya, Kirillov taking the blame for the murder of Shatov—are parodies of taking responsibility, cases of manipulative "authorship" in which others are forced into roles, and destructive roles at that. Stepan Trofimovich is doubled, not too seriously, with the vacuous Karmazinov, more seriously with Stavrogin's mother and with his son. We have noted that the end of the novel presents father and son alike in flight from the town. Stepan finally escapes from his imprisonment to Varvara's projections and muddled emotions and from his son's vortex of destruction; like Raskolnikov, he encounters an other—the Bible seller, Sofya—who has a horizon outside his own, not confined to being other simply to him.

This is perhaps the point that emerges most clearly: when the other is not just *my* other, there is a possibility of renewal and change. In *Karamazov*, the focus of the pairing technique seems to be Ivan above all: he has his diabolical double in nightmare; he has his "ape," Smerdyakov; there is, so some have read it, his younger self, Kolya; and there is Alyosha, who alone of these doubles is able to bring something other to him. As in the relation between Alyosha and Grushenka, there is something about the *sibling* relationship that ensures the two characters do not simply look at and relate to each other, but find a common space beyond the duality which allows both to move and develop, a common point of reference. Once again, the resonance of a certain kind of Christian trinitarianism are hard to overlook (some twentieth century Orthodox theologians, following through the language of patristic writers like St Gregory Nazianzen, have spoken of the transcendence of the "dyad" in the Trinitarian pattern and thus the overcoming of the mere logical complementarity of "opposition").[41]

In sum: responsibility is the free acceptance of the call to give voice to the other, while leaving them time and space to *be* other; it is the love of the other in his or her wholeness, that is, including the fact of their relatedness to more than myself; it is the acceptance of the labor of decentring the self and dissolving its fantasies of purely individual autonomy, and it is to be open to a potentially unlimited range of relation, to human and nonhuman others. It is the outworking of the ethic of Dostoevskian authorship itself, the confirmation that the tactics of narration in Dostoevsky's novels are inseparable from the vision that drives them. And, given the field in which Dostoevsky operates, a field in which it is the holy as well as simply the good that is in play, it remains to think through, in the final chapter, how the holy becomes visible in these narratives.

5

SACRILEGE AND REVELATION
The Broken Image

As we observed in the introduction to this book, the exact sense in which Dostoevsky could be called an "Orthodox" novelist is a teasing question, but there is no doubt that, to borrow Avril Pyman's term, he operates firmly in the Orthodox "semiosphere,"[1] at least in the major novels of his maturity. This is a world in which it is natural to visit monasteries—even to visit holy or reputedly holy recluses—to light lamps in front of icons, and to confess and receive Holy Communion at certain prescribed times, especially in serious illness. This last point has been rather understated in some commentaries on the fiction; because much of the explicit religious exhortation and reflection in the novels includes little or nothing about the fasts and feasts of the Church (a criticism which Leontiev did not fail to make), one can miss the unobtrusive but significant moments when the sacramental life of the Orthodox Church is invoked as something taken completely for granted. The outward and visible sign of moral or spiritual change is sacramental practice—Raskolnikov's Lenten Communion at the end of *Crime and Punishment* (when he is attacked by his fellow convicts who think he is an atheist), Stepan Trofimovich's reception of the last rites, Markel's Holy Week return to the sacraments. Interestingly, it is only *The Idiot* that is almost entirely lacking in reference to the sacramental practice of the Church: Myshkin, as we have noted, seems to have little firsthand knowledge of Orthodox practice, and his belief, while violently hostile to Roman Catholicism [632ff.], shows no sign of rootedness in any other church and is expressed solely in terms of *pochvennost'* in relation to the Russian soil.

The veneration of icons is, of course, a distinctive mark of Orthodox piety, perhaps of *Russian* piety above all. Recent work on the role of the Russian icon as a social and political symbol and about the correlation between political crisis in Russia and crises about the credibility of holy images has opened up a broad field of study and interpretation in connection with Dostoevsky's fiction. A relatively brief essay by Sophie Ollivier has begun to open up this subject, and her discussion of the role of the icon in Dostoevsky's early story, *The Landlady*, is of great interest, but, as she indicates, there is more to say about the part played by icons in the mature works.[2] In what follows, we shall look at two examples of this, in *Devils* and *The Adolescent*. Both have to do with violation and transgression in connection with holy images, and both suggest certain lines of reflection—very much in tune with some of what we have already said about irony—on the importance of blasphemy and parody in clarifying the nature of the sacred in these narratives.

Part 5, chapter 2 of *Devils*, "Before the Fete," is a strange mélange of events, none of them clearly connected at first reading with the main direction of the plot, except to illustrate that "The people of our town were in a strange state of mind at the time" [323], as they prepare for Mme von Lembke's celebrations: we are vividly shown an atmosphere of hectic and wild mockery directed at everyone and everything. But as the chapter proceeds, a theme emerges very clearly indeed. It is all to do with anxiety about images and representations, imitation and reality: what is visibly breaking down in the course of the chapter is the ability to tell true from false, representative image from *ersatz* substitute, fantasy, gossip, and burlesque from responsible communication. It is in fact about the loss of the skill to recognize things, words, images for what they are.

After two anecdotes about marital abuse (regarded as matter for great merriment among the young hangers-on of Mme von Lembke), the first "theologically" charged outrage occurs when a woman selling gospels—very like Sofya Matveevna whom Stepan Trofimovich meets at the end of the book—is cruelly humiliated when Lyamshin, the leading spirit in the irreverent young set, plants pornographic pictures in her bag. Lyamshin, we learn, has also composed a piano piece combining the Marseillaise with a popular German song, to illustrate the Franco-Prussian War: in this, the fierce idealistic strains of the French anthem are gradually silenced by the increasingly aggressive and vulgar declamations of *Mein lieber Augustin*. A horrible and bloody conflict has been reduced to a parlor game, and the sentiments of the Marseillaise are skillfully made to sound bombastic and petulant. Lyamshin is a skilled mimic as well, and can impersonate "all sorts of Jews [the Russian phrasing is rather grosser, reflecting partly Dostoevsky's prejudices but partly his narrator's], the confession of a deaf peasant woman, or the birth of a child" [327]—in addition to doing a much-appreciated impression of poor Stepan Trofimovich. "He had become indispensable." It is not surprising that he is suspected of having a hand in the second and very serious incident of sacrilegious mockery.

This involves the large icon of the Mother of God displayed outside one of the old churches in the town: the icon is stolen and several jewels are removed from its metal setting; and behind the broken glass of the case, someone (Pyotr, it seems, from later references) has released a live mouse. Crowds of townspeople gather to pray and lament, and a couple of young men push through to throw a derisorily small offering into the collection plate. But at the same time, Lizaveta Nikolaevna, whose increasingly complex relationship with Stavrogin is part of the background of the chapter, arrives, prostrates in veneration and donates her diamond earrings.

Two days later, she is part of a large group of fashionable young people who—at Lyamshin's instigation—are off to visit a local recluse with a reputation as a holy fool, Semyon Yakovlevich. Dostoevsky gives an unsparing portrait of Semyon, who is even more of a parodic and grotesque caricature of a holy hermit than Ferapont. His ludicrous eccentricities are given solemn interpretations by an attendant monk and received with awe by his peasant visitors. En route to Semyon, the party makes a brief diversion to view the corpse of a young man who has committed suicide: when one young man ventures very tentatively to ask why suicide is becoming more prevalent, Lyamshin distracts the group by helping himself to some of the grapes that still stand on the table in the dead man's room. Arrived at Semyon's, the young people witness a few of the "prophet's" buffooneries; then Lizaveta

urges Maurice, her escort, to kneel before Semyon. To everyone's sur-
prise, he does so and is pulled to his feet by a furious Lizaveta. As they
crowd out of the holy fool's room, there occurs the odd episode we
have already noted above in our third chapter, where Lizaveta encounters Stavrogin and appears to be getting ready to slap his face.

The final section of this chapter is a conversation between Stepan
and Varvara, a conversation in which she sets out to dismiss him: she
is tired of being patronized, and she has also clearly been stirred by
Pyotr's presence and the fashionable ferment in town to reexamine
many of her ideas. But here again, holy images are at the center of the
argument. Years before, she claims, Stepan did not want to discuss with
her what her impressions of the Sistine Madonna were ("As though I
was incapable of the same feelings as you" [342]). And now, Stepan is
proposing to talk about the same Sistine Madonna at the von Lembke
literary *conversazione*. Varvara tries to dissuade Stepan from making a
fool of himself by doing this: she is embarrassed by the old-fashioned
rhetoric of ideals and aesthetic perfection, having had the benefit, in
the preceding chapter [305] of Mme von Lembke's up-to-date judgment of the Sistine Madonna ("No one finds anything remarkable in it
now, neither Russians nor the English"). Stepan should confine himself
to being entertaining if he cannot actually be useful. But Stepan will
not be humiliated, and he is boiling up toward a declaration against
the fashionable, rational, utilitarian spirit he discerns around him; he
acknowledges that something has been broken in his relationship with
Varvara, and begins to gather his forces for the grand, disastrous tragic-
comic protest he will make at the literary gathering. He is about to
cross a kind of Rubicon (*Alea jacta est!* [345]).

The point of giving so detailed a synopsis of this chapter is to
illustrate just how many interwoven strands there are here of concern about images and the right response to images. Lyamshin and his
friends are radically incapable of recognizing authority or significance
in the images they literally and figuratively deface. They will make an
obscene or belittling joke of suffering, of suicide, of the innocent book
peddler's attempt to spread the divine Word; they mock the bereavement of the people for whom the theft of the icon is genuinely traumatic, and they sneer at the easy target of Semyon Yakovlevich's crude
nonsense, as if the sacred boils down to this kind of superstitious cha-

rade. In a word, they do not understand that they live in an environment of immense *loss*, not simply a "disenchanted" world but one that is locked into itself and shrinking. Instead of the icon, there is a blank wall, a cavity with a mouse scuttling inside; all they can see of the spiritual resource of a tradition of holiness is the insanity of Semyon, a spectacle that can be enjoyed on an afternoon out, along with the amusing debris from a suicide.

These are, compared with Pyotr, minor demons, but they are no less diabolical. They inhabit, or seek to inhabit, a world in which nothing is serious—in which nothing, that is to say, *signifies*, opens unexpected horizons, exhibits depth or suggests a narrative larger than that of themselves as rootless individuals. They are cut off from the risks of dialogue. What sets Lizaveta apart is that she has recognized something about loss; she knows what it means for the icon to be absent, even if she does not know quite what it would be for it to be present. And when she forces Maurice to kneel to Semyon, it is as if she is pushing her companions to make visible what it is they are truly serving, to enact a sacrament of their nihilism—kneeling before a void, an empty caricature that only reflects their own two-dimensional reality. Her impulse to strike Stavrogin and the fact that she does not actually do so reflect her intuition both that Stavrogin is in thrall to the same emptiness and that he is still capable of a seriousness that the others do not understand at all. She will ultimately discover that he cannot after all escape from the void into any human commitment, and it is left to the despised Maurice to offer her acceptance and grace [534].

The Sistine Madonna may not be an icon in any proper way,[3] but for Stepan it serves at least as an image of dimensions that are being rapidly lost, an image of what matters more than solutions and strategies for social harmony. Like Lizaveta, he has acknowledged that the climate in which he lives is becoming one of bereavement, which is steadily extinguishing the human in the name of a false humanitarianism: in his final, embarrassingly incoherent and ineffectual witness at the von Lembke party, he pleads for a recognition that beauty is more important than science or bread, because there is no impulse to invent anything in a world without beauty and nothing to live for if our only concern is to guarantee that we all stay alive [483]. It is by no means Dostoevsky's own voice that we hear in these words; Stepan is a thoroughly silly man, and his lack of responsibility, shown in his laying the foundations for a new generation's infidelity, and his total lack of concern for the actual specific victims of injustice means that his conversion will be necessary and painful. But we do know that he is on the side of the angels to the extent that he—like all those in Dostoevsky's fiction who resist the reduction of human possibility—has noticed that a humanity with its problems definitively solved is no longer human. The Sistine Madonna, canonized by a rather tired European good taste, may be a suitable icon for the agnostic, but its status as a conventional object of praise is not trivial. Nor, of course, is it an accident that its subject matter is exactly the same as the icon that has been stolen from the church porch. What Stepan confusedly speaks about in terms of "that ideal of humanity" [344] is as it happens a representation of humanity literally giving birth to God.

So this chapter of *Devils* provides an important moment of stock-taking within the narrative for some of its major themes. It situates Stepan's decision to make his doomed testimony at the fete against a background in which the demonic is busy not only with schemes of problem solving but with the dismantling of any acknowledgement of presence, authority or judgment outside the self. It depicts with painful intensity a mindset for which there are no losses that can be called tragic—whether the loss of a life in adolescent despair or the loss of a symbolic map in which a moral location can be plotted. The world it shows is one in which the mouse in the empty icon-case and the antics of Semyon Yakovlevich are all that is left—in the awareness of the fashionable young—of a subtle and resourceful symbolic world. In a novel pretty full of traumatically bleak passages, this chapter ranks among the most simply desolate. It "trails" a number of later events with great skill: Stepan's final, reconciling encounter with the Bible seller Sofya, Stavrogin's meeting with a true "holy fool" in Bishop Tikhon, and his eventual suicide; just as the heartless observers of the nameless suicide at the hotel declare that "the boy could not have done anything more sensible" [331], so after Stavrogin's death the doctors determine "that it was most definitely not a case of insanity" [669]. Lizaveta's sacrificial self-humbling and her generous gift may assist the restoration fund at the church, but they will not be enough to restore the missing "icon" that is God's image in Stavrogin. And just as Stepan Trofimovich cannot be absolved for his responsibility for the moral chaos of the younger generation, so we have been told [264; c.f. 484] that the criminal Fedka is a former serf of his, whom he has lost in a game of cards (or so Pyotr claims): all the future instruments of chaos in the book have their moral roots in poor Stepan's foolishness and selfishness, his unconverted failure to see human actuality for what it is.

Fedka the convict is, in a very Dostoevskian touch, allowed to confront Pyotr Verkhovensky later on, in something like a dramatized debate between honest sin and diabolical evil. Fedka is a thief and a murderer, but he is not an atheist; he is a believer like those Myshkin talks about to Rogozhin, quite confident of the existence of a God whom he nonetheless insults by his behavior. After all, he has only stolen the jewelry from the icon, not desecrated it. And he musters a finely Dostoevskian metaphysical conceit when he challenges Pyotr: "how do you know, maybe my tear, too, was in that moment turned into a pearl in the furnace of the Most High for the trials I've suffered in this world, seeing as I'm just an orphan child what has no proper place or refuge" [557]. Fedka is adept at mobilizing the sentimental rhetoric of criminal as victim, which Dostoevsky so effectively parodies in *Karamazov*, yet, when all's said and done, he has a point. He has been treated as subhuman and acts accordingly. But he still lives his life in relation to a larger picture: he acknowledges that he and his actions have a significance beyond his decisions and purposes. The tear transformed into a pearl is the sort of thing a parodist of Dostoevsky might have come up with, yet another instance of the writer's ironizing of serious issues—because it is always just possible that, in the last analysis or the Last Judgment, crimes *will* turn out to be the fruit of deprivation and suffering. No one, least of all Pyotr, who is getting very impatient with him, can say the last word about Fedka.

The difference is between someone whose evildoing "inhabits" a world in which acts have meanings because persons bear the image of God, and someone whose evil is—to refer back to our earlier discussion—essentially a refusal to belong in any world at all, to belong in bodies, histories and limits. If Fedka is put before us as sinner not devil, this is not because Dostoevsky is sentimentalizing him; he is a ruthless, depraved killer. But he is aware of what he relates to; his life has a meaning which he does not control, and in that sense he is a—hideously disfigured—image. The vandalized icon is a mirror of his own state.

✛   ✛   ✛

Some of these considerations are also at work in the second episode of symbolic desecration we shall (more briefly) be looking at, in *The Adolescent*—not a novel that figures largely in discussions of Dostoevsky's religious philosophy, but one that is nevertheless still saturated in the themes of the other major books in all kinds of ways. Here the icon in question is one that has belonged to Makar Dolgoruky, the saintly peasant who functions as the "good father" to the young narrator, Arkady, over against the young man's biological father, Versilov. Versilov is torn throughout the book—more and more tragically so as the melodramatic plot unfolds—between the world of enlightened progressivism, the world of Stepan Trofimovich, we might say, and the *pochvennost'* of the Russian people and their faith. His duality is played out in the indecision of his sexual life: he has fathered Arkady on Makar's wife, Sofya, but is obsessed by Katerina, who is also the object of Arkady's infatuation. At times, he voices some of Dostoevsky's central concerns, as when he describes turning stones into bread as a "very great" thought but "not the greatest" [211–12], in anticipation of the Inquisitor's challenge. As we have noted,[4] he is also capable of anticipating some of Ivan Karamazov's other views, notably that humanity cannot be loved but only despised. And he shares with his son [466–72] the haunting Golden Age dream which, in various forms, drifts through Dostoevsky's last novels:[5] he envisages a world from which belief has disappeared and in which the muted sense of bereavement caused by this would drive people closer to each other, loving each other "in order to extinguish the great sadness in their hearts" [471]. Yet at the last, Christ returns to them, saying "How could you have forgotten me?" and a "new and last resurrection" follows [472]. In all this tangle of themes and allusions, Versilov establishes himself as serious in the way Ivan Karamazov is serious and open to question in the way Ivan is open to question: is the price of universal love a universal bereavement? can there still be a role for a Christ who (as we can certainly say in this instance) has no God "behind" him? and what exactly is the "resurrection" that is foreseen?[6]

The point, narratively, is that we have been prepared for deeply contradictory responses and acts from Versilov, and the incident with the icon [part 3, chap. 10] is a culmination of these contradictions.

Makar has left the icon to Versilov, and his widow Sofya, Versilov's former mistress, has to give it to him. After an overwrought confession of his sense of torturing duality, Versilov seizes the icon and smashes it; "Don't take it as an allegory," he shouts at Sofya, immediately adding, "anyhow, why not take it as an allegory; it certainly must have been" [508]. The breaking of the image may not be (as he is eager to protest it is not) an outright repudiation of Makar, but it is a symbol, a rather obvious symbol, of his inner dividedness or brokenness—what Arkady eventually identifies, with the help of his medical encyclopedia, as a "serious mental derangement" [552]; in modern terms, Versilov's behavior is schizoid. Arkady, though, is still uncertain about whether it has moral content, and cannot stop thinking of it as "malicious" [552]. At the end of the novel, with Versilov disabled and bedridden after his failed suicide, we are left as uncertain as Arkady: he likes to think that the evil half of his father's personality has somehow disappeared, yet Versilov significantly refuses reconciliation with Orthodox practice on the grounds that he has been struck by "some amusing contrast," the kind of superficial absurdity that Lyamshin and his friends want to mock in their visit to Semyon Yakovlevich [553]. Arkady, one of the most unreliable of all Dostoevsky's narrators as far as his interpretation of events is concerned, is in search of a happy ending that his father will not allow.

If Fedka's stolen, stripped, and profaned, but still in some sense revered icon is an image of his conscious sinfulness, Versilov's broken icon is an image not only of his inner division but of the destructive effect of his inability to commit himself, to inhabit a single world of belief and relationship. He is, in that respect, a less nightmarish version of Stavrogin. The image is broken not just as an act of violence but as a sign of the frustration of a mind that cannot escape its own interior indeterminacy. One world may be as true or real as another; only arbitrary choice can settle it. But Versilov is reflective enough to know that this is no solution at all: we cannot love by deciding. The brokenness of the image in him is a function of this tragic dissolution of the functions of the mind into quasi-agents, as Evdokimov puts it,[7] so that there is no core from which unified agency can proceed. The broken icon represents a wholeness that Versilov cannot reach. It is also an heirloom, perhaps from the days before the Schism, certainly of the sort approved by the Old Believers; although Makar is not an Old Believer, Versilov seems to think the icon is one of theirs [506]. But Makar simply inhabits a continuity stronger than the Schism. And, as if the icon were not already sufficiently semantically overdetermined, we are told that it depicts *two* saints [504]: the commitment that makes us whole, which the icon symbolizes, is to a plurality—it is tempting to say "polyphony," in Bakhtinian mode—not a static or monolithic thing. The breaking of the icon is the tearing apart of a duality or plurality which God has joined together, so to speak.

❖   ❖   ❖

There is one more text in the novels that bears on the subject; although it does not involve the *actual* desecration of an image, it points to several of the issues discussed, around the rejection and absence of the icon and its implications for human agents. Fyodor Karamazov, in his drunken squabbling with Ivan and Alyosha in book 3, chapter 8, has been reminiscing about his second wife, the "shrieker," in the context of describing his methods of seduction. Women must be surprised, he says, surprised that anyone should think them worth troubling with, so surprised that they end up being ashamed "that such a *barin* [gentleman] should have fallen for a miserable little commoner like herself" [182]. With his wife, Fyodor surprises her by a display of exaggerated devotion, drawn out until she laughs; but the laugh, as Fyodor comes to recognize, is the sign of a coming hysterical fit. He does not believe he ever did anything to offend her, except once when he threatened to spit on her beloved icon of the Mother of God, to show her that it will not work any miracles. She is overcome with shock and falls to the floor.

Alyosha, as he hears this story, is also overcome, unconsciously reproducing his mother's reaction, so much so that Fyodor is disturbed. Almost certainly, we are meant to recall what is much earlier [30] described as Alyosha's first memory, of being held before the icon by his mother as she gives way to hysterical cries and screams. The combined memory of the icon and his mother's face is obviously an image of that place where love is secure, despite the overwhelming evidence of suffering; Fyodor's brutal threat is a threat to disrupt this safe place, the perfect repose *à deux* represented by the canonical image of mother and child. The whole scene is one of the most powerful proto-Freudian episodes in the novel. But that is not its sole significance. Fyodor is protesting that his wife invests her hopes and trust in a presence other than his—the sacred realm of the icon, but also, implicitly, his child or children, whom he wants to forget (as he has apparently "forgotten" in late years that Ivan and Alyosha share the same mother [184]). He wants his wife to exist solely for him, like the peasant women whom he seduces; he wants her to feel that she owes her worth to him, so that the mixture of indebtedness and shame that is produced will keep her entirely in subjection. He is out to establish himself as what we have been designating a diabolical "author," a controller of others, deliberately self-isolated. A wife and mother on her knees before an alien presence is a grave threat to this project. It is all of a piece with the observation, again related in the early pages of the novel, that he "had in all likelihood never placed so much as a five-copeck candle in front of an icon" [36].

Fyodor's confusion and disturbance are interrupted, as the next chapter opens, by the entry of a furious Mitya, who assaults the old man, believing that Grushenka is in the house. When he has gone and Alyosha, Ivan and Smerdyakov have got Fyodor to bed, the old man, delighted that Alyosha does not believe Grushenka will marry Mitya, tells his son to take his mother's icon with him back to the monastery. Although attempts have been made to interpret this as turning the once mocked icon into "an instrument of expiation,"[8] this seems a rather sanguine reading. It is more plausible to think of Fyodor, reassured in his erotic ambitions, unconsciously making a final effort to rid the house of the alien presence—now represented both by the icon and by Alyosha—as he pursues his manipulative game. The chapter ends with Ivan and Alyosha discussing Fyodor and Mitya; the fact that Alyosha asks his brother, "does any man really have a right to determine, just by looking at other people, which of them is worthy of living and which is unworthy" [190] strongly suggests that at this moment Alyosha's hatred for his father is as real as that of both his brothers, however much he is ashamed of it. It is as though Fyodor in the whole of this episode has been putting himself further and further outside the ordinary currency of mutuality and respect, and both the recollection of his threat to the icon and his offering of it to Alyosha (does Alyosha take it? we are not told) are visible correlates of this withdrawal. It is his last appearance alive in the novel.

✤   ✤   ✤

These stories of desecrated icons thus begin to outline for us something of what Dostoevsky is suggesting about the visible or recognizable forms of the holy. Holy images contain without simplifying the tensions of the actual world, and they offer a context of narrative and self-identification within which human agents may find a shape and a communicative significance for their activities. They are a measure of the potentially tragic in human agency, because they define the dimensions whose absence we know has the effect of defacing humanity itself. Holy images inform us that our lives are serious—that is, that they may succeed or fail in fulfilling a calling given by the creator, and that failure in this is a hideous and painful loss. And they are also a representation that neither distorts nor substitutes for an underlying reality, but is transparent to its workings—"true" images not because they reproduce something absent but because they express, and give a specific vehicle for, something present. The world depicted in "Before the Fete" is a world without "real presences." The world into which Dostoevsky's fiction intends to induct us is one in which human actions have communicative force because they are imbued with presence— the presence of a real agent, a free and immortal soul, and the presence of what that agent is itself "activated" by, the prototype of the image, the face of God.

This means, as has been hinted, that the broken icon remains in some sense a true icon, deserving of veneration. The person whose world is shaped by what the icon embodies is one who is significantly *vulnerable* to the impact of that frame of reference, and ultimately to the single decisive presence that underlies it. To be visibly affected by that presence, even in minimal ways, is to share in the representation of the presence, to be iconic—which is why Fedka remains an (appallingly damaged) "iconic" figure, not a diabolical one, and why Fyodor Karamazov is on the way to defining himself in diabolical terms, even if (above, p. 65) he is still not a major demonic force within the novel's action. The demonic appears when someone is for all practical purposes impervious to this framework: the face not seen or turned away (as in the anti-icon that is Holbein's dead Christ, a face that is seen only in profile, turned at an angle to any possible encounter). And the basic polarity in Dostoevsky's moral world is not therefore between good people and bad people but between those who acknowledge their iconic dimension and those who struggle to resist or extinguish it.

This makes sense of Raskolnikov's final prostration before Sonya [654] and—even more importantly—Zosima's prostration before Mitya [101]; the elder himself later explains to Alyosha that he "bowed down to the great suffering that is in store for him" [369], and this seems to mean that he sees this suffering as a sign of "iconic" significance. Mitya is "preparing for himself" terrible things, says Zosima [370], but it is clear that this is different from Tikhon's clairvoyant intuition that Stavrogin will commit a serious crime. Zosima is recognizing someone who will be broken by his own awareness of evil, not by his guilt—who will therefore be in some degree an icon, a mark of presence. The whole narrative of *Karamazov* is shaped by Mitya's fate, and the elder's prostration to him near the beginning of the novel indicates where we are going to see presence revealed. And so we do, in Mitya's joyful embrace of sacrifice; his is the most costly embrace of responsibility in the novel, and, despite its being rethought and moderated with the help of Alyosha and Grushenka, the important thing is that he has said yes to it. From one point of view, then, the most effective icon in this story is Mitya; Alyosha may be the paradigm of a Christian embrace of the world, Zosima of a mature love for all and a transforming compassion, but Mitya is the one to whom Zosima pays the kind of veneration that is given to icons. The icon as a cultic object shows brokenness healed and plurality reconciled, but translated into the terms of a human biography, the icon must be a story, a process, that shows the reality of a life that is disrupted by the awareness of loss or sin and still faithful to the world that the icon manifests, faithful enough to become answerable for that world's reality and power.

It is not an accident that Zosima explains his prostration to Mitya after Alyosha has made his customary reverence to him on entering the cell and before he begins his autobiographical musings. Zosima

is, of course, an iconic figure, a visible representation of holiness, surrounded by the customary veneration given to monks and elders, but
before his death he needs to share with Alyosha and the others some of
the history that has made him who he is, and so has made him capable
of recognizing what is going on in Mitya. Zosima, in relating his story,
is telling us to be wary of thinking that human "icons" come ready-
made; he is about to present himself in terms of a history of disruption and self-discovery. Again, it helps to set this alongside the Tikhon
episode in *Devils*, where it is clear that the Bishop, though evidently
meant to be "iconic," is not a timeless image of holiness. His history
is unclear—he has evidently retired from his diocese—and his reputation is mixed, even more so than Zosima's, it seems. Gossips claim
that he drinks, though the truth is simply that he has severe trem-
ors of rheumatic origin; he "had not been able to inspire any particular respect in the monastery itself" [673]. We have noted already the
fact that he has an "unsuitable" personal library. Although we have no
account comparable to Zosima's recollections of Tikhon's personal history, all these details provide that three-dimensionality to the portrait
that makes it a credibly *narrative* image, a study in flaws and disrup-
tions worked through over time. It is as characters who have a history
that Tikhon and Zosima are able to discern the secrets of those who
confront them.

The process by which these narrative images were formed is a fascinating and protracted one. Dostoevsky was determined, we know, to
produce a "positive" portrait of Orthodox holiness in his work. From
the time when he had begun planning the unwritten novel, *The Life
of a Great Sinner* (around the time he was beginning work on *Devils*),
he had intended to depict a close and warm relationship between his
hero and a figure representing the eighteenth-century saint, Tikhon
of Zadonsk.[9] He wrote in 1870 to Maikov and Katkov[10] to announce
his intention of tackling a kind of figure generally ignored in contemporary literature, the figure of a genuinely holy person. The relation
between this figure and the "Great Sinner" as sketched in Dostoevsky's
notes plainly foreshadows that between Alyosha and Zosima, but St.
Tikhon is just as plainly in the background of *Devils* as well. Dostoevsky had written to Maikov that he did not want to invent anything,
simply to show "the authentic Tikhon"; and this is pretty much what

he achieved in *Devils*—though of course this rendering was never published in his lifetime. The original Tikhon was obliged to retire early from his diocese, although he continued his large output of spiritual and theological writing, and the monastery where he spent his later years did not treat him with any great respect. He exhibited acute nervous symptoms and suffered from what we should now regard as severe depressive episodes. He evidently struggled with a difficult, hypersensitive temperament. Tikhon in *Devils* is an unmistakable portrait, far more so than Zosima, and his fascination for Dostoevsky seems to have been not only in his writings and teachings but in these aspects that are so strongly hinted at in the interview with Stavrogin, the flaws and struggles constantly present and constantly overcome.

Georges Florovsky, who wrote insightfully about St. Tikhon,[11] noted the essential thing that must have secured Dostoevsky's loyalty: the saint was unquestionably a *modern man*. Educated, self-aware in a contemporary way, experiencing the divided self unavoidable for a committed Christian in an Enlightenment culture, Tikhon moves through the eighteenth-century environment (complete with the German Pietist devotional rhetoric that had spread among educated Russians) toward a rediscovery of the Paschal and transfigurational mindset of Byzantine spirituality.[12] And much of what Leontiev summarily dismissed in Zosima, says Florovsky, is actually Tikhon. Zosima's cosmic vision, as described in the autobiographical sections, has close analogues in Tikhon, as does his understanding of hell as the rejection of love.[13] In short, Tikhon presented to Dostoevsky just the sort of model Dostoevsky's characters have offered to so many readers—an unequivocally modern subjectivity (with all its weaknesses and potential or actual neuroses) that is still capable of interpreting itself within the "iconic" world.

By the time *Karamazov* was written, the biographical particularity of Tikhon has come to matter a good deal less. Zosima's teaching may be largely rooted in that of Tikhon,[14] but there are no points of contact with Tikhon's life or with his temperament; Zosima may be a modern man, but he is not as complex and neurotic as the Tikhon of history or of *Devils*. This certainly reflects Dostoevsky's contact with the celebrated Optina monastery, one of the major centers of spiritual revival in nineteenth-century Russia, where the institution of elders was strongly rooted. As is well known, Dostoevsky made a pilgrimage in the company of Vladimir Solovyov to Optina in 1878, not long after the devastating death of the novelist's three-year-old son Alexei (Alyosha). He spent time with the leading elder of the day, Amvrosii, and spoke with him about his bereavement: the meeting was reflected in the description of Zosima receiving pilgrims in book 2, chapters 3 and 4 of *Karamazov*, and, according to Dostoevsky's widow in her reminiscences, some of Amvrosii's advice to him is quoted directly.[15] As a result of this, Amvrosii rather than Tikhon of Zadonsk has been claimed as the "model" for Zosima.[16] It is true that the monastery described in the novel and the ambience of Zosima's cell are recognizably—if rather loosely—based on Optina, and even that Zosima's physical characteristics are strongly reminiscent of descriptions and photographs of Amvrosii. But the real elder's life bore no relation at all to the fictional one's. Amvrosii had been a blameless provincial schoolteacher before taking the habit; and it is difficult to see anything distinctive in his teaching corresponding to Zosima's ideas. The question is in any case a silly one: as Frank says, "Dostoevsky never modelled a character on just one real-life figure."[17] And while there may be one or two cases to give us pause—including Bishop Tikhon and perhaps Karmazinov—the general point is valid. We shall not understand Zosima simply by tracing him to Father Amvrosii.

But it is worth observing that, as Salvestroni suggests, the figure of Tikhon of Zadonsk has retreated a little under the impact both of the contemporary reality of Optina and of the fuller awareness of classical Eastern spirituality that was developing in monasteries like Optina (where there was active interest and involvement in translating some of the Eastern spiritual classics into contemporary Russian). The importance in particular of the eighth-century Isaac the Syrian is very clear. Zosima's injunction to love the whole creation, including birds and animals, is an echo of a famous passage in the thirty-eighth of Isaac's discourses, and the same holds for Zosima's warnings against judging others[18]—though this is a very widely instanced theme in monastic literature. And the association of hell with loss of love, found in the teaching of St. Tikhon as well as of Zosima, has a common root in Isaac's theology.[19] Salvestroni, who has traced these textual allusions to Isaac and some other Eastern spiritual authorities with great care,[20] concludes that Dostoevsky is intentionally locating his explicitly religious characters more in the Orthodox mainstream than ever. Leontiev's complaints are dramatically off-target, as are the comments of those who have reduced Zosima's language to "pantheism"; and the degree of dependence in Zosima's teaching upon non-Orthodox sources—St. Francis, the Bishop in *Les misérables*[21]—seems less important (though not negligible) in the light of the evidence of such a conscious use of traditional Orthodox material.

The interest of all this is that it shows Dostoevsky carefully finding his way between tradition and modernity in his depiction of his most overtly saintly characters. St. Tikhon and his very lightly fictionalized portrait in *Devils* are both deeply complex and flawed figures, and their rootedness in the fullness of Orthodox tradition is a little questionable. They are in one sense very "Western" characters. It is important to Dostoevsky to underline this, so as to show that even those who have been through the crucible not so much of general religious doubt but of Western *self*-doubt and the psychological unsettlement this brings are capable of "iconic" transparency. But the thrust of the narrative in *Karamazov* is different from that in *Devils*: Mitya is destined for conversion, not disaster, and for this he needs not just a fellow sufferer, someone who understands his modern angst, but someone who more clearly demonstrates a degree of achieved integration. Zosima, as the spiritual lodestone of the novel, thus needs to be less of a tortured or tragic soul than Tikhon, but he still needs to be someone who has grown into holiness, a "narrative icon," if he is to function in the novel as he must—that is, as the one person who recognizes from the first that Mitya is going to be the bearer of some kind of transformative suffering and who can give a wholly credible account of what the taking of responsibility for all must mean. Zosima has to be more solid than the fictional (and perhaps even the real) Tikhon; and so Dostoevsky locates him in far greater detail against the backdrop of a robust theological tradition—not by any means beyond controversy, but the controversy is less about Zosima as an individual, who is generally revered in the monastery [44], than about the institution of eldership. He even takes the trouble to give us a whole chapter [book 1, chap. 5], which makes a great deal of use of one of the standard Optina biographies,[22] to fill out the backdrop and explain the controversy.

Dostoevsky's statement in his letter to Pobedonsostsev[23] about book 6 as the "reply" to the Inquisitor has for many critics highlighted what are argued to be the artistic failures of book 6—certainly as compared to the unquestioned and sustained intensity of the Inquisitor fable. But what has emerged in this chapter and its predecessor is that it works as a reply to the Inquisitor not by attempting a parallel exercise in concentration and vividness but by offering the imaginative tools that will enable us to understand Mitya's fate—already, in the earlier parts of the narrative, flagged as a, or the, coordinating theme of the novel. If we are to understand what Mitya suffers and accepts, we need to understand not just Mitya as a character but the very nature of conversion to "responsibility." He is to become iconic, but for that to happen, someone with unquestionable iconic authority has to provide the interpretative context for this to make sense. Zosima's prostration to Mitya requires the exegesis that book 6 provides. And because the "answer" to Ivan is not a theory but the actuality of life lived in responsibility, that is what needs explication—not in Zosima's life and teachings as something in themselves, but in that record read as the key to the events of the rest of the novel. For that to work as Dostoevsky needs it to, the figure of Zosima demands both the rounding-out of a narrative background and a degree of explicit spiritual perspective that he has not yet elaborated. The icon not only reveals the mystery it portrays; it reveals what is hidden in the person who is confronted by it. The more depth and fullness in the depiction, the more the capacity to unveil the beholder. Thus Zosima, as the "narrative icon" who will reveal the mystery of Mitya's vocation and potential, needs to be as well-resourced as possible, heavily charged with the meanings authorized by his faith and practice.

This may serve as a bit of a corrective to the appealing notion, already referred to more than once, that the Dostoevskian saint is a "face on the wall," casting revelatory light on events but not contributing to how they turn out. There is, as we have granted, some real truth in this, but if it is read as suggesting that the iconic presence literally makes no difference, we have misunderstood the nature of that presence. The unveiling is also a gift of the potential for encounter: the icon is itself an invitation into a dialogical world. As a cultic object, it is both clearly defined in relation to persons and events and to the disciplines of painting within a tradition, and also, by means of a range of sophisticated conventions, such as the famous reversal of visual perspective, presented as a question to the limits of the world occupied by the beholder. It does not leave the world unchanged. Response to what the icon opens up draws more out of the icon itself: it is not something that we can *finish* with, interpretatively or imaginatively. Thus the narrative icon, the holy character, is bound to open doors for those who are engaged by it (Stavrogin is unambiguously presented with a specific and unforeseen *choice* by Tikhon). Iconic presence is neither a passive *marginale* nor an intrusion of some fixed point that will dictate to others or coercively organize other realities around itself. To return to the language of Gary Saul Morson about the background assumptions of religious narrative (above, p. 143), the icon makes visible the "assumption of plenitude," the excess of possible meaning and resource that maintains the narrative itself as a symbol of possible reconciliation.

Inexorably, the Christological question returns. The icon that is recognizably anchored in the actual world of decision and change, yet carries an abundance that inducts us into a larger world is—as the theologians of the Christian East consistently argued—an appropriate sign of the primordial icon, the eternal image of God which is embodied in time in the flesh and blood of Christ. As we have seen, this Christological reference brings with it an inescapable "kenotic" dimension: the coexistence of infinite abundance with historical limitation is only thinkable in connection with a divine self-withholding, a voluntary absence that most powerfully testifies to loving presence. The author becomes a character; the unrepresentable becomes a visible phenomenon. And when that authorial self-emptying is represented, it is in the form of an image that is, inevitably, caught up in processes of seeing and not-seeing, understanding and not-understanding, reverence and contempt, like all other phenomena in the world, which are all vulnerable to being made sense of in diverse ways. Even the eternal, finally authoritative image, when it is manifested in history, is subject to rejection and disfiguring; the Word of God is not naturally and visibly the last word in history as it proceeds.

So just as the authority of the divine Word has to establish itself, in and through the unceasing continuation of dialogue, as that which continually offers excess or abundance which may be healing, so the divine image establishes itself not by universally compelling attraction but by its endurance through disruption and defilement. Fyodor Karamazov offers to spit on his wife's beloved icon, as if the lack of any visible sanction or punishment that would prevent him doing this is a demonstration of the lack of "real presence" in the image, but he has failed to grasp the fundamental fact—to which all Dostoevsky's stories of desecrated images point—that it is in the nature of images to be capable of desecration, and that what makes images sacred is not some magical invulnerability or supernatural protection but their capacity to retain in themselves the real energy of another world, transmitted into the world of isolated and death-bound agents. The icon is in this sense a "powerless" image, in that it is not safe from what history may do to it; the crucifixion of the fully incarnate image of God lets us know that. But a vulnerable image is not an empty one.

What comes into focus here is the same theme that is discernible in the discussion of the dialogic nature of our reality. The presence of an otherness that is ultimately quite inaccessible to me and resistant to my control, the otherness that makes unceasing dialogue possible, is not a presence that simply denies my identity, a threat to my security and ontological stability, an enemy never to be overcome. It is an offer and an invitation: it is an otherness that seeks itself in me, and enables me to seek myself in it, not a diminution of my own solidity but the condition for it, because what is utterly without foundations is a self-hood cut off from dialogue, from the active presence of the other. And the "iconic" other, the holy image either in the literal form of the icon or in the translation of the icon into narrative in a holy person, is likewise not a kind of impenetrable surface repelling my identity, nor a solid presence invading my weak and under defended territory, but a presence that offers to nourish and augment what I am. In the world of human relations, in which we all have some iconic function in regard to each other, what expresses this is precisely the mutual answerability and taking responsibility we have examined at length. And although we do not literally contribute to the cultic icon, let alone to its prototype, our relation with it continually augments what it is able to give us, augments its concrete presence in history.

This may be the point for a brief word about the metaphysical theory that was being evolved by Dostoevsky's friend Vladimir Solovyov in the years leading up to the publication of *Karamazov*. What came to be called "Sophiology" was a schematic vision of the universe in relation to God in which the pivotal concept was that of "Holy Wisdom," *sophia*, understood as a quasi-personal energy diffused throughout creation, reflecting the imminent power and wisdom of God—a sort of hidden impulse in things toward order and beauty and union with the creator. For Solovyov, this *sophia* was conceived in strongly mythological terms, virtually an "eternal Feminine" in the universe, and he believed that he had three times been granted a direct vision of her/it.[24] In the "Lectures on Godmanhood" which he delivered in Petersburg in 1878, this scheme receives an early airing; it was to be much elaborated by him and by the next generation of Russian religious philosophers, and to be the subject of fierce controversy well into the twentieth century.[25]

But its relevance here is that language about pervasive hidden harmonics in creation and about the overcoming of individualistic, mutually impenetrable definitions of identity is central in the sophiological scheme. Solovyov understood the notion of "Godmanhood," *bogochelovechestvo*, as that transformed human identity that Christ made possible, a humanity of perfect mutuality, reflecting the otherness without alienation that is eternally real in the life of the Trinity and in the union without confusion of humanity and divinity in the incarnate Christ. The distinction between the "God-man," Christ incarnate, and the "man-God" who is the hope of certain kinds of radical activist is made in so many words in Stavrogin's conversation with Kirillov [244]; it is hard to believe that Solovyov intended no allusion to this in his lectures. But the further question of whether Solovyov in turn influenced Dostoevsky is a harder one. Dostoevsky's widow claimed that Ivan Karamazov owed a good deal to the young philosopher, and it is true that Ivan's argument for the convergence of Church and state as presented to his monastic audience in book 2, chapter 5 has strong echoes of Solovyov's advocacy of a "free theocracy"[26]; Solovyov himself wrote that he and the novelist had discussed these matters during their trip to

Optina.[27] It is possible, even likely, that these conversations, following on the lectures (which Dostoevsky had attended), bore fruit in some of the shaping of Ivan's discourse in the novel. Beyond this, it is harder to be sure. Although the "cosmic" spirituality evident in *Karamazov* is very much in tune with Solovyov's thinking, its sources, intellectual and stylistic, go back well before the late seventies in Dostoevsky's reading and writing. And while some have made much of the fact that the name "Sofya" seems invariably to be associated in Dostoevsky's novels with saving or holy presences,[28] the only such figure to appear after Dostoevsky and Solovyov came to know each other is perhaps the least persuasive, Alyosha's mother. There is no way in which the sophiological vision can have informed the earlier instances, and in spite of valiant attempts to show that sophiology has roots much further back in Russian Christianity, there is nothing in Dostoevsky's notebooks or recorded reading that would support the idea that he was drawing on some buried theological tradition. Solovyov himself, in developing his system, made extensive use of Gnostic and Cabbalistic Jewish speculation rather than any overtly Orthodox sources, and it was left to the next generation of sophiological thinkers, notably Pavel Florensky and Sergei Bulgakov, to provide a somewhat more respectable theological pedigree. Reluctantly, we must conclude that it is unlikely that Dostoevsky deliberately invested the name with special significance.

What is pretty evident is that there was a real convergence between the two men in their intuitions about mutuality and mutual answerability as the key elements in a God-oriented universe. For Dostoevsky, naturally, this expresses itself as a set of assumptions about *speech* and representation; this is what novelists concern themselves with. For Solovyov, it is a more theoretically ambitious matter; how far his ambitions succeed is debatable, given his almost complete disregard for the conventions of ordinary philosophical argument, but his scheme remains a monument of imaginative comprehensiveness. And the consequence both draw from their basic notion is that the essence of any challenge toward human maturity is to come to understand an otherness that is not threatening. Dostoevsky's characteristic insistence on the acceptance of limit, and therefore of suffering, as against the diabolic temptation to seek for an identity not bound by limit and therefore supposedly invulnerable, is a translation of the principle of mutuality into the most uncompromising terms of narrative risk, self-venturing, and self-loss.

Holy images presuppose that there is something to be imaged, a form that can be rendered in different modes or media. And this means that we can distinguish between a religious sensibility for which images are radically inappropriate, a sensibility for which the interplay of images is in an important sense arbitrary and various in its combinations, and one in which there are canonical images which act as focal points of reference. It is obvious that Dostoevsky as an artist of religious conviction has nothing to do with any "aniconic" spirituality (a different matter, as we shall see, from a spirituality that takes negation and absence seriously), but there have been quite a few commentators who, as we noted in the Introduction, would argue that he belongs more with the second than the third category—that is, that in spite of his declared dogmatic loyalties he presents a world in which specifically Orthodox or even specifically Christian categories are not finally determining. A very careful and typically insightful version of this has been argued by Malcolm Jones, making use of the notion of "minimal religion" outlined by Mikhail Epstein in essays on the contemporary religious consciousness emerging in Russia—the environment of "post-atheism."[29] In essence, the argument is this: Russian Christianity has always had within it a deeply "negative" impulse, the apophatic concern to deny that God can be captured by word, image or concept; this generates an anti-intellectualism in Russian religion, which has had some very varied and strange effects, but which can also be seen as part of the climate in which nineteenth-century nihilism and Soviet atheism were able to grow; after the death of official atheism, what survives of the old religious impulse is, paradoxically, just that obscure sense of the sacred that evades controlling definitions, discernible in folk religion, in some more self-conscious styles of neopaganism, in what Epstein calls "minimal religion," the religious sense separated from any specific marks of doctrinal identity.

Jones' case is that, whatever Dostoevsky's intentions, he ends up leaving the door clearly open to "minimal religion"; "It is as if, at the level of ideal author, his text is telling us that a situation has arisen out of the conflict between belief and unbelief in the modern age in which the richness of that tradition has to be put aside in order that personal faith may be allowed to blossom again."[30] Because the conflicts of the novels are not (and cannot be) resolved simply in the terms of the Orthodox Christian tradition, we are actually left as readers with an indeterminate invitation to faith, left in a "semiotic space" quite other than the ecclesial home the novelist actually occupied, though still one that houses a sensibility that "preserves the image of Christ to guide it."[31] The fact that in his "Cana" experience, Alyosha can only say that "something" or "someone" visited his soul bears out the argument that the specificity of Orthodox commitment is being—just how deliberately we cannot know—marginalized.[32] And even Zosima's own recollections represent "[m]inimal religious experience . . . channelled through the Orthodox tradition, as though in a kaleidoscope in which, just occasionally, fragments suddenly and unexpectedly come together."[33]

"Minimal does not mean superficial and certainly not trivial," Jones insists,[34] but, granted that this is a reading that takes the religious dimension with complete seriousness and depends upon careful exegesis of the narrative, does it quite do justice to what Dostoevsky is doing? The answer to this is not to be found simply in detailing explicit Orthodox and patristic allusions in, say, Zosima's discourses, though this is not insignificant. It is rather in understanding how the actual method, not merely the content, of the fiction requires to be understood in reference to a set of focal processes and images. To argue this is not to demand that the novels be read as transcriptions of Orthodox doctrine, let alone as compellingly persuasive transcriptions; it is to acknowledge that our reading of the fiction is best resourced when we are able to trace some of its dominant themes and tropes in relation to a determinate central narrative and image.

Thus it is not decisive in reading Dostoevsky that the visions of Zosima or Alyosha are theologically inexplicit, to a degree that will doubtless continue to cause unease to some devout readers. The idea that there should be a "full" Orthodox and Christian idiom employed for these passages rather begs the question of what is novelistically possible or appropriate, as though the only way in which the text could reflect Dostoevsky's theological conviction were by the direct incorpo-

ration or citation of theological material. He is, after all, writing immediately for an audience that, while it is vaguely familiar with Orthodox
practice, is likely to be indifferent or hostile to explicit credal profession. What is to be communicated from a doctrinal standpoint is
pretty well bound to be less than fully spelled out if such an audience
is not to be lost. And, at a deeper level, the theological subtext cannot
be presented as definitive, for all the reasons we have discussed already
in connection with the dialogic and polyphonic register of the fiction.
Yet this does not mean that the subtext is absent or that it is to be simply relativized in reading. As we have seen, the very fact of this dialogic
method points ultimately to theological questions: we cannot forget or
ignore Bakhtin, surely one of Dostoevsky's most committed and subtle
readers, returning constantly to those Christological categories that
enable him to give proper weight to the novelist's own wrestling with
the nature of authorship and freedom. The myth—using the word, for
the moment, neutrally—of a single and foundational act of transfer-
ring responsibility, the mythical figure of a "liminal" person inhabit-
ing the frontier between complete vulnerability and limitless excess
of resource, these categories are, for Bakhtin, inescapable in the work
of interpretation in general and interpreting *this* author in particular.[35]

What should make us pause before accepting the thesis about
"minimal religion" as it stands is that Dostoevsky's fiction overall has
two characteristics that do not easily fit the model of an ultimate "formal" detachment within the work itself from doctrinal specificity.
First, very simply, they are about life and death, and the life in question
has a face and a particularity. So that, second, they are among other
things protracted reflections on images of definitive symbolic power.
We have seen what it is for figures in the books to be "life-bound"
or "death-bound": this does not depend on their capacity to find or
inhabit *some* or *any* system of meaning; it depends on their capacity to
be brought into the pattern of mutual responsibility. Death is, again
very specifically, the refusal of a certain relation with the truth represented by mutuality and exposure. Thus the engagement with life
has to be represented as somehow bound to engagement with a figure embodying the reality of freedom within the limits of history and
mutual answerability; it is bound to what the icon is about, what the
icon pictorially embodies. There is one and only one kind of "presence"

that sustains a possible future from within the nightmare of deformed and deforming human interaction, the nightmare both of the rampant sadism illustrated by Ivan's terrible anecdotes and of the no less terrible vacuity, frivolity and casual inhumanity of the demon-haunted society of *Devils*, and that is the presence of Christ. But we need to clarify. *Pace* Malcolm Jones, this is more than the claim that any future religious awareness stemming from Dostoevsky's fiction will "preserve the image of Christ to guide it." This would be dangerously close to that focus on Christ as inspiration and teacher which the *Devils* notebooks warn us against. As this chapter has attempted to show, it is the shape of the narrative of the incarnate Christ that allows us to make sense of the particular kind of imaging that is going on in both the saints and the sinners of Dostoevsky's world. That narrative is not simply the ensemble of stories about Jesus recorded in Christian Scripture; it is also the narrative of the self-displacement of God that occurs when the eternal Word becomes human and historical. It is thus a narrative of vulnerability accepted: whatever images this embodying of the eternal image is bound to be subject to the possibility of violent disfiguring, in varying degrees. A true image of it will necessarily be something that can be broken or spat upon; a narrative image is one that has endured something of the self-disfiguring of rebellious individualism. Take away the "kenotic" story at the center, and the complex unfolding of true images in narratives of sin and forgiveness, rupture or suffering and enduring presence, loses its logic.

Of course Dostoevsky leaves us with the option of accepting or not accepting this core narrative as a basis on which—or a presence in dialogue with which—we as readers may establish our identities. It is open to us to follow paths that approximate to "minimal religion" or any number of other options: the last word has not been said as far as the history of reading the texts is concerned—not by the author, not by any one interpreter. But a "minimal" response will, on Dostoevsky's terms, leave us with a problem. A system of representations without a defining center, a core image/narrative, is no less problematic than a world without presence at all, because such a system implies that visible and narratable images are ultimately exchangeable for one another. There is no image that provides the capacity for all others, no voice that definitively sustains the possibility of dialogue, that is never silenced. If the minimal option reduces the scope of the fiction to a range of possible meanings for the individual reader to choose from, what is lost is the sense of any possible presence in the text that lays a claim on the reader (whether or not such a claim is judged finally acceptable or intelligible). In short, it is by no means obvious that what Dostoevsky's fiction is "really" telling us is that the conflicts of belief and skepticism offer us no alternative but to revise our expectations of what can be honestly affirmed in faith as a result of reading this fiction, and to be content with an unsystematic and largely unfocused sensibility, detached from any "interpretative tradition"[36] of doctrine or practice. The manifest fact that the conflict between faith and its opposite in the fiction is not decisively resolved should not mislead us. It is in the nature of the enterprise that no final theoretical solution is given: only the reader can decide what kind of life it is desirable to live as a result of engaging with the dialogue, what is concretely made possible for him or her. As Myshkin remarks, atheists usually seem to be talking about something other than what believers think they are saying, and—as several commentators have underlined[37]—the belief-unbelief standoff resists being rendered in terms of a detached inquiry about some third party (God). Yet the decision for belief is clearly, for Dostoevsky, a matter of deciding for a structure of moral life authoritatively shaped by the central icon that is the narrative and presence of Christ.

Before moving on, there is one further—putatively nonfictional—anecdote about the desecration of the holy that bears in a number of ways on what we have been discussing. This is the essay "Vlas" contained in Dostoevsky's *A Writer's Diary* for 1873.[38] The piece turns upon a story which Dostoevsky presents as having been told to him by an elder in a monastery; this, incidentally, gives him an opportunity of some ironic disclaimers: far be it from him to say anything about elders or monasteries, about the education and insight of elders and the transforming force of their counsel and example—"But since we are living in the real world as given, one cannot throw even a monk out of the story if the whole thing is based on him."[39] The elder relates an encounter with a peasant pilgrim who is still after many years seeking to atone by his suffering for a blasphemy many years before. He was dared by a neighbor to take his Communion but not swallow it, keep the consecrated morsel and then put it on a stick and fire a gun at it;

as he aimed, he suddenly saw the figure of the crucified in front of him and lost consciousness. Since then, he has been a wanderer, despairing of salvation and inviting suffering in reparation for his crime.

This leads Dostoevsky into musing on the distinctive features of the Russian psyche—its extremism in good and evil, the impulse that turns someone from the abyss of destructiveness toward penitence, the urge toward suffering among the Russian people and the fact that at least Russian sinners are never complacent in their sins but recognize their baseness. This may lead them to push their fury at themselves outwards in violence against others as a way of coping with the suffering that their self-knowledge brings, but it means that if and when they repent they will exact "terrible vengeance" on themselves. The actual dare, Dostoevsky suggests, must have its origins in buried hostility between the young man and the friend who prompts his crime; the friend forces him to carry out what must have been a secret diabolical fantasy, attractive in its very extremity. And the extremity is real because "[p]erhaps the only love of the Russian People is Christ, and they love His image in their own fashion, that is, to the point of suffering."[40] As the young man prepares for his act of sacrilege, what was going on in his soul? A sense of "mystical horror," certainly, but also a hardening that enabled him to go up for Communion even with his purpose of defiling the sacrament. The young man must therefore have been of unusual spiritual strength and resourcefulness, especially as he still does not know exactly what outrage his friend has planned. And then at the last moment, the inner falsehood and cowardice "burst forth from his heart" in the image of the crucified: it is not, Dostoevsky emphasizes, that there is a divine intervention, a parting of the clouds, only a voice from within. What finally happens to the sinner we do not learn—nor, Dostoevsky says, do we know what became of the other young man, who "did not see the vision, after all."[41]

The moral of the piece is, it turns out, to do with what is being said about the Russian peasantry in the wake of the emancipation of the serfs in 1872—Dostoevsky wants to reassure his readers that at the crucial moment, whatever extremes of violent and drunken behavior are reported, the people will show themselves faithful: "the falsehood, if indeed it is falsehood, will burst forth from the People's hearts and confront them with incredible accusatory power."[42] The potential of the people to save the drifting and faithless educated classes is unaffected by incidents of barbarity or depravity, because there remains a solid ground of self-knowledge in the presence of God that will keep the Russian peasant from ultimate apostasy and self-deceit. The conclusion is of a piece with so much of the *Writer's Diary*, with its aggressive defense of the uniqueness of Russian sensibility and spirituality and its messianic confidence in the Christian peasant. But the interest of this little essay for our purposes does not lie in the conclusion. It is rather that the story casts a good deal of light on all we have been considering in this chapter. Real blasphemy—to state a truism—is possible only where belief is strong, and, as Dostoevsky notes, the paradox is that it takes a certain kind of spiritual strength to perpetrate a blasphemy or sacrilege in a context of unquestioning belief. But this means that the sacrilege is inescapably an act of colossal violence against oneself. If it is true that Christ is the sole abiding object of the people's love (yes, of course a sentimental bit of Slavophil mythology if you like), violence against the Holy Gifts of the Eucharist is a denial of what is most formative and definitive in a Russian life; it is not surprising that the young man's despair is so acute. But because he does not minimize the gravity of what he has done or planned to do, he is—to go back to the distinction made earlier—a sinner, not a demon.

And the desecration takes a very clear "iconic" form. The holy elements are not seen as just objects surrounded with a generalized *mana*: they represent the crucified Christ, with all that this signifies about the acceptance of expiatory suffering. They are an image that (as is spelled out more fully in the narrative pattern of *Karamazov*) opens on to the horizon of responsibility and mutuality. What is important for our argument here is that this anecdote, like all Dostoevsky's stories about desecrated images, relies for its meaning upon the absolute authority of the image, grounded as it is in the incarnational paradigm. Whatever "religious consciousness" Dostoevsky imagines for the future, it cannot be one in which images like this have no authority; to understand what kind of religious awareness he believes to be necessary for our social and spiritual salvation is to understand why blasphemy or sacrilege looks like *this*. A spirituality detached from this might appeal to fragments of Dostoevskian citation but would not represent what the actual fictions insist upon.

✵   ✵   ✵

We began this chapter by looking in detail at a section of *Devils* which seems designed to highlight anxiety about images or representations and reality. The world of that section is one in which nothing is sacred: if an icon can be stolen and mocked, it is not surprising that the dead body of a young suicide prompts little except frivolous and callous response. But there is an underlying problem: not every image of the holy is obviously authoritative or credible. Semyon Yakovlevich is, so to speak, the icon reduced to a cartoon. We are in a world where the callousness and casual blasphemy of the young generation is confronted only by a mindless and superstitious religiosity. There are no narrative icons around, and so the cultic icon is in danger of being seen as equally an empty sign, without power. And when the image, in painted wood or flesh and blood, is experienced as vacuous and ineffectual, the potential for realizing the image of God in actual human beings disappears: no icon, no human compassion or self-questioning.

So Dostoevsky is not confronting the world of Lyamshin with a triumphant reassertion of Orthodox ecclesiasticism or a requirement for unreasoning submission to traditional authority. He recognizes that in a certain sense the icon has to vindicate its authority, and that therefore there must be narrative transcriptions of what the icon presents which can have some claim to restore that authority—though he also recognizes that, in this ambiguous and ceaselessly "dialoguing" world, such a claim can still be resisted and countered. Tikhon's role in *Devils* as originally conceived was evidently to sketch what this strategy might look like in practice, with Tikhon exhibiting the questionable, ambiguous personal character of a saint whose holiness is at best a fragile achievement over time. Tikhon's fate at the hands of the censor meant that the challenge of communicating holy presence in fictional form remained on the table for Dostoevsky. Makar, in *The Adolescent*, is at best an outline, rather skewed by Dostoevsky's hope to produce a Dostoevskian rival to Tolstoy's Platon Karatayev. But the interwoven stories of Zosima, Markel, Alyosha and Mitya are his mature essay in imaging the holy—not simply in one "achieved" character, despite the pivotal significance of Zosima, but precisely in the interaction and mutual mirroring of these lives. Which suggests that, despite what Dostoevsky seems to claim, book 6 *alone* is not the response to the

Inquisitor. But neither is that response a completely unfulfilled promise relegated to the unwritten continuation of *Karamazov* and embodied in the future of Alyosha. The presence and effectiveness of the holy is already imaged in what we have of the novel.

And it works in part through the way in which, in the stories of young Zinovy and of Mitya, the turning point is identified with a moment in which some sort of depth is acknowledged in the other, especially the victim. Zinovy/Zosima's shame at his violence toward his servant is related to Mitya's dream of the burnt-out village and the hungry baby: something is *offended*, not just assaulted, in the suffering that violence causes. It is the awakening of a sense of what is blasphemous; and this brings Zinovy and Mitya closer to Fedka and to the "Vlas" of Dostoevsky's 1873 essay. Something has been insulted and defaced and the observer is responsible for restoring it or making reparation for it. Alyosha's advice to Mitya not to take on more suffering than he can bear is a wise modification of the "maximalist" response illustrated by the peasant in "Vlas," reminding the sinner that mercy overtakes literal reparation, a message that "Vlas" cannot hear. But mercy is effective in the human heart only when the recognition has occurred that prompts the first response of an appalled longing for expiation. Dostoevsky is walking a familiar theological tightrope between "cheap grace" and salvation by works alone—a particularly difficult tightrope in an Eastern Christian context which is suspicious of Augustinian formula about the sovereignty of grace and strongly committed to the importance of ascetic labors in order to remain in God's grace.

The cultural situation evoked in *Devils* illuminates that teasingly repeated formula in *Karamazov* about everything being permitted if God does not exist. What happens "if God does not exist" is not that a particular item is withdrawn from the sum total of actual things, nor that a crucial sanction against evildoing is taken away, so that no punishment for evil can be guaranteed. It is that we are no longer able to see violence against others as somehow blasphemous, an offense against an eternal order; no longer able to see our dealings with each other as opening on to a depth of interiority that we cannot fathom or exhaust. In a world deprived of such possibilities, it is reasonable enough to respond to a suicide by saying "it was the best solution" [331]; there is nothing definably insane about taking one's life [669]. Neither, of course, is there any reason to think that any other human subject has any more absolute a reason to live than oneself. Kirillov's suicide is prompted by a kind of passion for the life of others, and that is what sets him apart from Pyotr and most of the group. But Pyotr is happy to use this suicide as a useful tool to manage the results of a murder.

The essential problem, though, is *not* that the disappearance of the sacred licenses murder, although that is the presenting symptom both in *Devils* and in *Karamazov*. This is the extreme conclusion that needs to be faced and narrated, but which is not actually the root of the matter. The fundamental issue is what is exemplified in Stavrogin: there is nowhere and no one to which or to whom fidelity can be given, no source outside the will from which difference, otherness, can be absorbed in a renewal of life or energy. Everything depends on choice, and what is chosen today need have no relation to what is chosen tomorrow or what is chosen by anyone else. There is no rationale for *narrative* itself, since these choices need not in any way be seen in terms of growth, of the aggregation of an identity. From the point of view of the timeless choosing ego, all moments are equal; there is no sense that what is done now shapes what is possible in other circumstances, when of course a completely different or contradictory option may be taken. This is why Stavrogin's associates regard him with such desperate frustration and disappointment: he has said this or that, he has commended this or that course of action, but he has moved on, and those who have tried to take his belief or policy at a certain point as authoritative have found themselves abandoned. And because of this equivalence in all choices, the choosing ego is more and more reduced to paralysis: if one act is much like another, why act at all? What is depicted as *Devils* moves toward its conclusion is the process by which the elevation of choice increasingly produces an evacuation of desire.

We are back with the theme of our second chapter, the identification of the diabolical with the end of narrative. The world without credible images portrayed in *Devils* is equally a world in which there is no context for relating stories or constructing ways of speaking about an identity; it is therefore also a world without dialogue. As Stavrogin's example again shows, dialogue is not possible with an absent interlocutor, an other who refuses to *inhabit* their acts and words. What the holy image represents is profoundly connected with the possibility of language itself, as a communal and dialogical reality, and as something that embodies the inextinguishable freedom to go beyond what is given. Paradoxically, to emphasize the absolute liberty of the choosing ego is finally to eradicate that freedom to go beyond the given: because the isolated will can only ever return to itself and is impervious to otherness, it cannot transcend its own moment by moment agenda.

Whether in relation to language, to narrative or to images, Dostoevsky's fiction insists upon an anthropology, a coherent conception of the human, and the anthropology he outlines is consistently one in which the human operates in recognizably human fashion only in an imaginative world where human persons are seen as bearing significance beyond themselves, and particularly beyond their self-understanding as individuals. The well-known instances where he deliberately underscores the unpredictability of some action, the absolute and urgent reality of all possible options,[43] are not examples of a romanticism of arbitrary decision but illustrations of how little we know of the characters before us and how little they themselves know. Rather than pointing us toward a solitary and context-free choosing will, these moments show the strangeness that accompanies the formation of identity. As Morson argues in his introduction to the *Writer's Diary*, comparing Mitya's indecision as he picks up the pestle with which he *might* be going to attack his father with the real-life case of a woman charged with attempted murder, " [i]f their only choice was whether to carry out their plan, then time merely enacts or fails to enact what was there from the outset, but it does not shape anything and does not possess a developing plurality of possibilities."[44] In short, what is revealed in these moments of poised indecision and multiple options is not the simplicity of a bare will that can decide quite arbitrarily but the immense complexity of an embodied and embedded self, upon which countless lines of force converge.

And it is this sense of a crowded background to the acts of the will that gives us a further clue in understanding how holy images work in the Dostoevskian world. We noted earlier how Epstein's concept of minimal religion appealed to the history of apophatic theology in Eastern Christianity. This in effect to read the history of apophaticism in a rather undialectical way, as if the point were the inculcation simply of a *suspicion* of image or concept. There is in the theological tradition and in modern Orthodox discussion[45] a distinction between saying that the ultimate truth of God is incapable of being captured definitively by any picture or idea and saying that the truth of God is radically *different* from what is represented. It is not that the image is somehow untruthful; or rather it becomes so only if it is regarded as final or comprehensive. Images are not unilaterally discarded in this tradition, but seen as truthful though imperfect vehicles for the active presence of what they represent. They neither deliver a complete grasp of the underlying reality nor act only as a trigger to wordless contemplation; they create a relationship in which discovery occurs, and continues to occur as the contemplation of the image goes on. The negativity is less a matter of an absolute "this is not it"—which might suggest that there could in principle be a standard by which the accuracy of a proposition about God could be measured—than of "this is not, and can never be, all"— since there is an infinity of excess in the being of God beyond what can ever be expressed. But without the continuing or recurring reference to the truth that the image imperfectly communicates, contemplation of the truth represented is undermined.[46]

This is a negative theology that depends—again—on the "assumption of plenitude"; the negative moment is the recognition of excess, not absence or privation. It is true that Russian Christianity inherited aspects of the apophatic tradition, especially through the "hesychast" disciplines received from Mount Athos from the fifteenth century onward and central especially to the monastic ethos of Optina. But it is not very safe to conclude that this fed so directly into popular religion or even intellectual culture that it paved the way for nihilism and the repudiation of faith under Communism. The characteristic problem of Russian religion in the early modern period (though that designation is not really very helpful where Russia is concerned) was an *over*-identification with religious forms, as shown in the seventeenth-century Schism: any relativizing of the external vehicles of faith was seen as an attack on the fundamentals of Orthodox and Russian integrity. And it was the failure of protests against the new forms that prompted the emergence of that apocalyptic radicalism that did indeed affect some of the revolutionary spirit of the nineteenth century. If the images fail or are destroyed, there is nothing to hope for in history, and the options are either quietism or suicidal violence.[47] This is recognizably the same "semiosphere" that Dostoevsky is working in: passionate and apocalyptic violence against oneself or others (Kirillov) is one response to the failure or absence of authoritative "icons"; and another is the antihumanist indifferentism of Lyamshin or, more sinisterly, Pyotr Stepanovich, a violence of a different and more spiritually troubling kind. And it is telling that in *The Idiot*, with the anxiety it constantly hints at as to whether Myshkin is positively a vehicle of transforming grace or not, a novel, in fact, that again threatens a loss or occlusion of images, we should find—if in slightly burlesque form—a self-proclaimed expert in the exegesis of the Apocalypse, the slippery and untrustworthy Lebedev. He is a figure whose inner solidity is manifestly in question, someone who lives in a world where images have lost their anchoring power and the complex symbols in Holy Scripture are at the mercy of unreliable interpreters.

We are back once more with the recurrent point that the tension in Dostoevsky is not straightforwardly between belief and unbelief—as if it might be possible for a modified and less straitened form of belief to arise as a resolution of sorts—but between the world in which image, word, and presence are realities that create transformation by addressing the human subject from outside their own frame of reference and one in which there is no such dimension to reality and no such register for speech. In an odd way, he suggests (in, for example, Tikhon's remarks to Stavrogin about atheism), the utterly committed atheist has more in common with the believer than the indifferent, since the committed atheist fully acknowledges what it means to deny the register or dimension of the holy, and declines to create sentimental substitutes. Both know what a world that is informed by "presence" looks like and what a world looks like that is without this. It is true that the importance of the Russian traditions of religious dissent and radicalism for Dostoevsky needs more exploration; not because it will show us a novelist more at odds with mainstream Orthodoxy or closer to some "dark" and apocalyptic dimensions of Russian religiosity than we had supposed, but because this tradition has so much in it that bears precisely on the matter of this chapter, on the crisis that arises when images are evacuated of their force. Dostoevsky's novelistic response to the mounting crisis of a secularized and trivialized imagination in educated Russia is not to suggest that we relax a bit more about the importance of images in our faith, but to do what the theologians of his church, in one way or another, had long been doing—to create images, narrative or conceptual or visual, that had a claim to be credible, while insisting that they represented a moment in the continuing dialogue rather than its end; and also, vitally, to remind us at every point of the nature of the image around which all other Christian images are organized, the image of the self-emptying of God which springs "out of his own heart" for the sacrilegious peasant in "Vlas."

This approach to the image of the sacred means that any fiction which takes this as its methodological principle is going to be a high-risk venture. The image created in the narrative must not be one that forces the reality around it to bend to its shape, and so it risks losing manifest presence in the discourse of the whole novel. Dostoevsky's decision to cast some of his Zosima material in a rather churchy devotional idiom was one that was obviously suggested both by the nature of the material and by the need not to make Zosima a character competing for imaginative force with the others. He has to be marked out, yet not in a way that reduces his distinctiveness. And this runs the risk—which to some extent is realized in the Zosima dossier, in the eyes of many readers—of making the image less immediate or credible in stylistic terms. How can such a "weakness" be connected with the essential vulnerability of the incarnate image of the holy? That is, how can it be read as a sign of depth not shallowness, fullness of realization rather than imaginative failure? What has been proposed here in this chapter and its predecessor is that the connection of Zosima's image and story with Mitya's offers a partial answer. Read Zosima in this context and you may be able to put the devotional idiom in proper perspective. But all this heightens the risk, as Dostoevsky was well aware, and to think about what he is doing in terms like these does not simplify the job of making aesthetic and stylistic judgments about the result; it is hard to deny that his success is uneven.

Yet, all that being said, we cannot simply judge the enterprise a failure. As we noted in the Introduction, the goal is to portray the meaning of holiness—necessarily incomplete in mortal subjects, necessarily involving a web of human narrative connections and thus necessarily concluding with the invitation to the reader to "complete" the picture, ideally by a response that acknowledges the presence discernible in this narrative interaction and is prepared to occupy along with these characters the space created by the author. If the holy in Dostoevsky is not an inaccessible realm "elsewhere" but that which sustains an infinite perspective on the worth or dignity of every other, it is bound to have this invitatory character. And the cliché of the Dostoevskian "holy sinner" is accurate to the extent (and no more) that the sinner who is conscious of sin and suffers because of it becomes a vehicle of the holy, an "iconic" figure, through that act of conscious self-referral to the holy, both as source of judgment and as possibility for the future.

Examining how Dostoevsky treats images of the holy has cast light both on what he understands as an image or icon and what he has to say about holiness itself. We have seen some reason to emphasize in his treatment the particularity of what holiness means. Despite the lyrical cosmic spirituality of Markel and his brother, and of Alyosha after his dream, the sacred cannot be reduced in these fictions to a generalized occasion for awe and wonder. In keeping with Dostoevsky's almost life-long absorption with the person of Christ (rather than with any general religious sense), these elements of spiritual experience have to be read in the context of both the fundamental anchorage of all visible signs of the holy in the Word who became incarnate and the requirement laid on those who experience "cosmic reconciliation" to make it concrete in the choice of responsibility for the sin and suffering of the world we see. The visions of Markel or Alyosha are not Myshkin's or Kirillov's moments of heightened awareness thinly disguised and reworked; they are about the call to an engagement with what is broken or defaced. Even the controversial bowing down to the earth, commended to assorted sinners, practiced by Raskolnikov and Alyosha, which has raised some Orthodox eyebrows, becomes more intelligible when seen in the context of a conviction that sin is in itself a defacement of the entire material environment: that is, that the earth is another defaced icon, whose inner and nonnegotiable dignity is secured only when its relation to the creator is acknowledged. The image is inexorably associated with the possibility of its suffering and defilement because it is the image of an inescapable vulnerability.

To say that we grasp what the holy means only when we see it defiled when we can articulate what blasphemy means, is not a commendation of blasphemy as a deliberate path to holiness. What Dostoevsky observes is that what the genuine blasphemer or profaner does exhibits in radical form what is involved in acknowledging the holy. The blasphemer, like the wretched young peasant of "Vlas," has *decided* to treat the visible image of the holy as if it is not what he knows it is and what he and his entire culture daily acknowledge it to be (Dostoevsky, remember, gives every possible benefit of the doubt to the young man in respect of the reality of his religious belief; it would not be real blasphemy if that belief were weak or nominal—which is why there are probably few real blasphemers). Thus the true profaner has elevated his or her will against reality, chosen isolation from what is commonly known and acknowledged. Blasphemy becomes a sort of trial of strength between the will and the real. And the effect of this spiritually suicidal act is what the elder has described to Dostoevsky in depicting the despair of the peasant, crawling on the ground and crying that he is damned. Only when both the will and the real are fully in play can this sort of thing happen: the essence of the diabolical is, in this connection, that it simply dissolves the real, as Ivan's Devil does with his solipsism and agnosticism.

So blasphemy brings us to see that the holy is manifest in the material world apprehended as transmitting and embodying eternal reality —but doing so in the only way in which eternal reality as Christians see it can be so embodied, that is, in habitually hidden and always questionable form. The labor of image-formation, which for the novelist is the labor of narrative, is to do with following through that embodiment, and so it is itself a risk-laden and vulnerable matter, always open to contest and denial; if it seeks greater clarity or closure, it steps outside the reality of the world in which it is operating—in this instance the "world" of the fiction itself. And in the novelist's difficult negotiation of authorial presence and *kenosis*, of a distinctive imaging of the holy and an immersion in the matter and interrelation that is the finite world, it becomes possible to discern a particular sort of discipleship, an *imitatio* or imaging in its own right.

CONCLUSION

The Dostoevsky we have been reading in these pages does not fit comfortably into the terms of modern religious debate as usually phrased. As we have repeatedly noted, he is not really interested in arguing the question—in general terms—of whether God exists. This does not mean that the reality of God is a matter of indifference to him or that he can be claimed for some form of contemporary nonrealism. But the difference between the self-aware believer, the self-aware sinner and the conscious and deliberate atheist is not a disagreement over whether or not to add one item to the sum total of really existing things. It is a conflict about policies and possibilities for a human life: between someone who accepts the dependence of everything on divine gratuity and attempts to respond with some image of that gratuity, someone who accepts this dependence but fails to act appropriately in response, and someone who denies the dependence and is consequently faced with the unanswerable question of why any one policy for living is preferable to any other. Kirillov's atheism is probably closest to what Bishop Tikhon has in mind when he says to Stavrogin that "[t]he absolute atheist stands on the last rung but one before most absolute faith (whether he steps higher or not)" [679]. Kirillov is intensely aware—at least as much as Nietzsche—that the death of God is not a rational conclusion which will allow humanity to pursue its proper goals and attain its proper happiness at last without interference. It is a terrifying gap in the coherence of the human mind: what "must" exist does not as a matter of fact exist. To recall Simone Weil's phrase (above, p. 9), we should in such a case have to believe that our desire or love *is* illusory—unless we can fill the gap with a God who is identical with the human self. And if the supreme source of value is the unconstrained will of the self, so Kirillov argues, that can only be demonstrated by the highest possible expression of the will's power, the power to overcome itself in voluntary death.

Dostoevsky is not claiming simplistically that all atheism ought to lead to suicide, though his tracing of Kirillov's argument is a powerful bit of polemic. He is saying that the question of the context from which we derive values is the most serious, life-and-death question we could possibly articulate. Committed believer and committed atheist agree about this; the committed and self-conscious unbeliever grasps at once that the absence of God poses the question urgently. The problem is with half-believers and unconscious unbelievers. The half-believer—like Stepan Trofimovich in his heyday as a local liberal guru [51]—is content with a God who does not exist fully and consciously except in relation to human subjectivity, a God whose evolution toward self-awareness is tied to history. The unconscious unbeliever assumes that the absent God can be compensated for by a clear assessment of material human need and the correct policies to deal with this. But the former inverts the proper order of dependence, making God depend on the contingencies of our story; and the latter takes it for granted that, in the absence of God, we can still give a credible account of "what human beings owe each other." Both are self-deluded; while both the sinner and the true (Kirillovian) atheist are not. The rare atheist who has faced the full implication of God's absence and still managed to discover and own a consistent policy will be able to do this only at the cost of a quite conscious decision to alter the terms of human living itself. Thus the Inquisitor accepts as a task the guaranteeing of security and happiness for the majority of humanity, fully understanding that, in the absence of God, this must involve a massive exercise in frustrating or diverting those areas of human desire that pull toward the sacred and—where necessary—a violent and decisive repression of dissent. If the Inquisitor too stands on the next rung to faith it is not because he has compassion on the multitude, but because he has not concealed from himself the cost of the divine absence. He has taken a kind of responsibility—not "for all," but for whatever majority can be managed; and not because of any conviction about the Body of Christ or whatever but out of the need to ease a subjectivity (irrationally?) troubled by human suffering.

As we saw in the first chapter, Dostoevsky in effect challenges the reader to explain exactly *what* the truth outside or without Christ would be, and stakes the claim that truth about the human world is not going to possible if faith is removed from the equation. The world without the sacred is not just disenchanted but deprived of some kind of depth—that is, of the sense that what we encounter is already part of a complex of interrelation before it is part of our world of perception.[1] Perhaps this is connected with what Zosima means in his undeniably odd phrase about God taking "seeds from other worlds" to begin creation in our world, so that "what grows lives and is alive only through the feeling of its contact with other mysterious worlds" [415]. In the depthless world that emerges in the absence of God, the lack of any sense in the world we encounter of this prior relation with what cannot be seen leaves our own capacity for relation with it deprived and distorted. We are en route to regarding and treating it as related only to the individual will, and thus as, ultimately, only instrumental to that will's purposes. It is, as Zosima indicates, bad enough in respect of the merely material or animal world; it is a far more serious matter where the human world is concerned.

Here is the heart of Dostoevsky's concern, and it is something unquestionably urgent in a cultural setting where depthlessness looks like becoming normal. At the very beginning of this book, we noted some of the issues that arise in Dostoevsky's fiction and their uncomfortably contemporary feel. Because all of them are in one way or another grounded in the question of what we owe to each other, they are all of them connected to the problem of lack of depth and the instrumental mentality that flows from this. Owing something to another is a recognition that what my relation with that other properly involves cannot be reduced to what I *decide*, to what I choose to "grant" to the other. And the inaccessible or inexhaustible hinterland of the other is precisely what exceeds my choice and has no need of my license. For Dostoevsky one of the characteristic motives in planned violence, individual or political, is the determination to extinguish dimensions in the other that exceed what is chosen and granted. And the contemporary cultural scene is one which strongly suggests that there is more than one style of violence directed against these rebel dimensions in humanity: to take the most obvious example, the global economy works on the assumption that local solidarities and patterns of shared meaning are all accidental to the fundamental practice of human beings in the world, which is the unrestricted exchange of commodity and currency. All particulars are leveled or assimilated to each other on the principle that everything has an exchange value that can be clearly determined. And the principle is applied equally to objects and to practices or skills: hence it becomes possible to quantify quite strictly the value of activities that were formerly regarded as given meaning by their intrinsic human worthwhileness, and surrounded accordingly by informal cultures and disciplines. The point at which the activity of nursing the sick can be expressed in terms of a producer supplying a customer is the point at which the *culture* of nursing the sick begins to disappear. It is replaced by contractual negotiations of power between the two interests represented, producer or supplier and consumer: whose will is going to be secured and protected? What do I need to concede in negotiation so as to secure the maximum amount of liberty for my future choices? And when such contracts cease to be satisfactory, there is no relation left; the other has ceased to be properly instrumental to my will and can be safely discarded.

"Since human beings perpetually exceed themselves in the surplus known as culture, they become inhuman when they are stripped to no more than themselves."[2] Yet the violence of that condition where human beings are stripped of cultural identities is potentially something that can trigger varieties of self-recognition. This may throw light on what Dostoevsky means by Tikhon's comments on atheism: for Dostoevsky, atheism is effectively the end of culture, since it is bound to reduce human practices to the level of arbitrary constructs. At this point, one grasps the nature of the choices that now lie ahead: to work for the most consistent and least painful of arbitrary constructions, fully aware that it will entail a level of untruth and further violence (the Inquisitor's option), or to make a commitment to "order" at the deeper level, even when that order does not appear to be vindicated by the way the world runs. Thus a crucial element in moral and spiritual pedagogy must be the presentation of what the dissolution of culture means. At its extreme point, such a dissolution portends an "end of history," a collapse of the possibility of making any meaningful narratives of individual or corporate experience; which is why Dostoevsky's fictions repeatedly introduce us to the diabolical, understood as that which seeks to end history and speech.

This critical point is at the same time a crisis for our understanding of freedom. Faced with the choices that are presented by the "post-cultural" vision of humanity, we cannot evade their seriousness by pretending that the will on its own can recreate vanished values. Absolute freedom is never further away than in the post-cultural moment. And this is why circumstances in which our fantasies of freedom are dispersed offer opportunities of insight—Raskolnikov in the camp, the homeless Stepan facing his death, Mitya arrested and threatened with unjust imprisonment. These are characters who have been brought to their own individual post-cultural moment, brought to a situation in which they are isolated and powerless, where they cannot create any meaning out of their own resources. They have moved outside the world of defensible and predictable order; even if they can be said to be suffering "justly," like Raskolnikov, they have no means of making sense of what is happening to them. They have no reason to trust the social environment they are used to, they have nothing to say: *J'ai menti toute ma vie*. The choice left them is whether or not to embrace their personal post-cultural deserts, to abandon the egotistical dreams of making sense by force of will and to decide whether or not the resulting condition is one that can be lived with—whether suffering at this level could conceivably be an induction into some other sort of human living. This means a conscious setting aside of inner and outer protections, the discovery of new and unflattering self-images, the abandonment of whatever feeds the dream of isolation or self-sufficiency. It is an invitation to self-emptying.

Simone Weil uses *malheur* to describe the state of humiliating, unheroic desolation in which the nature of human freedom may be clarified because there are no defenses left. It is commonly translated—with a nod to George Herbert, perhaps—as "affliction."[3] Something exactly parallel is contained in the way Dostoevsky uses *misère* when Lebedev, in *The Idiot*, defends himself against his nephew's mockery. The young man has made fun of the fact that Lebedev has been praying for the repose of the soul of Mme. Du Barry; and Lebedev responds by telling the story of the once-great countess being dragged to the guillotine after the Revolution. Her pathetic pleas ("Wait just one little moment, Mr. Executioner, just one!" [231]) are the mark of a soul utterly overcome by *misère*. She has no defense left, not even self-respect; she is a figure of fun, sentenced not only to die unjustly but to be laughed at as she does so. And for this, says Lebedev, no stranger to the loss of self-respect, "perhaps the Lord will forgive her." Self-emptying need not be a noble and deliberate act of self-sacrifice; how should we know what hidden egotism might be buried in that? It may be the sheer abandonment of oneself to animal terror and childlike wretchedness. What matters is the defenselessness. Somehow, or so Lebedev implies, a soul that has long lost touch with ordinary human mortality is being reacquainted with it in terrible ways, and that reacquaintance may have a saving dimension. It uncovers a hidden face.

Somewhere in all this is a troubling but crucial imaginative proposal: what if it is true that there are some sorts of suffering that stubbornly refuse to be seen in anything like a neutral fashion? Some sorts of suffering that inescapably demand the recognition that an order greater than what we have agreed on or chosen is being offended? Lebedev senses this in the comprehensive humiliation of Mme Du Barry, but it is this point that also underlies Ivan's "Mutiny" (the little girl locked in a freezing privy by her parents, crying to "dear, kind God" for protection sounds an echo of Du Barry's desperation). The sufferings of children are not capable of reduction to instrumental terms; they cannot be written off, either ignored or justified. And one of the central paradoxes of the Dostoevskian universe comes into view: the awareness of a depth that cannot be negotiated, an offense against universal order that cannot be mitigated, arises most authoritatively in a context where it simultaneously raises the question of what sense or beauty can possibly be seen in an "order" that makes such offenses possible as well as condemning them. Ivan's anguished narratives are not simply about how human suffering makes the existence of God incredible but about how certain sorts of suffering draw out from us the most unchallengeable intuitions we have about the transcendent value of human persons, and how that morally all-important intuition can be held together with any sort of "acceptance" of the depth of the actual outrage. This is the dilemma from which Ivan recoils in "returning his ticket." "The world rests upon preposterous things, and indeed it's possible that without them absolutely nothing would ever have come into existence," says Ivan excitedly [318], anticipating some of what his diabolical visitor will say later. Is this absurdity more or less livable with than the absurdity of the Inquisitor—or Shigalyov— enforcing the suppression of humanity as it is for the sake of humanity as it might be in his plan?

In other words the rediscovery of depth in the human and nonhuman world comes at a price. If there were a way of saying that the suffering of children did not matter, it would be immeasurably easier to give our allegiance to the notion of a universal moral order and a just and loving God, but it is precisely the conviction of order and divine love that makes the suffering of children beyond justification or mitigation, because it is this conviction that anchors the "depth" of the child's being in a way that nothing else does. Faith, in this context, is anything but consoling. If the only possible reply to Ivan's catalogue is Alyosha's admission that he could not imagine torturing a single child for the sake of cosmic harmony, what becomes of the possibility of anything like reasoned faith? How can we articulate a belief in a God on whom everything is dependent, to whom everything is related, without simultaneously treating this God as a source of explanation? Can we find a way of speaking about a creation in which human persons are so clearly seen as having irreducible value incapable of being translated into functional terms that they cannot even be seen as having an "instrumental" function in securing universal harmony? Alyosha is right in refusing the idea that any particular suffering can be seen as a means to someone else's purpose (even God's). But what kind of creation is it that produces personal identities that are so valuable for their own sake or in their own right that their value is totally detached from whatever fate lies in store for them?

The implied answer is that it is a creation in which the creator's responsibility for what is made means that created subjects mirror the gratuity of God's own being; they exist so that God may delight in them and they in each other, although none of this is necessary for any goal. To quote Terry Eagleton once more, "There was no more point to us

than there was to God" in classical Christian theology.[4] Thus our creat-
edness does not entail that our fate is predetermined in the simple sense
that at any temporal point God "foresees" what is going to happen to us
so that we have no true choice (we noted above, p. 148, the misunderstandings that can arise over this), and what prevents this from being a
kind of deism (God makes the world and then leaves it to run according
to its laws) is the assertion of divine presence or fidelity to what is made,
a fidelity that is most decisively expressed in the complete indwelling of
God in human flesh in the person of Christ. And this is the context in
which the specific work of the novelist becomes theologically significant. Dostoevsky works on the basis that the novelist is able to show
in some degree what divine creation might be like: that is, by creating a
world in which the unexpected and unscripted is continually unfolding,
in which there is no imposed last word. The novelist attempts what is in
one way an obviously impossible task—a self-emptying in respect of the
characters of the fiction, a degree of powerlessness in relation to them.
Impossible it may be (given that there is only one actual subject—the
writer—making choices here), the approach to it or the intimation of
it may also be an intimation of the work of a creator who does bring
actual separate agents with choices into being.

This book has argued that we best read Dostoevsky as working
through this analogy between writing and divine creation; the point
being not to *assimilate* human creativity to the divine but to introduce
to the imagination a model of making that is directed toward freedom
and not control. The analogy is imperfect, and even the ultimate theological framework does not offer a tidy theoretical resolution of the
imaginative problem facing both Ivan and Alyosha—how to believe in
a God who is both the necessary condition for unconsoled outrage at
human suffering and the source of the world in which such suffering is
permitted. Pictorially and narratively, the resolution lies in Alyosha's
freedom to offer Ivan such reconciliation as is in his power—the kiss
which echoes Christ's for the Inquisitor. This is simply the reaffirma-
tion of the ultimate presence of creative love within the narrative. And
because it is theoretically helpless, the decision to offer what Alyosha
offers becomes itself another moment of "emptying," the acceptance
of a freedom that is both unquenchable and strictly finite, and the
use of that freedom to make one gesture that carries the appropri-

ate meaning—not unlike the onion of Grushenka's little folktale. The novel cannot reassure us about anything except that the creator of the narrative world has created a real and indissoluble otherness and relates to it in unbroken respect for its otherness. But because that tells us nothing about the future except that it will happen, and that the creator will not be absent from it, the response it proposes is necessarily risky. One *can* read without that response; the only thing the novelist has to say then is that the question still lies on the table: how much can you live with? The issue over the anchorage of values is not going to go away just because the response of Orthodox (or any other) Christianity, for whatever reason, fails to persuade. And the refusal of the freely admitted paradoxes of Christian belief does not absolve you from paradox and struggle. If you cannot live with the tension Ivan so unforgettably depicts, the tension around the way in which suffering both questions what we mean by God and intensifies our sense of a human value that can only be grounded in God, you will have to live with another kind of tension, the recognition that such a ground of value is indispensable for a recognizably human life, yet at the same time an illusion depending on the human will.

What makes Dostoevsky so emphatically not a voluntarist at the end of the day, despite his intense commitment to the freedom of the will, is that he cannot see any possible way of saying simultaneously that we create value and that we are obligated to it. A value that we have *decided* should be honored is one whose observance finally depends on someone's power to enforce it: it cannot be defeated but still real, hidden but still present, paradoxically surviving the denials of history; if it is not enforced, it is not there, except in someone's subjective preferences. Part of the concern that underpins Dostoevsky's nuanced and complex views about images and holiness is the insistent belief that value and depth in persons (as in the world at large) have to be shown as actual, even when not triumphant: hence the recurring tropes of defaced or desecrated images and of holiness marginalized or seemingly compromised. And that is also why his theology of creation and incarnation is finally "realist," in the sense that he is repeatedly directing us toward a pattern of divine action that is outside our heads or hearts. The incarnate Christ would be the divine Word in human flesh even if no human soul acknowledged him, even if (to allow a Kierkegaardian echo) his incognito was never pierced. Only as such can Christ offer us an authoritative liberation. As the Stavrogin of the notes for *Devils* insists, it is this or nothing: Christ the teacher will not interrupt the deceits of the human world in any way that will change the terms of reference for human possibility. Equally, a Christ who, in the manner of twentieth-century Christian existentialism, is simply the occasion for a divine summons to authenticity to be heard is not what Dostoevsky envisages. We relate as believers not to the abstract proclamation of a divine Word calling us to abandon our self-justifications, but to the narrative particularity of the story of God the Son taking flesh and living in a certain definable, imageable way. And our own holiness is not a matter of successive detached moments of "authentic" reception of the divine challenge, but the cumulative labor of taking responsibility—knowing at every turn that we shall in important respects fail and can only depend on the persistence of grace in the depth of all kinds of defeats, the persistence of the icon despite its desecration or occlusion.

In a searching essay on Dostoevsky and Kierkegaard, George Pattison sums up the "dialogical" concern of both in these terms: "the account of freedom's dangerous dialogue does not lead us to indeterminacy but requires choices that neither author can make for us, because we can only make them for ourselves."[5] And those choices are not the self-projection of the will in the void; they are recognitions that the world is finally like this and not like that: that the world is either the product of divine abundance, marked above all by excess, by new possibility, by grace or mercy in simple theological terms, or the product of chance or even of an all-generating subjectivity, in which there is no more in the way of ultimate resource than can be provided by an unconstrained capacity for self-assertion. Which you choose determines what you think is possible not only for yourself but for the human world as you engage its full complexity. Dostoevsky had turned away decisively from one sort of political activism after his term in prison, but he remained an unashamed political activist in another mode as a writer. His fears of what we should now call totalitarianism are fears about the corruption and eventual disappearance of politics itself. When dialogue fails, when history is supposed to be over, when certain aspects of the human mind have been recatalogued as pathologically generated illusions, there is no more politics: there is nothing to entertain dialogue *about*; nature, in the guise of a definitive account of what human beings timelessly need and how to meet those needs, has defeated culture.

As a good number of commentators have noted in recent years, the opposition, now canonical in the public language of many governments, between the "freedom" of the North Atlantic cultural milieu and the nightmare of terrorism and fundamentalism that exists outside this enclave is more and more vacuous. Freedom as a designation for maximal consumer choice (including the consumerizing of public service and personal care) combined with an economic *jeu sans frontières* is an indifferent rallying point for moral conviction, conviction about the goodness or justice rather than simply the comfort of a society. A concept of freedom divorced from—at the very least—a serious tradition of public debate about social good is only a transcription of that fantasy of "absolute freedom" that Dostoevsky has in his sights. Faced with a global ideology of resentment, as wholly modern in its formation as is Western secularism, an ideology equally determined to end history in its preferred way for the sake of an absolutely manifest social good, our rhetoric of defending freedom does not make a very persuasive showing. One of the things that makes Ivan's Inquisitor such a perennially haunting figure is that his voice is clearly audible on both sides of the current global conflict. He is both the manager of a universal market in guaranteed security and comfort for a diminished human soul and the violent enforcer of a system beyond dialogue and change. And we may feel a similar unease at the way in which the profiles of terror are sketched in *Devils*: the selfless fanatic and the solipsistic libertarian are pushed together, at the mercy of anyone with the material and communicative resources to manipulate them. Repeatedly, he insists to his readers that this is what a world without icons, without presence, will mean.

He wants us to choose that humanity will survive—not merely as a biological but as a cultural reality. And the culture he identifies as human is one in which we do not have to lie about what we are in relation to our environment; a culture that insists upon a recognition of mortality and fallibility, of limit, of mutual indebtedness for our nurture and psychological growth, of the inaccessibility of our souls to one another and of the gratuitous and creative nature of what we say to one another. His fictions tell us, with intensifying urgency, that this culture is more at risk than we might have thought, that the restless concerns of secular and instrumentalist thinking are fast eroding it, so that we may wake up and discover we no longer know how to respond with either respect or compassion to each other, and so have literally nothing to say.

The American novelist Marilynne Robinson, in an eloquently polemical essay about Darwinism,[6] has anatomized at length the contradictions of an intellectual style determined to show that its own cultural sophistication is only the byproduct of natural processes. She is neither attacking theories of evolution as such nor defending creationism (she very properly remarks that "[c]reationism is the best thing that could have happened to Darwinism, the caricature of religion that has seemed to justify Darwinian contempt for the whole of religion."[7] Her target is the response of awe and fascination that is evoked in the contemporary intellectual milieu by theories designed to deny the distinctiveness of humanity. And that distinctiveness, she argues, is most evident in the free corporate elaborations of human existence that characterize social life—religion, art, celebrations of mutuality, indeed science itself. Science ought to be regarded as an aspect of culture—an aspect of that gratuitous exploration of the limits of what we can say to each other about our environment that is typically human; yet it has so constructed itself in much modern argument that it has appeared not only as a rival of humanistic discourse but as a dissolvent of culture itself, attacking its own rational and persuasive methods by reducing causality to mechanism. Robinson does not enlarge on this, but her point is echoed by those who see the disappearance of religious belief not as the triumph of reason but as the harbinger of reason's collapse, and it is significant that Evdokimov's reading of Dostoevsky (and this is some six decades ago) identifies the crisis of reason in the wake of the reductionist turn in science and psychology as an illustration of the novelist's prescience and claims that a revivified understanding of *communion* as a fundamental category is needed for the recovery of reason.[8] In our current climate, Robinson continues, the antihumanism that is so popular, deriving from aspects of Freud and Nietzsche as much as aspects of Darwin, is marked by a kind of resentment against culture itself as something that "has prevented survival from being a pressing consideration for many people most of the time."9 The Adam we have pensioned off was at least a symbol of liberty, sociality, and intelligent—if sometimes disastrous—self-determination.

> The old mystery of subjectivity is dispelled; individuality is a pointless com-
> plication of a very straightforward organic life. Our hypertrophic brain . . .
> which was so long believed to be the essence of our lives, and a claim on one
> another's sympathy and courtesy and attention, is going the way of every
> part of collective life that was addressed to it—religion, art, dignity, gracious-
> ness. Philosophy, ethics, politics, properly so called. It is a thing that bears
> reflecting upon, how much was destroyed, when modern thought declared
> the death of Adam.10

Dostoevsky's fiction is a sustained imaginative protest against the death of Adam. He is innocent of the refinements of vulgarized Nietzsche, Freud, or Darwin, but he knows very thoroughly the seduction, the paradoxical "charm" (the term is Wittgenstein's in this connection, from his lectures on psychoanalysis)11 of reductive and determinist anthropology; Raskolnikov's muddled reflections and Rakitin's attempt to persuade Mitya Karamazov that there is no such thing as criminal responsibility both show how clearly Dostoevsky conceived the issue at stake. Rakitin wants Mitya to agree that he has no soul, that there is no "image and likeness" in him that grounds his intelligence, and Mitya's response, confused but serious and ironic enough ("It is magnificent, Alyosha, this science! The new man is coming, that I understand . . . But all the same I'm sorry for God!" [753]), is finally to do with his inability to reduce his compassion for the homeless child in his dream to an instinctual or automatic thing, no better in itself than whatever impulse tempted him to kill his father. There *is* a "new man" coming, but it is one who understands his freedom to create the pattern of mutual answerability and to set aside his own interest; that is who will decide Mitya's future [763], the new man who is in the likeness of the Second Adam, Christ.

Dostoevsky's use of the biblical language of "image and likeness" here is an index of the importance of these categories in his imagination. If humanity is in God's image, there is something that it is *like* to be human, something beyond any negotiation or contingency. In this sense, Adam cannot wholly die. Yet if every individual is of incalculable value, a situation in which large numbers of human beings are liable to suffer the obscuring or defacing of the image is an insupportably tragic one. Adam will not wholly die, but this does not mean that the death—morally or spiritually—of any one child of Adam is tolerable. It is still necessary to write, in the effort to bear credible witness to the reality of Adam in a world where he is becoming invisible. It is necessary to go on talking, narrating, in the attempt to discover whether what is said or told can be recognized, which also means that a novel that closed down the possibility of intelligent dissent would have failed.

A constant theme in these pages has been the complexity and delicacy of creating a fiction that both clearly speaks the truth and yet provides the material on which a refusal or refutation can be based. This is the enterprise of *Karamazov* above all, and it has manifestly succeeded to the extent that readers have continued to protest and argue, with the ammunition the author has provided. Dostoevsky has been frequently accused of an obsessive concentration on extreme personalities and situations; Gary Saul Morson has written perceptively about the problems of the ethic that Dostoevsky seems to be advocating in some of his journalism—and perhaps implicitly in some of the fiction: an ethic that demands to be judged only by its adequacy to the most extreme of dilemmas.[12] "Most decisions of life take place in a continuum of time, in an open time of side shadowing, where imponderable long-term effects in multiple possible futures also need to be taken into account and answered for."[13] And (as Morson stresses) this extremism sits ill with Dostoevsky's clear statement of the need for a morality growing from the prosaic aggregation of practical wisdom, for what we earlier called attention to the particulars. Certainly the extremism of Dostoevsky's convictions about the Balkan crisis of the seventies (and his savage polemic against Tolstoy's treatment of this in *Anna Karenina*) shapes what he has to say in this context, and the *Writer's Diary* discussions are redolent of precisely the utopian, apocalyptic register which the fiction generally warns us against so eloquently. There is no salvaging of this part of his journalism for common sense or religious coherence.

But, granted that the contradiction in Dostoevsky is real, and that the urge to make all decisions apocalyptic is a thoroughly bad recipe for ethics, some note of extremism is unavoidable in the context of his overall strategy as a narrator. What we picture to ourselves as possible when we are faced with a decision tells us (and others, if we share it with them) essential things about where we are on the moral landscape. Could we imagine living with the consequences of a great act of renunciation? Then, as with Mitya Karamazov, we have conceived something as possible for ourselves that would be a dramatically "iconic" policy. Could we imagine living with the consequences of a fully conscious refusal to contemplate suffering that we might alleviate? Then we have a problem; we are allowing that our responsibility has limits: not just practical limits, as that is granted in Alyosha's encouragement to Mitya to abandon his initial extremism, but imaginative limits. We have shown ourselves capable of a deliberate reduction of what we will contemplate as real; what are the possible consequences of that?

The extreme situation invites us to affirm something about what we regard as unconditional: we may well be able to imagine—indeed, be compelled by uncomfortable experience to imagine—circumstances where we might fail to live in a way that adequately manifested this unconditionality. But if we could imagine justifying this or deliberately setting out to ignore what was required, then any sense of an iconic dimension to our behavior would have disappeared. My decision would not be an attempt (successful or unsuccessful) to reveal some dimension of the truth that did not depend on circumstance or on my individual disposition: it would show only that I had, in this particular situation, elected to behave in a certain way. And ethics, for Dostoevsky, has to concern itself with something more than what an individual will determines. Thus, in the example Morson uses, Dostoevsky's complaint about Tolstoy is less about a specific decision than the refusal to see that a decision has to be made: fairly or unfairly (mostly the latter), Dostoevsky reads the struggles of Levin over the Balkan question at the end of *Anna Karenina* as leading only to a "too difficult" verdict. This tells us nothing; it is the opposite of a revelatory decision. Or rather it tells us that there is nothing in Levin's consciousness that exacts unconditional obedience. And Levin—and the rest of us—ought to worry about that.

Imagining extremes can be self-indulgent and melodramatic. In many situations, all anyone could say is that he does not know how he might decide, but Dostoevsky is insistent that at least we recognize that a decision will be necessary, and that we cannot "go home to Kitty," to borrow his derisive summary of Levin's conclusion. We need both the imagination that is prepared to face the test of extremity and the humility to realize that we cannot be sure of ourselves in the face of this. What we cannot do is to think as though the terms of our moral commitment could be revised when things get difficult. And it is this facing of extremity that shapes the kinds of narrative Dostoevsky consistently presents us with. Decisions, moral trajectories, are life-bound or death-bound; they cannot be other than iconic in the sense we have outlined. But this means that our commitments need repeated imaginative testing. A little earlier in this chapter, the challenge of the fiction was expressed in the question, "How much can you live with?" We are invited to think through what it might be like to believe *this* in *these* circumstances—whether the "this" is Christian commitment or atheist commitment. And in developing these experiments in extremity, the narrator of fictions is bound to be giving ammunition to the case for the other side. Dostoevsky's "extremism" is thus bound up inseparably with the dialogical principle: to state a position and stake one's fidelity to it requires as complete an honesty as possible about the circumstances and ideas that would most severely test its credibility. Stating it honestly entails invoking its possible denial, and thus inviting or provoking an interlocutor to explore just such circumstances and ideas.

It is this fusion of a surrender to the claims of an independent truth and a surrender to the actual risks and uncertainties of asserting this truth in word and action that makes the entire enterprise of spiritual—and specifically Christian—life one that is marked by the decentring and critique of the unexamined self. What is so distinctive about Dostoevsky's narrative art is that he not only gives us narratives in which this difficult fusion is enacted; he also embodies the fusion in his narrative method, in the practice of his writing, risking the ambitious claim that the writing of fiction can itself be a sort of icon. In depriving itself of the right to close down imaginative possibilities, in obliging itself to confront the most extreme stresses to which belief can be exposed, in simply giving imaginative space for the continued exchanges of real mutual difference, Dostoevsky's fiction presents a

Christocentric apologetic of a unique kind. It brings together issues around creation and imagination, representation and the real, incarnation, power, and absolution that are too seldom grasped in their interconnectedness. And, finally and most importantly, on the basis of all this it continues to interrogate its readers, asking them whether they can conceive that humanity is only itself when it a sign of what is other —and, following from that, what the cost is of continuing to affirm such a humanity in a world that will constantly appear to deny it. That is a question which is at once literary, theological and political, and unmistakably contemporary.

NOTES

Introduction

1   From his letter of 1854 to Natalya Fonvizina, where he says that he is "a child of this epoch, a child of disbelief and doubt up to now and even (I'm quite sure of it) to the day of my death" (full text in *Pol'noe sobranie sochinenii*, 30 vols. [Leningrad: Nauka, 1972–1990] 28.2: 176). The text is often quoted; it can conveniently be found in English in Malcolm Jones, "Dostoevskii and Religion" (148–74 in *The Cambridge Companion to Dostoevskii*, ed. W. J. Leatherbarrow [Cambridge: Cambridge University Press, 2002]), 155–56.

2   William Hamilton, "Banished from the Land of Unity: Dostoevsky's Religious Vision through the Eyes of Dmitry, Ivan and Alyosha Karamazov," in *Radical Theology and the Death of God*, ed. Thomas J. J. Altizer and William Hamilton (Harmondsworth: Penguin Books, 1968), 65–94.

3   Hamilton, "Banished," 94.

4   Lawrence's wildly idiosyncratic "Preface to Dostoevsky's The Grand Inquisitor" can be found in *Dostoevsky: A Collection of Critical Essays,* ed. Rene Wellek (Englewood Cliffs, N.J.: Prentice-Hall, 1962), 90–97.

5   For a survey of discussion of Dostoevsky in the Russian émigré world, see Vladimir Seduro, *Dostoevski's Image in Russia Today* (Belmont, Mass.: Nordland, 1975), 387–459, an indispensable bibliographical guide. The most significant studies are Nicholas Berdyaev, *Dostoievsky: An Interpretation* (London: Sheed & Ward, 1934 [Russian original 1923]); Nikolai Lossky, *Dostoevskii i ego khristianskoe miroponimanie* [Dostoevsky and His Christian

World-view] (New York: Izdatel'stvo imeni Chekhova, 1946); Konstantin Mochulsky, *Dostoevsky: His Life and Work* (Princeton: Princeton University Press, 1967 [Russian original 1947]). These belong in the same general intellectual frame as a number of important pre-Revolutionary works, especially Lev Shestov, "Dostoevsky and Nietzsche: The Philosophy of Tragedy," in his *Dostoevsky, Tolstoy and Nietzsche* (Athens: Ohio University Press, 1969 [Russian original 1903]), 141–322; and Sergei Bulgakov's two essays on Dostoevsky, "Ivan Karamazov kak filosofskii tip" ["Ivan Karamazov as a philosophical type"] in *Ot marksizma k idealizmu* [From Marxism to Idealism] (St. Petersburg: Obshchestvennaia Polza, 1903), 83–112, and "Venets ternovyi: pamyati F.M.Dostoevskago" ["A Crown of Thorns: In Memory of F. M. Dostoevsky"] in *Dva grada* [Two Cities] (Moscow, 1911), 223–43, a lecture originally delivered in 1906. A very substantial and original study that has been sadly neglected is Paul Evdokimov, *Dostoevski et le problème du mal* (Lyon: Ondes, 1942; repr. Paris: Desclée de Brouwer, 1978); some of the themes of this lengthy work are recapitulated—and occasionally modified or reworked—in the same author's *Gogol et Dostoievski. La descente aux enfers* (Paris: Desclée de Brouwer, 1961 [2nd ed., 1984]). An important Roman Catholic essay is Romano Guardini, *Der Mensch und der Glaube: Versuche über die religiöse Existenz in Dostojewskijs grossen Romanen* (Leipzig: J. Hegner, 1933). Eduard Thurneysen's *Dostojewski* (Munich: Chr. Kaiser, 1921 [English trans., London, 1964]) represents the world of "dialectical theology."

6 Barth's enthusiasm for Dostoevsky, most marked in his first commentary of Romans (1918) is still very evident in several passages in the second (1921), massively revised edition and subsequent editions (*The Epistle to the Romans* [London: Oxford University Press, 1933]); see, e.g., 67, 122, 238, 253 (on the experience of dread in religion and the places where demons appear), 300 (on Ivan Karamazov), 332 (the Grand Inquisitor), 354 (*The Idiot*), 393 (the Inquisitor again and Christ's reply with his silent kiss), 501–2 (sanctity and the ineradicable possibilities of evildoing), and 520 (the Inquisitor and the ambiguities of Christian freedom). There is still work to be done on Barth's reception of Dostoevsky.

7 There are some eyebrow-raising essays by Philip Rahv and Derek Traversi, for instance. For the general critical reception, see Colin Crowder, "The Appropriation of Dostoevsky in the Early Twentieth Century: Cult, Counter-cult, and Incarnation," in *European Literature and Theology in the Twentieth Century: Ends of Time*, ed. David Jasper and Colin Crowder (London: Macmillan, 1990), 15–33; and Peter Kaye, *Dostoevsky and English Modernism, 1900–1930* (Cambridge: Cambridge University Press, 1999).

8   Seduro, *Dostoevski's Image*, is the best guide to this in English, a fascinating overview of the intellectual contortions necessary in the Soviet era to conduct serious critical discussion and of the risks run by some literary scholars in pursuing their tasks.

9   Seduro, *Dostoevski's Image*, chaps. 6 and 7, outlines the history and impact of the successive critical editions of 1956–1958 and 1995 onward.

10 To mention only two books from ecclesiastically connected presses in Russia, there is a useful collection under the title *F. M. Dostoevskii i Pravoslavie* (Dostoevsky and Orthodoxy), ed. A.nStrizhev andnV. Sechina (Moscow: Izdatel'stvo "Otchii dom," 1997), which contains extracts from the books of Lossky and Mochulsky, as well as a section representing less friendly Orthodox assessments of Dostoevsky, including the famous critique by Leontiev; and more recently, Archpriest Dmitrii Grigor'ev's *Dostoevskii i Tserkov: u istokov religioznykh ubezhdenii pisatelya* [Dostoevsky and the Church: At the Sources of the Religious Convictions of a Writer] (Moscow: Izdatel'stvo Pravoslavnogo Sviato-Tikhonovskogo Bogoslovskogo Instituta, 2002), is a lucid summary of the novelist's religious and theological sources and of the response to his work of a number of influential theological writers (it also has a valuable appendix on Dostoevsky and Pasternak). Two collections of essays edited by V.nZakharov include many excellent pieces on Dostoevsky's religious world: *Evangel'skii tekst v russkoi literature XVIII–XX vekov* (Petrozavodsk: Izdatel'stvo Petrozavodskago universsiteta, 1994), and *Novye aspekty v izuchenii Dostoevskago* (Petrozavodsk: Izdatel'stvo Petrozavodskago universiteta, 1994).

11 *Dostoevsky and the Christian Tradition* (ed. George Pattison and Diane Oenning Thompson [Cambridge: Cambridge University Press, 2001]) is a generally first-class collection; and there is much intereting material in the recent Festschrift for Malcolm Jones, doyen of British Dostoevsky scholars, *Dostoevsky on the Threshold of Other Worlds*, ed. Sarah Young and Lesley Milne (Ilkeston, Derbyshire: Bramcote Press, 2006).

12 See the comments of Abbot John Chapman, *The Spiritual Letters of Dom John Chapman*, 2nd ed. (London: Sheed & Ward, 1935), e.g., 47: in the seventeenth and eighteenth centuries, the greatest spiritual trial was the belief that God had turned his back on the believer, "[b]ut the corresponding trial of our contemporaries seems to be the feeling of not having any faith; not temptations against any particular article (usually), but a mere feeling that religion is not true."

13 Simone Weil, *Notebooks*, trans. Arthur Wills (London: Routledge & Keegan Paul, 1956), 127; for a full discussion of this and related themes in her work, see R. Williams, "The Necessary Non-existence of God," in *Simone*

Weil's Philosophy of Culture: Readings towards a Divine Humanity, ed. Richard H. Bell (Cambridge: Cambridge University Press, 1993), 52–76.

14 Stewart Sutherland, *Faith and Ambiguity* (London: SCM Press, 1984), 25.

15 See the discussion in chapter 10 of *God, Jesus and Belief* (Oxford: Blackwell, 1984); his *Atheism and the Rejection of God: Contemporary Philosophy and The Brothers Karamazov* (Oxford: Blackwell, 1977) is also a particularly suggestive and helpful treatment of the difference between lack of belief and repudiation of belief, and of the diverse registers in which the question of "the existence of God" can be articulated.

16 Terry Eagleton, *Holy Terror* (Oxford: Oxford University Press, 2005), 71.

17 Malcolm Jones, *Dostoevsky and the Dynamics of Religious Experience* (London: Anthem Press, 2005) one of the best recent studies, although I have some points of disagreement, 139–46, discusses different kinds of silence in Dostoevsky's fiction.

18 Aleksei Khomyakov's theological reflections on the Church, defining Orthodoxy as standing for spiritual consensus rather than externalized authority are summarized in his *L'Eglise latine et le protestantisme au point de vue de l'Eglise d'Orient* (Lausanne: B. Benda, 1872); Ivan Kireevsky supports Khomyakov, accusing Roman Catholicism of rationalism and an authoritarian and legalistic spirit, shown in the Inquisition (*Polnoe sobranie sochinenii*, ed. M. Gershenzon [Moscow, 1911], e.g., 1:112–14, 226–28, 245–49; 2:291–96, etc.); Vladimir Solovyov's *Lectures on Godmanhood* (Poughkeepsie, N.Y.: Harmon Printing House, 1944, with an introduction by P. P. Zouboff) characterize Western Catholicism as demanding subjection to an external power rather than growth into spiritual harmony (92, 220–21, etc.). Dostoevsky was in the audience when these lectures were first delivered in 1878; see Joseph Frank, *Dostoevsky: The Mantle of the Prophet, 1871–1881* (Princeton: Princeton University Press, 2002), 386–89.

19 Samuel Taylor Coleridge, *On the Constitution of the CHURCH and STATE According to the Idea of Each*, ed. John Barrell (London: Dent, 1972; originally published in 1830), 115–27, on the papal idea as a fundamental politicizing distortion of the true character of the Church.

20 The most important text is Dostoevsky's Pushkin memorial speech of 1880; Frank (*The Mantle of the Prophet*, chaps. 27 and 28) gives a full account of the speech and the reactions to it. James Scanlan (*Dostoevsky the Thinker* [Ithaca: Cornell University Press, 2002], chap. 6) discusses Dostoevsky's understanding of the Russian vocation with exemplary clarity.

Chapter 1

1 Above, n. 1 to Introduction.

2 See, e.g., Jones, *Dostoevsky and the Dynamics*, 26–27. Hamilton's essay "Banished" comes close to this.

3 See, e.g., Rudolf Bultmann, *Essays Philosophical and Theological* (London: SMC Press, 1955); idem., *Kerygma and Myth*, 2 vols., ed. H. W. Bartsch (London: SPCK, 1953/1962).

4 From the extensive list of Cupitt's publications, *The Sea of Faith* (London: BBC Books, 1984) and *The Long-legged Fly* (London: XPress, 1995) offer a good orientation to his views, though those views have continued to develop.

5 See, e.g., "The Peasant Marey," in *A Writer's Diary*, vol. 1, *1873–1876*, trans. and annotated by Kenneth Lantz (Evanston, Ill.: Northwestern University Press, 1993), 351–55; the text and its setting are discussed in chapter 9 of Joseph Frank (*Dostoevsky: The Years of Ordeal, 1850–1859* [Princeton: Princeton University Press, 1983]), including the scene setting for Easter Communion that can be found in *From the House of the Dead*.

6 Dostoevsky seems to have stopped taking the Sacrament in the forties during the time of his involvement with radical circles, though he clearly regarded himself as some sort of a Christian still, and there is evidence that he did go to Communion between 1847 and 1849, in the period after his break with Belinsky (Evdokimov, *Gogol et Dostoievski*, 198). He shared in the corporate sacramental life that was part of the discipline of the prison camp, as *From the House of the Dead* makes plain, but it is not clear how regular he was in his sacramental life in the years immediately after his release.

7 On this, see Scanlan, *Dostoevsky the Thinker*, 70ff.

8 Edward Wasiolek, *Dostoevsky: The Major Fiction* (Cambridge, Mass.: M.I.T. Press, 1964), 12–13.

9 See Scanlan, *Dostoevsky the Thinker*, 77–80, esp. 78.

10 *Pol'noe sobranie sochinenii*, 28.2: 73; see Joseph Frank, *Dostoevsky: The Stir of Liberation, 1860–1865* (Princeton: Princeton University Press, 1986), 320ff.; also Maria Nemcova Banerjee (*Dostoevsky: The Scandal of Reason* [Great Barrington, Mass.: Lindisfarne, 2006], 67–69), who rightly notes that Dostoevsky's decision not to restore the censored passage is "consistent with the intrinsically Christian thrust of the text," since the aim is to depict a character who has in effect chosen self-isolation, hellish enclosure with his grievances.

11   Cf. Evdokimov, *Dostoievski et le probleme du mal*, 218–20.

12   See Joseph Frank, *Dostoevsky: The Miraculous Years, 1865–1871* (Princeton: Princeton University Press, 1995), 305, on the parallels between this and the philosophy of Proudhon.

13   A. Boyce Gibson, *The Religion of Dostoevsky* (London: SCM Press, 1973), 187.

14   See, e.g., *Gogol et Dostievski*, 88–89.

15   See W. J. Leatherbarrow, *A Devil's Vaudeville: The Demonic in Dostoevsky's Major Fiction* (Evanston, Ill.: Northwestern University Press, 2005) (a study of great subtlety and importance), 168, drawing on the work of Victor Terras (*A Karamazov Companion* [Madison: University of Wisconsin Press, 1981]) in tracing the connections; c.f. V. Strada, "Il diavolo di Dostoevskij tra metafisica e metapolitica," in *L'autunno del diavolo*, ed. E. Corsini and E. Costa (Milano: Bompiani, 1998), 1:609–17, esp. 616.

16   Dostoevsky, *The Scandal of Reason*, 112. Compare the observations of Eric Ziolkowski, "Reading and Incarnation in Dostoevsky" (156–70 in Pattison and Thompson), 167, though in speaking of "incitement" to forgiveness or reconciliation, he may be slightly underselling the empowering force being ascribed to Christ's action.

17   Though it would not be sensible to underrate its importance, as we shall see later in this book.

18   The idea, eloquently expressed by D. H. Lawrence, that the kiss is an admission of defeat, a sign of Christ's agreement with the Inquisitor (and Ivan's with Alyosha), is perverse, but still finds its exponents.

19   Frank, *The Stir of Liberation*, 298; the whole of chapter 20 contains exensive quotation and is an invaluable discussion of these notes.

20   Frank, *The Stir of Liberation*, 305.

21   Frank, *The Stir of Liberation*, 306.

22   Frank, *The Stir of Liberation*, 306.

23   In *Fyodor Dostoevsky: The Notebooks for The Possessed*, ed. Edward Wasiolek, trans. Victor Terras (Chicago: University of Chicago Press, 1968), see, e.g., 252–53; for Dostoevsky's own views, see Jones, *Dostoevsky and the Dynamics*, 17. On his early passionate loyalty to the person of Jesus, even during his most radical days, we have the well-known passage about Belinsky's mockery of Dostoevsky for having tears in his eyes whenever he spoke of Christ (*A Writer's Diary*, 1:128–29).

24   Including Jones, *Dostoevsky and the Dynamics*, 61.

25   The most extended and sophisticated statement of the case is Sergei Hackel, "The Religious Dimension: Vision or Evasion? Zosima's Discourse in *The Brothers Karamazov*," in *New Essays on Dostoevsky*, ed. Mal-

colm Jones and Garth M. Terry (Cambridge: Cambridge University Press, 1983), 139–68.

26 Jones, *Dostoevsky and the Dynamics*, 64.

27 Steven Cassedy, *Dostoevsky's Religion* (Stanford: Stanford University Press, 2006).

28 See above, n. 15 on the intertextual relationships; I am greatly indebted to Dr. John Arnold for conversation on this question.

29 In *A Writer's Diary* I (ed. cit., 332–39), Dostoevsky discusses the possibility of the diabolical inspiration of spiritualistic phenomena and offers a comparably ironical comment on how devils will want to avoid providing conclusive proof of a non-material realm; if they are indeed behind spiritualistic manifestations, it is with the deliberate intention of leaving the question unresolved by providing unconvincing evidence. If complete evidence of preternatural power were available, it would enable people to sort out a range of practical problems and to arrive at perpetual peace, "stones turned into bread," but the innate dissatisfaction of humanity with such an outcome, the perversity of which the Underground Man speaks, would ultimately guarantee a decisive revolt against the diabolical. So it is in the interests of the devils to keep us uncertain. Dostoevsky is in fine, tongue-in-cheek form in this piece, claiming that he does not believe in devils, but also that his theory only works if you do. There is plenty of anticipation of *Karamazov*, and of the statement in *Devils* that many who don't believe in God still believe in devils (334).

30 The French phrase about the weather (*C'est à ne pas mettre un chien dehors* ["You wouldn't put a dog out in this"] [853]) which Ivan uses, talking to Alyosha, has already been used by the Devil [830], as if to alert us to the fact that Ivan cannot distinguish between what he says in his own right and what the Devil has said.

31 See above, n. 29, and cf. other mentions in vol. 1 of the *Diary* of the question (420–22, 457–64).

32 Thus Dostoevsky could not agree with a theologian such as Bultmann that the historically specific character of Christ's human life was irrelevant to the proclamation of the saving force of the cross: it matters that Jesus lived in a particular way, recreating a shape for human life and decision.

33 Quoted by Frank, *The Mantle of the Prophet*, 712 (*Polnoe sobranie sochinenii*, 27:57).

34 Frank, *The Mantle of the Prophet*, 713 (*Polnoe sobranie sochinenii*, 27:86).

35 Frank, *The Mantle of the Prophet*, 713.

36 Jones, *Dostoevsky and the Dynamics*, 93, 141.

37 In a late notebook entry (*Pol'noe sobranie sochinenii*, 27:65), he speaks of realism "of a higher sort," as his aim, by means of the description of the depths of the soul; similarly he can talk about the apparent "extremism" of his subject matter as the key to a more accurate depiction of reality than that of the mere reporter. On this, see W. J. Leatherbarrow's introduction to *The Cambridge Companion to Dostoevsky*, ed. Leatherbarrow (Cambridge: Cambridge University Press, 2002), 1–20, esp. 4–8; also, Jones, *Dostoevsky and the Dynamics*, 92–99.

38 Hackel, "The Religious Dimension," 152.

39 For the "perfectly beautiful man," see, e.g., his letter to Apollon Maikov in January 1868 (*Pol'noe sobranie sochinenii*, 28:240–41), quoted in the introduction to the 2004 Penguin translation, xxiii. The apparent assimilation of Myshkin to Christ first appears in the notebooks for the novel under the date of April 10, 1868. Great care is needed in assessing how far this represents the novelist's settled purpose, let alone how far it was modified in the actual execution of the novel.

40 The introduction to David Magarshack's 1955 Penguin translation provides a good brief guide to the chaotic history of the planning of *The Idiot*. The full story can be read in *Fyodor Dostoevsky: The Notebooks for The Idiot*, ed. and trans. Edward Wasiolek (Chicago: University of Chicago Press, 1967).

41 (Princeton: Princeton University Press, 1977), chap. 4 ("The Gaps in Christology"), esp. 106–11.

42 Simonetta Salvestroni, *Dostoevski et la Bible* (Paris: Lethielleux, 2004), 109.

43 There are very significant intertextual echoes in these "Golden Age" evocations; see Boyce Gibson, *The Religion of Dostoevsky* (London: SCM Press, 1973), chap. 6.

44 *Dostoevski et la Bible,* 117; and see chap. 2 in general, esp. 107–24. See Gibson, *The Religion of Dostoevsky*, chap. 6, on these and other "utopian" passages.

45 Salvestroni, *Dostoevski et la Bible*, 121.

46 Salvestroni, *Dostoevski et la Bible*, 131: *Il [Myshkin] refuse de grandir, d'accepter le douloureux processus de la connaissance* ["He refuses to grow, to accept the painful process of acquiring knowledge"].

47 Wasiolek, *The Major Fiction*, 106.

48 Adam Weiner (*By Authors Possessed: The Demonic Novel in Russia* [Evanston, Ill.: Northwestern University Press, 1998]), discussed by Leatherbarrow, *A Devil's Vaudeville*, chap. 3 ("The Abbot Pafnuty's Hand: *The Idiot*").

49 Leatherbarrow, *A Devil's Vaudeville*.

50 Mikhail Bakhtin, *Problems of Dostoevsky's Poetics*, ed. and trans. by Caryl Emerson and Wayne C. Booth (Minneapolis: University of Minnesota Press, 1984), 173.

51 Bakhtin, *Problems of Dostoevsky's Poetics*.

52 Diane Oenning Thompson, "Problems of the Biblical Word in Dostoevsky's Poetics" (69–99 in Pattison and Thompson), 76.

53 Leatherbarrow, *A Devil's Vaudeville*, 108.

54 George Steiner, *Tolstoy or Dostoevsky*, 2nd rev. ed. (Harmondsworth: Penguin Books 1967), 141.

55 Discussed by Holquist, *Dostoevsky and the Novel*, 108–9.

56 Jones, *Dostoevsky and the Dynamics*, 93.

57 Many instances in Seduro, *Dostoevsky's Image*; e.g., 14–15, chap. 10, *passim*.

58 Jones, *Dostoevsky and the Dynamics*, 93.

59 *Dostoevski et le probleme du mal*, 386–87.

Chapter 2

1 Victor Terras, "The Art of Fiction as a Theme in *The Brothers Karamazov*," in *Dostoevsky: New Perspectives*, ed. Robert Louis Jackson (Englewood Cliffs, N.J.: Prentice-Hall, 1984), 193–205.

2 Leatherbarrow, *A Devil's Vaudeville*, 140.

3 Leatherbarrow, *A Devil's Vaudeville*, 23–26, 148.

4 See below, p. 199.

5 The title of the memoir of Zosima in book 6 of the novel refers to him as *ieroskhimonakh*, a priest and "schema-monk," the latter referring to the taking of extra vows of prayer and fasting taken by senior monks in the Orthodox Church (Father Ferapont complains that Zosima did not obseve the proper disciplines of the great habit [434]); these vows are signaled by the adoption of a more elaborate version of the monastic habit, worn on special occasions, and—as the novel lets us know—a different version of the burial liturgy. Dostoevsky had taken some care in checking the variations of the monastic funeral service. The term "schema-monk" (in its more colloquial Russian version, *skhimnik*) is also used by Ivan, in affectionate mockery, for Alyosha during their conversation in book 5, chap. 4 [319].

6 See Marcia A. Morris, *Saints and Revolutionaries: The Ascetic Hero in Russian Literature* (New York: SUNY Press, 1993), 120ff.

7 Morris, *Saints and Revolutionaries*, 122–23.

8 On Dostoevsky's anti-semitism, Scanlan (*Dostoevsky the Thinker*, 209–11) has a candid and sensible discussion, focused on the March 1877 article in

A Writer's Diary in which Dostoevsky (disastrously) tries to defend himself against the charge of prejudice against the Jews; Scanlan does not attempt to minimize or excuse the disturbing character of some of Dostoevsky's rhetoric, here and elsewhere, though he does note that at least the novelist does not seek to limit or attack their civil liberties.

9   *Dostoevski et le probleme du mal*, 118–21.

10 Leatherbarrow, *A Devil's Vaudeville*, 170ff.

11 See, e.g., Leonid Ouspensky and Vladimir Lossky, *The Meaning of Icons*, 2nd ed. (Crestwood, N.Y.: St. Vladimir's Seminary Press, 1982).

12 Evdokimov, *Dostoevski et le probleme*, 307; cf. 161–64.

13 Leatherbarrow, *A Devil's Vaudeville*, 148.

14 A good and exhaustive discussion in Scanlan, *Dostoevsky the Thinker*, 16–17, 19–40. See also Ya. E. Golosovker (*Dostoevski i Kant* [Moscow: Izdatel'stvo Akademii nauk SSSR, 1963]) on the philosophical context of this, though Scanlan (22) is sceptical about the degree of Dostoevsky's direct knowledge of Kant.

15 See Scanlon, *Dostoevsky the Thinker*, 29–30, 34–35.

16 *Pol'noe sobranie sochinenii*, 30.1: 10–11; see Scanlan, *Dostoevsky the Thinker*, 29–32.

17 1:732–36.

18 Raskolnikov's fevered dream in prison, related in the epilogue to *Crime and Punishment* [651–52], is a sort of final "dramatization" of his thinking: practically the whole of humanity has been possessed by a sort of alien spiritual parasite, and only an elect few will survive, though no one knows who they are. The dream (with its foreshadowing of the themes of *Devils* and other works) portrays humanity as subject to absolutely meaningless, self-inflicted suffering, combined with an absolute conviction of human rationality; there can be no assurance for anyone that they have escaped the infection. The hidden remnant of the uninfected make no sign and cannot be recognized. The point of the dream—though Raskolnikov himself doesn't see it at first—is that no one can safely or sanely identify himself as exempt from the universal mania and chosen to redeem others because of their spiritual superiority. It is the beginning of Raskolnikov's realization of why Sonya is essential to his healing.

19 See Scanlan, *Dostoevsky the Thinker*, chap. 6.

20 Scanlan, *Dostoevsky the Thinker*, 228.

21 They met in 1873. Frank (*The Mantle of the Prophet*, 387–89) has a helpful survey of the interaction of the two men, as do Andrzey Walicki, *Legal Philosophies of Russian Liberalism* (Oxford: Clarendon Press, 1987), 170ff. and David Cunningham, "*The Brothers Karamazov* as Trinitarian Theol-

ogy" (134–55 in Pattison and Thompson), 142–43. Jonathan Sutton (*The Religious Philosophy of Vladimir Solovyov: Towards a Reassessment* [London: Macmillan, 1988]) is the best and fullest recent discussion of Solovyov.

22 Scanlan, *Dostoevsky the Thinker*, 198–99.

23 Scanlan, *Dostoevsky the Thinker,* 201–4, discusses in this connection the 1862 essay, "Two Camps of Theoreticians."

24 There is a very lucid account of this in Paul Vallière, *Modern Russian Theology. Bukharev, Soloviev, Bulgakov: Orthodox Theology in a New Key* (Grand Rapids: Eerdmans, 2000), 127–37; and cf. Evdokimov, *Dostoievski et le problème*, 408–9.

25 Frank (*The Mantle and the Prophet*, 627–28) also notes the connections with the social reflections of the young Zosima's Mysterious Visitor in *Karamazov*, book 6, chap. 2(d) [393–94].

26 Auden's *Spain* (London: Faber & Faber, 1937): "the conscious acceptance of guilt in the necessary murder."

27 Above, p. 21ff..

28 Salvestroni, *Dostoevski et la Bible,* 185–86.

29 See, e.g., the seventh and eighth of the *Lectures on Godmanhood*.

30 Evdokimov, *Dostoievski et le problème*, 322.

31 Salvestroni, *Dostoevski et la Bible*, 211, though she seems to miss the Gethsemane resonances.

32 D. I. Chizhevskii (*Gegel v Rossii* [Paris: Dom knigi, 1939]) traces the process by which these two thinkers (along with Schiller) came to be almost canonical philosophical and ethical authorities in mid-nineteenth-century Russia. See 36–49 on the influence of Schelling in particular, 127–41 on Belinsky's ultimate repudiation of Hegel. Richard Freeborn (*Furious Vissarion. Belinskii's Struggle for Literature, Love and Ideas* [London: School of Slavonic and East European Studies, 2003], 33–34, 54–55) gives some flavor of the impact of Hegel on the generation of the forties, and of the subsequent disenchantment felt by some; Stepan Trofimovich has remained in the speculative and aesthetic world opened up in that first moment of impact.

33 For Dostoevsky's views on Sand, see *A Writer's Diary*, 1:505–14—a striking and rather surprising defense of Sand as a fundamentally Christian artist (comparable in that respect to Dickens, 514). On the general issue of Dostoevsky's indebtedness to Romantic writers, see Jones, *Dostoevsky and the Dynamics*, 3–4, 31, and also 151–52 of "Dostoevskii and Religion," 148–74.

34 Frank, *The Mantle and the Prophet*, 398–400. Robert L. Belknap (*The Genesis of The Brothers Karamazov. The Aesthetics, Ideology and Psychology of Making a Text* [Evanston, Ill.: Northwestern University Press, 1990], 66–68) notes

also the influence of Sand's novel, *Mauprat*, on the treatment of Mitya, as well as on the final encounter between Svidrigailov and Dunya in *Crime and Punishment*—a connection first demonstrated by V. L. Komarovich.

35 *A Devil's Vaudeville*, 119–20; Leatherbarrow also notes the significant number of indeterminate qualifiers in the description—"like," sort of"—as if Pyotr is never quite brought into focus. Cf. below, p. 122–24.

36 This is preferable to seeing Stavrogin alone as a "double" to Myshkin, as René Girard proposes in *Resurrection from the Underground: Feodor Dostoevsky* (New York: Herder & Herder, 1997), 81–84, though his contrast between Stavrogin and Myshkin as "two contrasting images of the novelist" (narrative detachment as innocence, narrative detachment as mastery) is very suggestive.

37 Holquist, *Dostoevsky and the Novel*, 135.

38 In 1845 a man claiming to be the son of Tsar Nicholas II's elder brother Konstantin had appeared, calling himself the Tsarevich Ivan; but the title has far more resonance than this alone, as the hero of countless Russian folktales (like the story of the Firebird) is "Ivan-Tsarevich." In other words, the title has something like the combined associations of "Prince Charming," "King Arthur" and "Bonnie Prince Charlie." See also Frank, *The Miraculous Years*, 451.

39 *The Religion of Dostoevsky*, 150–53.

40 Holquist, *Dostoevsky and the Novel*, 128.

41 Holquist, *Dostoevsky and the Novel*, 144–45.

42 Seduro (*Dostoevski's Image*, 148–50) gives a brief sketch of the complex publishing history of the suppressed chapter.

43 Holquist, *Dostoevsky and the Novel*, 151.

44 Holquist, *Dostoevsky and the Novel*, 152.

45 *Rog* is a horn; it may be worth noting too that *tavro* is a brand, perhaps hinting at the "mark of Cain." Like Dickens, Dostoevsky can make a name carry multiple echoes and suggestions.

46 Steiner, *Tolstoy or Dostoevsky*, 285.

47 Steiner, *Tolstoy or Dostoevsky*, 286–89.

48 Bakhtin, *Problems of Dostoevsky's Poetics*, chap. 5, esp. 237ff.

49 Bakhtin, *Problems of Dostoevsky's Poetics*, 241.

50 Bakhtin, *Problems of Dostoevsky's Poetics*, 242–46.

51 Bakhtin, *Problems of Dostoevsky's Poetics*, 244.

52 Bakhtin, *Problems of Dostoevsky's Poetics*, 246.

Chapter 3

1 Bakhtin, *Problems of Dostoevsky's Poetics*, 93.

2   In a curious way, this has parallels with Ivan Karamazov's approach to suffering; for him too, it is something that has happened, and whatever sense participants or victims might be able to make of it is irrelevant to the observer's point of view, for which it remains an unhealable and unfogiveable horror.

3   Bakhtin, *Problems of Dostoevsky's Poetics*, 97. On the whole question of how a "picture" works to counter an argument, Sutherland, *Atheism and the Rejection of God*, remains an indispensable study.

4   Sutherland, "The Philosophical Dimension: Self and Freedom," in Jones and Terry, 169–85.

5   Bakhtin, *Problems of Dostoevsky's Poetics*, 112–19 on the characteristics of Menippean drama and narrative.

6   Bakhtin, *Problems of Dostoevsky's Poetics*, 135.

7   Gibson, *The Religion of Dostoevsky*, 187, 95, 102; the "what if?" with which Raskolnikov, in effect, signs off is profoundly hopeful, and Dostoevsky refers to a "great heroic deed" that lies ahead for him, but the reader still has to fill in the blanks. See also Stewart Sutherland ("Language and Interpretation in *Crime and Punishment*," *Philosophy and Literature* [1978]: 225) on the open character of the conclusion.

8   Wasiolek, *The Major Fiction*, 76.

9   Sutherland, "Language and Interpretation," 180–81.

10   Bakhtin, *Problems of Dostoevsky's Poetics*, 238.

11   Evdokimov, *Dostoievski et le problème*, 62.

12   For examples, see part 2, chap. 2 (139–40), chap. 6 (203, 210); part 3, chap. 6, 328–30; Svidrigailov's nightmare in part 6, chap. 6, also uses the theme of the confusing yet deceptively clear or familiar topography of the city—a theme which many other Russian writers deployed.

13   Bakhtin, *Problems of Dostoevsky's Poetics*, 215.

14   Bakhtin, *Problems of Dostoevsky's Poetics*, 214.

15   Sutherland, "Language and Interpretation," 180.

16   Bakhtin, *Problems of Dostoevsky's Poetics*, 53.

17   Bakhtin, *Problems of Dostoevsky's Poetics*, 53.

18   Noted by Evdokimov, *Dostoevski et le problème*, 338, n. 1. Throughout the notebooks for *Devils*, Dostoevsky refers to the Verkhovensky figure as "Nechaev," and the crime for which Nechaev himself became notorious was one of the startingpoints for the plot of the novel; for further background, Frank (*The Miraculous Years*, chap. 23) is invaluable (esp. 447 on the cult of more or less random violence).

19   *A Devil's Vaudeville*, 119–20 (cf. above, n. 35 to chap. 2).

20   Evdokimov, *Dostoievski et le problème*, 347.

21 Part 2, chap. 5 of *The Idiot*, which follows Myshkin's reverie as he is drawn
    back towards Nastasya's house. He avoids asking himself what he is doing
    and why: "He did not feel like thinking anything over" [263]; "To reflect
    any further on his 'sudden idea' at once seemd to him horribly repulsive
    and almost impossible" [266]. The point is noted by Boyce Gibson, *The
    Religion of Dostoevsky*, 121.

22 "The saintly characters . . . do not advance the action," says Avril Pyman
    in "The Prism of the Orthodox Semiosphere" (103–15 in Pattison and
    Thompson), 111.

23 "Pavel Smerdyakov and Ivan Karamazov: The Problem of Temptation"
    (189–225 in Pattison and Thompson), including a translator's afterword by
    Caryl Emerson, 220–24.

24 "Pavel Smerdyakov and Ivan Karamazov," 208.

25 Evdokimov, *Dostoievski et le problème*, 379–80, citing a study by S. Hessen
    ("La Trinité du bien dans les Frères Karamazov," Annales contemporaines
    35).

26 Bakhtin, *Problems of Dostoevsky's Poetics*, 252.

27 Frank, *The Stir of Liberation*, 194–96.

28 Frank, *The Stir of Liberation*, 194.

29 Frank, *The Stir of Liberation*, 195–96.

30 "Problems of the Biblical Word in Dostoevsky's Poetics" (69–99 in Pat-
    tison and Thompson).

31 Bakhtin, *Problems of Dostoevsky's Poetics*, 284.

32 Bakhtin, *Problems of Dostoevsky's Poetics*, 285.

33 See especially Alexandar Mihailovic, *Corporeal Words: Mikhail Bakhtin's
    Theology of Discourse* (Evanston, Ill.: Northwestern University Press, 1997);
    Ruth Coates, *Christianity in Bakhtin: God and the Exiled Author* (Cam-
    bridge: Cambridge University Press, 1998); and the important symposium
    on *Bakhtin and Religion: A Feeling for Faith*, ed. Susan M. Felch and Paul J.
    Contino (Evanston, Ill.: Northwestern University Press, 2001). We shall
    be looking in more detail at some of Bakhtin's theological echoes in the
    next chapter.

34 Despite the burgeoning literature on the theological background of
    Bakhtin's work, it is dismissed as a retreat from engagement with
    "the roles and identities which flow from human institutions" by Ken
    Hirschkop, *Mikhail Bakhtin: An Aesthetic for Democracy* (Oxford: Oxford
    University Press, 1999), 6–7. "Here history has no place," according to
    Hirschkop, and he is critical of American readers of Bakhtin like Morson
    and Emerson for "provincializing" the idea of dialogue so that it no longer
    impinges on the public sphere. This detailed and vigorously argued Marx-

ist reclamation of Bakhtin is not, in fact, as far from the concerns of at least some of Bakhtin's "religious" readers as Hirschkop supposes.

35 Thompson, "Problems of the Biblical Word," 94–95.

36 Thompson, "Problems of the Biblical Word," 69.

37 Thompson, "Problems of the Biblical Word," 70.

38 *Dostoevsky and the Dynamics*, 32–33.

39 Thompson, "Problems of the Biblical Word," 70.

40 Thompson, "Problems of the Biblical Word," 71–73.

41 Especially Isacc the Syrian and Simeon the New Theologian; see below, chap. 5, n. 20.

42 Thompson, "Problems of the Biblical Word," 95.

43 Thompson, "Problems of the Biblical Word," 95.

44 The conservative journalist Aleksei Suvorin claimed after Dostoevsky's death that he had planned a continuation in which Alyosha would assassinate the Tsar (Frank, *The Mantle of the Prophet,* 727).

45 Gary Saul Morson in his afterword to Felch and Contino (189).

46 Thompson, "Problems of the Biblical Word," 95.

47 Freud's article on "Dostoevsky and Parricide" can be found in the standard edition of *Freud's Collected Works*, vol. 21 (London: Hogarth Press, 1964–2001), 177–94; 177 has the remarks referred to on Dostoevsky's attitude to morality. Freud's reading is heavily influenced by some rather distorting presentations of Dostoevsky's career, suggesting that he himself deliberately courted the morally degrading in his experience. The essay can charitably be described (not unlike the more famous study of Leonardo da Vinci) as not showing Freud at his best.

48 *Tolstoy or Dostoevsky*, 286.

49 *Dostoevski et le problème*, 147–48; n. 3 on Schelling is significant in underlining the difference between Schelling's tendency to associate evil with the processes of "cosmogony," the formation of the universe, as opposed to the Christian insistence that it is essentially bound up with the freedom of intelligent subjects.

50 "Conclusion: Reading Dostoevskii" (212–34 in *The Cambridge Companion*).

51 "Conclusion," 229.

52 "Conclusion," 228.

53 "Conclusion," 232.

54 "Conclusion," 219–20.

55 "Conclusion," 217.

56 "Conclusion," 216.

57 "Conclusion."

58 "Conclusion," 229.

Chapter 4

1 It is odd that Thompson, in her essay on the "biblical word" in Dostoevsky, does not discuss the episode of Sonya's reading of the Lazarus story,
surely the most explicit appeal in the whole of Dostoevsky's fiction to the
force of biblical narrative.

2 Leatherbarrow, *A Devil's Vaudeville*, 170–77.

3 See Frank (*The Mantle of the Prophet*, 621–23) on this issue of style; on the
models for Zosima's idiom in book 6, see, for example, Hackel, "The Religious Dimension" on Dostoevsky's use of the writings of the monk Par-
feny from earlier in the nineteenth century.

4 See Thomas Dormandy, *The White Death: A History of Tuberculosis* (New
York: New York University Press, 2001), chap. 8, "The Romantic Image."

5 In addition to the obvious patterns of deathbed edification in the fiction
of the period, there seem to be hints of the Farewell Discourses of Christ
in St. John's Gospel as well in the "wonderment" and incomprehension of
Markel's family: "no one was able to understand this at the time" [375] is
a very Johannine comment.

6 Frank, *The Mantle of the Prophet*, 628.

7 "The people will go to meet the atheist and they will conquer him, and
there will arise a united Orthodox Russia" [407], "May it come to pass,
may it come to pass!" [409]. The latter quotation (*Budet! budet!* in the
Russian) reproduces the title of book 2, chap. 5, which is Father Paissy's
response to Ivan's vision of the state becoming a church. The Russian can
equally mean, "may it be!" or "it will be."

8 The routine epithet for the earth in Russian folk poetry and popular
epic.

9 Evdokimov, *Dostoievski et le probleme*, 333–34.

10 See, e.g., Hamilton, "Banished," 87.

11 Coates, *Christianity in Bakhtin*, 101.

12 Mihailovic, *Corporeal Words*, 58.

13 Mihailovic, *Corporeal Words*, 75.

14 Mihailovic, *Corporeal Words*, 214–20; cf. *Christianity in Bakhtin*, 95–98.

15 For a brilliant and searching treatment of this, see Gillian Rose, *Mourning Becomes the Law: Philosophy and Representation* (Cambridge: Cambridge
University Press, 1996), chap. 3, "The Comedy of Hegel and the Trauer-
spiel of Modern Philosophy," 63–76.

16 "Bakhtin and the Hermeneutics of Love" (25–45 in Felch and Contino); see
also Alan Jacobs, *A Theology of Reading: The Hermeneutics of Love* (Boulder:
Westview Press, 2001), 101–12, notably 106: "The evacuation of the self in
favour of Being, or of the other, actually prevents a genuinely answerable

and self-active 'I-for-another.'" On the risks of interpreting kenosis in completely self-cancelling ways, see Gillian Rose, "Angry Angels—Simone Weil and Emmanuel Levinas," in her *Judaism and Modernity: Philosophical Essays* (Oxford: Blackwell, 1993), 211–23; and Rowan Williams, "The Necessary Non-existence of God."

17 On the divine "ecstasy" in incarnation and the consequent reconstruction of human understanding of the divine through Christ, see especially Alain Riou, *Le monde et l'église selon Maxime le confesseur* (Paris: Beauchesne, 1973).

18 David S. Cunningham (*"The Brothers Karamazov* as Trinitarian Theology," [134–55 in Pattison and Thompson]) offers some original and suggestive thoughts on trinitarian patterns and models in the novel.

19 *Resurrection from the Underground* (New York: Herder & Herder, 1997); and see Pattison's discussion of Girard on Dostoevsky in "Reading Kierkegaard and Dostoevsky Together" (237–56 in Pattison and Thompson), 241–48.

20 Susanne Fusso ("Dostoevskii and the Family," [175–90 in *The Cambridge Companion*]) includes a good account (184–86, 188–90) of Dostoevsky's treatment in the *Diary* of the question of whether family loyalty and affection has to be "earned."

21 Fusso, "Dostoevskii and the Family," 183–84.

22 *Dostoevski et le problème*, 406–7 (and cf. Evdokimov, *Gogol et Dostoievski*, 205–18).

23 *Dostoevski et le problème*, 407.

24 Leonard J. Stanton, *The Optina Pustyn Monastery in the Russian Literary Imagination: Iconic Vision in Works by Dostoevsky, Gogol, Tolstoy and Others* (New York: Peter Lang, 1995), 196–201.

25 The Russian text of Leontiev's article, "On Universal Love," can conveniently be found in *F. M. Dostoevskii i Pravoslavie*, 261–97 (there are useful extracts in the iintroduction to the current Penguin translation); see 263–64 on the definitions of love.

26 "On Universal Love," 275.

27 "On Universal Love," 276–77.

28 See *The Descent of the Dove: A Short History of the Holy Spirit in the Church* (London: Religious Book Club, 1939), esp. chap. 1 and 234ff.

29 See Frank, *The Mantle of the Prophet*, 472.

30 Chapter 6 of Georges Florovsky's *Puti russkogo bogosloviya* (Paris: YMCA Press, 1937); 64–70 in vol. 2 of the English translation, *Ways of Russian Theology*, trans. R. L. Nichols (Belmont, Mass.: Notable's Academic Books, 1987) (vol. 6 of Florovsky's *Collected Works*; the text also appears as "The

Evolution of the Dostoievskian Conception of Freedom" in Florovsky, *Theology and Literature*, vol. 11 of the *Collected Works*, 1989, 82–89).

31 Florovsky, *Puti russkogo bogosloviya*, 66.

32 Florovsky, *Puti russkogo bogosloviya*, 67.

33 Florovsky, *Puti russkogo bogosloviya*, 68.

34 Florovsky, *Puti russkogo bogosloviya*, 69.

35 *Fyodor Dostoevsky: The Notebooks for The Possessed*, 366.

36 "Geroizm i podviznichestvo," 176–222 of *Dva grada*; translation in Rowan Williams, *Sergii Bulgakov: Towards a Russian Political Theology* (Edinburgh: T&T Clark, 1999), 69–112.

37 Florovsky, *Puti russkogo bogosloviya*, 124.

38 Florovsky, *Puti russkogo bogosloviya*, 127–30.

39 See David McDuff's introduction to his Penguin translation, xxiv.

40 There may also be a hint of some kind of "salvific" doubling in the figure of the workman Nikolai, who, in part 4, chap. 6, confesses to Raskolnikov's crime as a way of inviting humiliation. As Porfiry later tells Raskolnikov [542–43], the workman turns out to be an actual Raskolnik, a sectarian who longs for expiatory suffering: "Have you any conception, Rodion Romanovich, of what the word 'suffering' means to some of them? They don't do it for the sake of anyone in particular, but just for its own sake" [543].

41 E.g., Vladimir Lossky, *The Mystical Theology of the Eastern Church* (Cambridge: St. Vladimir Seminary Press, 1957), 46–47.

Chapter 5

1 Pyman, "The Prism of the Orthodox Semiosphere" (103–15 in Pattison and Thompson), esp. 104–5.

2 "Icons in Dostoevsky's Works" (51–68 in Pattison and Thompson). See also Konstantin A. Barsht, "Defining the Face: Observations on Dostoevskii's Creative Processes," in *Russian Literature, Modernism and the Visual Arts*, ed. Catriona Kelly and Stephen Lovell (Cambridge: Cambridge University Press, 2000), 23–57—a very suggestive essay which notes some of the significance of desecrated icons in the novels [e.g., 35–37], pointing out that "the violations of icons which occur so very frequently in Dostoevskii . . . are not so much blasphemous as anti-human in their import" [37]. Unfortunately, he does not discuss any episodes in detail, and (on 35) attributes to Stepan Trofimovich a judgment on the Sistine Madonna that is actually Mme. von Lembke's. Nonetheless, this is an important essay in underlining the general significance of the visual for Dostoevsky, the importance of the connection between the human face and the image of

God, and the role of unattached and underdetermined visual images in his creative processes as evidenced in the notebooks.

3 It is interesting that Sergei Bulgakov describes his first encounter (in 1898) with the Sistine Madonna as a profoundly significant moment in his return to Christian faith; see his *Avtobiograficheskie zametki* [Autobiographical Notes], (Paris: YMCA Press, 1946–1991), 63–64. There is no evidence as to whether he had read *Devils* at this point.

4 Above, p. 181.

5 Cf. above, pp. 51, 56, 103, 252, n. 43.

6 It is possible that there are echoes here of the ideas of Nikolai Fyodorov, an eccentric "freelance" philosopher and essayist who impressed both Tolstoy and Dostoevsky. His work on *The Philosophy of the Common Task* (a posthumous collection of pieces, published in two volumes [Verny, 1906 and Moscow, 1913]; English translation in *What Was Man Created For? The Philosophy of the Common Task* [London: Honeyglen Publishing, 1990]) outlined a project for the literal resurrection of the dead as part of the ultimate renewal of human society.

7 Evdokimov, *Dostoevski et le probleme*, 212–14.

8 Sophie Ollivier, "Icons in Dostoevsky's Works," (51–68 in Pattison and Thompson), 64.

9 1724–1782, briefly Bishop of Voronezh and a prolific author. The best study is still Nadejda Gorodetzky, *Saint Tikhon of Zadonsk: Inspirer of Dostoevsky* (London: SPCK, 1951 [repr. Crestwood: St. Vladimir's Seminary Press, 1976)].

10 Relevant passages in Salvestroni, *Dostoevski et la Bible*, 174–75; see also Frank, *The Mantle and the Prophet*, 455–57.

11 Georges Florovsky, *Ways of Russian Theology*, part 1 (Belmont, Mass.: Nordland, 1989), 157–59.

12 Florovsky, *Ways of Russian Theology*, part 1, 159; cf. his short review article, "*The Brothers Karamazov*: An Evaluation of Komarovich's Work," reprinted in his *Theology and Literature*, 91.

13 Frank, *The Mantle of the Prophet*, 454; also Salvestroni, *Doestoevski et la Bible*, 292.

14 Gorodetzky argues this convincingly and at length in the last part of her book. It is noteworthy, though, that some Orthodox writers who are content to allow St Tikhon a high level of authority are resolutely unpersuaded about the Orthodox character of Zosima's teaching: a signal example is the late Archimandrite Seraphim Rose, who, in a letter of 1972, declares that Zosima "is actually a false elder and will only lead people astray" (*Letters from Father Seraphim* [Richmond Springs: Nikodemos Orthodox Pub-

lication Society, 2001], 39), but is also appreciative of Tikhon (and of Ivan Kireevsky as ally and interpreter of the Optina tradition).

15 Frank, *The Mantle of the Prophet*, 385; the detail comes from from Anna Grigorievna Dostoevsky's memoirs, *Vospominaniya A. G. Dostoevskoy,* ed. Leonid Grossman (Moscow: Khudozhestvennaia literatura, 1925), 232–33.

16 John B. Dunlop, *Staretz Amvrosy* (Belmont, Mass.: Nordland Publishing, 1972 [also London 1975]) allows for the influence of several models, including St. Tikhon, but adds that "one of the reasons Zossima is a far more successful figure than the Staretz Tikhon . . . in the novel *The Devils* is that Dostoevsky had a living rather than purely literary model to draw upon" (60).

17 Frank, *The Mantle and the Prophet*, 386.

18 See e.g., the famous text of Isaac quoted by Lossky, *The Mystical Theology*, 111. The flavor of Isaac's writing can be gauged from the brief but excellent selection from his works translated and introduced by Sebastian Brock, *The Wisdom of Saint Isaac the Syrian* (Oxford: Fairacres Press, 1997), with its suggestions for further reading.

19 Salvestroni, *Dostoevski et la Bible*; Lossky, *The Mystical Theology*, 234.

20 In addition to her book, see her articles, "Isaaco il siro e l'opera di Dostoevskii," *Studia monastica* 44 (2002): 45–56, which has some material about the impact of Dostoevsky's use of Isaac on the reception of the novelist by Thurneysen and Barth; and "Fedor Dostoevskii, Silvano dell'Athos, Simone il nuovo teologo e la voluntaria disceso agli inferi," *Studia monastica* 45 (2003): 61–72.

21 Leontiev accused Dostoevsky of being dependent on models of holiness in Western literature, including Victor Hugo's work, and he has been followed by Sergei Hackel and Sven Linner, *Starets Zosima in The Brothers Karamazov: A Study in the Mimesis of Virtue* (Stockholm: Almquist & Wiksell, 1975). See also Valentina Vetlovskaya, "Ob odnom iz istochnikov Brat'ev Karamazovykh" ["On One of the Sources of Brothers Karamazov"], *Izvestiya Akademeii Nauk; seriya literatury i yazyka* 40 (1981): 436–45, noted by Robert Belknap, *The Genesis of The Brothers Karamozov*, 21.

22 Kliment Zedergol'm, *Zhizneopisanie optinskogo startsa, ieromonakha Leonida (v skhime L'va)* [The Life of the Elder of Optina, Priest-monk Leonid (in the Great Habit, Lev)] (Moscow, 1876). The literary dependence of Dostoevsky's chapter about *startsy*, elders, is traced in detail by Stanton (*The Optina Pustyn Monastery*, 164–78).

23 Frank, *The Mantle and the Prophet*, 457.

24 Solovyov described his visions of Sophia in his poem of 1898, "Three Meetings" (*Tri svidaniya*); see Valliere, *Modern Russian Theology*, 112–13.

25 On the controversies around the subject in the 1930s, see Williams, *Sergii Bulgakov*, 172–81; see also Antoine Arjakovsky, *La génération des penseurs religieux de l'émigration russe* (Kiev-Paris: L'Espirit et la Lettre, 2002), 358–70.

26 See above, n. 23 to chap. 2.

27 Frank, *The Mantle and the Prophet*, 387

28 Sonya Marmeladova in *Crime and Punishment*, Sofya Matveevna, the Bible seller, in *Devils*, Sofya Andreevna, Makar's wife and Arkady's mother, in *The Adolescent*, Sofya Ivanovna (Fyodor Karamazov's second wife, mother of Ivan and Alyosha) in *Karamazov*. Wendy Wiseman, in an article ("The Sophian Element in the Novels of Fyodor Dostoevsky," *St. Vladimir's Theological Quarterly* 49 [2005]: 165–82) bravely attempts to show the pervasiveness of a "sophian" theme throughout the major novels, but this is in terms less of any argument about dependence on Solovyov than of a general thesis about Dostoevsky's understanding of cosmic harmony and reconciliation and the role of the feminine in this.

29 Epstein, "Minimal Religion," in *Russian Postmodernism: New Perspectives on Post-Soviet Culture*, ed. Mikhail Epstein, Alexander Genis and Slobodanka Vladiv-Glover (New York: Berghann Books, 1999; originally published in Russian in 1982), 163–71; and idem., "Post-atheism: From Apophatic Theology to 'Minimal Religion'" 345–93 in the same collection. I am indebted to Jonathan Sutton for allowing me to read his essay on Epstein ("'Minimal Religion' and Mikhail Epstein's Interpretation of Religion in Late Soviet and Post-Soviet Russia") delivered in December 2003 at the School of Slavonic and Eastern European Studies in London.

30 Jones, *Dostoevsky and the Dynamics*, 45 (cf. 80).

31 Jones, *Dostoevsky and the Dynamics*, 45.

32 Jones, *Dostoevsky and the Dynamics*, 80.

33 Jones, *Dostoevsky and the Dynamics*, 126.

34 Jones, *Dostoevsky and the Dynamics*, 132.

35 Mihailovic, *Corporeal Words*, 75–80.

36 Jones, *Dostoevsky and the Dynamics*, 132.

37 Especially Sutherland, *Atheism and the Rejection of God*; and cf. Golosovker, *Dostoevskii i Kant* for a similar argument.

38 *A Writer's Diary*, 1:156–69.

39 *A Writer's Diary*, 1:158.

40 *A Writer's Diary*, 1:164.

41 *A Writer's Diary*, 1:168.

42 *A Writer's Diary*, 1:168.

43 See Gary Saul Morson, "Conclusion: Reading Dostoevskii," in *The Cambridge Companion*, 212–33; and his "Introductory Study" in Kenneth Lantz's translation of *A Writer's Diary*, 1–117, esp. 82–97, 101–5.

44 Morson, "Introductory Study," 93.

45 A classical discussion is Vladimir Lossky, "Apophasis and Trinitarian Theology," in *In the Image and Likeness of God* (Crestwood: St. Vladimir's Press, 1974), 13–29; see also "Darkness and Light in the Knowledge of God," 31–43 in the same volume.

46 For a first class discussion of these issues, see Denys Turner, *The Darkness of God: Negativity in Christian Mysticism* (Cambridge: Cambridge University Press, 1995), esp. chaps. 2 and 11.

47 The seminal work on all this is Oleg Tarasov's brilliant *Icon and Devotion: Sacred Spaces in Imperial Russia* (London: Reaktion Books, 2002). This traces the importance during the period of the seventeenth-century Schism of unease and confusion around the canons for painting icons, the extreme scandal caused by the official destruction of ancient icons judged to be doctrinally misleading, and the connection between these scandals and anxieties and the conclusion drawn by some of the most intransigent of the dissidents not only that God had given over the Russian Church to the power of Antichrist, but that God's grace had been effectively withdrawn from the world, so that there could no longer be priests and sacraments. The mass suicides of some dissident groups were a dramatic witness to the extreme version of this conviction that all images had lost their power and presence. Many have noted Dostoevsky's profound interest in the byways of Russian dissent, and (as we have seen) the sectarian presence, half-offstage, is imaginatively significant in several of the novels. On icons and the Schism, see esp. chaps. 2 and 3 of Tarasov's study. For a picture (taken from a popular Old Believer book printed in the early twentieth century) showing the reforming Patriarch Nikon breaking icons on the floor of a church see p. 195.

Conclusion

1 This is intriguingly hinted at—though from a deeply anti-theistic perspective—by Philip Pullman in the third volume of his remarkable *Dark Materials* trilogy. In *The Amber Spyglass* (London: Scholastic, 2000), Mary Malone, the ex-nun, describes her sensations in the wake of losing faith: "[W]hat I miss most is the sensation of being connected to the whole of the universe. I used to feel I was connected to God like that, and because he was there, I was connected to the whole of his creation. But if he's not there, then . . ." (471). The chapters that follow attempt to suggest what

might take the place of that kind of connection, by way of the elusive but omnipresent image of the "Dust" that pervades the intelligent universe, and the task given to human beings of safeguarding the connectedness that Dust makes possible. The point is simply that any claim for the end of theistic religion still has to work through the implications of the loss of this dimension of unchosen and unsought connection.

2 Eagleton, *Holy Terror*, 136.

3 For Simone Weil's understanding of *misère*, see, for example, *Waiting on God* (London: Routledge & Kegan Paul, 1951), 76–94, and the texts on 72–76 in *Gravity and Grace* (London: Routledge & Kegan Paul, 1952).

4 Eagleton, *Holy Terror*, 69.

5 George Pattison, "Freedom's Dangerous Dialogue: Reading Kierkegaard and Dostoevsky Together" (237–56 in Pattison and Thompson), 251–52.

6 Marilynne Robinson, *The Death of Adam: Essays in Modern Thought* (Boston: Houghton Mifflin, 1998).

7 Robinson, *The Death of Adam*, 40.

8 Evdokimov, *Dostoievski et le problème*, 413–15, 419.

9 Robinson, *The Death of Adam*, 62.

10 Robinson, *The Death of Adam*, 74–75.

11 Ludwig Wittgenstein, *Lectures and Conversations on Aesthetics, Psychology and Religious Belief*, ed. Cyril Barrett (Oxford: Blackwell, 1970), 24.

12 Morson, "Introductory Study," 101–5.

13 Morson, "Introductory Study," 105.

BIBLIOGRAPHY

Primary Sources

The Adolescent. Translated by Richard Pevear and Larissa Volokhonsky. New York: Vintage, 2004.

The Brothers Karamazov: A Novel in Four Parts and an Epilogue. Translated by David McDuff. New York: Penguin Classics, 1993.

Crime and Punishment. Translated by David McDuff. New York: Penguin Classics, 1991.

The Devils; or, The Possessed. Translated by David Magarshack. New York: Penguin Classics, 1971.

The House of the Dead. Translated by David McDuff. New York: Penguin Classics, 1985.

The Idiot. Translated by David McDuff. New York: Penguin Classics, 2004.

Notes from the Underground; The Double. Translated by Jesse Coulson. New York: Penguin Classics, 1972.

Pol'noe sobranie sochinenii. 30 vols. Leningrad: Nauka, 1972–1990.

A Writer's Diary. Translated and annotated by Kenneth Lantz. Evanston, Ill.: Northwestern University Press, 1993.

Secondary Sources

Arjakovsky, Antoine. *La génération des penseurs religieux de l'émigration russe.* Kiev-Paris: L'Esprit et la Lettre, 2002.

Auden, W. H. *Spain*. London: Faber and Faber, 1937.

Bakhtin, Mikhail. *Problems of Dostoevsky's Poetics*. Edited and translated by Caryl Emerson and Wayne C. Booth. Minneapolis: University of Minnesota Press, 1984.

Banerjee, Maria Nemcova. *Dostoevsky: The Scandal of Reason*. Great Barrington, Mass.: Lindisfarne, 2006.

Barsht, Konstantin A. "Defining the Face: Observations on Dostoevskii's Creative Processes." 23–57. In *Russian Literature, Modernism and the Visual Arts*. Edited by Catriona Kelly and Stephen Lovell. Cambridge: Cambridge University Press, 2000.

Barth, Karl. *The Epistle to the Romans*. London: Oxford University Press, 1933.

Belknap, Robert L. *The Genesis of The Brothers Karamazov: The Aesthetics, Ideology and Psychology of Making a Text*. Evanston, Ill.: Northwestern University Press, 1990.

Berdyaev, Nicholas. *Dostoevsky: An Interpretation*. London: Sheed and Ward, 1934.

Brock, Sebastian. *The Wisdom of Saint Isaac the Syrian*. Oxford: S.L.G. Press, 1997.

Bulgakov, Sergei Nikolaevich. *Avtobiograficheskie zametki* [Autobiographical notes]. Paris: YMCA Press, 1946/1991.

———. *Dva grada: issledovaniia o prirode obshchestvennykh idealov* [Two Cities: Investigations on the Nature of Public Ideals]. Moscow: Tovarishchestvo tipografii A. I. Mamontova, 1911.

———. *"Ivan Karamazov kak filosofskii tip"* ["Ivan Karamazov as a Philosophical Type"]. In *Ot marksizma k idealizmu* [From Marxism to Idealism]. St Petersburg: Obshchestvennaia Polza, 1903.

Bultmann, Rudolf Karl. *Essays Philosophical and Theological*. London: SMC Press, 1955.

———. *Kerygma and Myth: A Theological Debate*. 2 vols. Edited by H. W. Bartsch. London: SPCK, 1953/1962.

Cassedy, Steven. *Dostoevsky's Religion*. Stanford: Stanford University Press, 2006.

Chapman, John. *The Spiritual Letters of Dom John Chapman*. 2nd ed. London: Sheed and Ward, 1935.

Chizhevskii, D. I. *Gegel' v Rossii*. Paris: Dom knigi, 1939.

Coates, Ruth. *Christianity in Bakhtin: God and the Exiled Author.* Cambridge: Cambridge University Press, 1998.

Coleridge, Samuel Taylor. *On the Constitution of the CHURCH and STATE According to the Idea of Each.* 1830. Edited by John Barrell. London: Dent, 1972.

Crowder, Colin. "The Appropriation of Dostoevsky in the Early Twentieth Century: Cult, Counter-cult, and Incarnation." 15–33. In *European Literature and Theology in the Twentieth Century: Ends of Time.* Edited by David Jasper and Colin Crowder. London: Macmillan, 1990.

Cunningham, David S. "'The Brothers Karamazov' as Trinitarian Theology." In Pattison and Thompson, 134–55.

Cupitt, Don. *The Long-legged Fly: The Theology of Longing and Desire.* London: SCM Press, 1995.

———. *The Sea of Faith.* London: BBC Books, 1984.

Dormandy, Thomas. *The White Death: A History of Tuberculosis.* New York: New York University Press, 2000.

Dostoevsky, Anna Grigorievna. *Vospominaniya A. G. Dostoevskoy.* Edited by Leonid Grossman. Moscow: Khudozhestvennaia literatura, 1971.

Dunlop, John B. *Staretz Amvrosy.* Belmont, Mass.: Nordland Publishing, 1972.

Eagleton, Terry. *Holy Terror.* Oxford: Oxford University Press, 2005.

Epstein, Mikhail, Alexander Genis, and Slobodanka Vladiv-Glover, eds. *Russian Postmodernism: New Perspectives on Post-Soviet Culture.* New York: Berghahn Books, 1999.

Epstein, Mikhail. "Minimal Religion." In Epstein, Genis, and Vladiv-Glover. 163–71.

———. "Post-atheism: From Apophatic Theology to 'Minimal Religion.'" In Epstein, Genis, and Vladiv-Glover, 345–93.

Evdokimov, Paul. *Dostoïevski et le problème du mal.* Lyon: Ondes, 1942; reprinted Paris: Desclée de Brouwer, 1978.

———. *Gogol et Dostoïevski, La descente aux enfers.* Paris: Desclée de Brouwer, 1961.

Felch, Susan M., and Paul J. Contino, eds. *Bakhtin and Religion: A Feeling for Faith.* Evanston, Ill.: Northwestern University Press, 2001.

Florovsky, Georges. *Puti russkogo bogosloviya*. Paris, 1937.

―――. *Theology and Literature*. Edited by Richard S. Haugh. *Collected Works of Georges Florovsky*. Vol. 2. Vaduz, Europa: Büchervertriebsanstalt, 1989.

―――. *Ways of Russian Theology*. Translated by R. L. Nichols. Belmont, Mass.: Notable & Academic Books, 1987.

Frank, Joseph. *Dostoevsky: The Mantle of the Prophet, 1871–1881*. Princeton: Princeton University Press, 2002.

―――. *Dostoevsky: The Miraculous Years, 1865–1871*. Princeton: Princeton University Press, 1995.

―――. *Dostoevsky: The Stir of Liberation, 1860–1865*. Princeton: Princeton University Press, 1986.

―――. *Dostoevsky: The Years of Ordeal, 1850–1859*. Princeton: Princeton University Press, 1983.

Freeborn, Richard. *Furious Vissarion: Belinskii's Struggle for Literature, Love and Ideas*. London: School of Slavonic & East European Studies, 2003.

Fusso, Susanne. "Dostoevskii and the Family." In Leatherbarrow, *Cambridge Companion*, 175–90.

Fyodorov, Nikolai Fedorovish. *What Was Man Created for? The Philosophy of the Common Task*. London: n.p., 1990.

Gibson, A. Boyce. *The Religion of Dostoevsky*. London: SCM Press, 1973.

Girard, René. *Resurrection from the Underground: Feodor Dostoevsky*. New York: Herder and Herder, 1997.

Golosovker, Ya. E. *Dostoevskii i Kant*. Moscow: Izdatel'stvo Akademii nauk SSSR, 1963.

Gorodetzky, Nadejda. *Saint Tikhon of Zadonsk: Inspirer of Dostoevsky*. London: SPCK, 1951. Reprint Crestwood: St. Vladimir's Seminary Press, 1976.

Grigor'ev, Dmitrii. *Dostoevskii i Tserkov; u istokov religioznykh ubezhdenii pisatelya* [Dostoevsky and the Church: At the Sources of the Religious Convictions of a Writer]. Moscow: Izdatel'stvo Pravoslavnogo Sviato-Tikhonovskogo Bogoslovskogo Instituta, 2002.

Guardini, Romano. *Der Mensch und der Glaube: Versuche über die religiöse Existenz in Dostojewskijs grossen Romanen*. Leipzig: J. Hegner, 1933.

Hackel, Sergei. "The Religious Dimension: Vision or Evasion? Zosima's Discourse in *The Brothers Karamazov*." In Jones and Terry, 139–68.

Hamilton, William. "Banished from the Land of Unity: Dostoevsky's Religious Vision through the Eyes of Dmitry, Ivan and Alyosha Karamazov." In *Radical Theology and the Death of God,* by Thomas J. J. Altizer and William Hamilton. Harmondsworth: Penguin Books, 1968, 64–94.

Hirschkop, Ken. *Mikhail Bakhtin: An Aesthetic for Democracy.* Oxford: Oxford University Press, 1999.

Holquist, Michael. *Dostoevsky and the Novel.* Princeton: Princeton University Press, 1977.

Jacobs, Alan. "Bakhtin and the Hermeneutics of Love." In Felch and Contino, 25–45.

———. *A Theology of Reading: The Hermeneutics of Love.* Boulder: Westview Press, 2001.

Jones, Malcolm. "Dostoevskii and Religion." In Leatherbarrow, *Cambridge Companion,* 155–56.

———. *Dostoevsky and the Dynamics of Religious Experience.* London: Anthem Press, 2005.

Jones, Malcolm, and Garth M. Terry, eds. *New Essays on Dostoevsky.* Cambridge: Cambridge University Press, 1983.

Kantor, Vladimir. "Pavel Smerdyakov and Ivan Karamazov: The Problem of Temptation." In Pattison and Thompson, 189–225.

Kaye, Peter. *Dostoevsky and English Modernism, 1900–1930.* Cambridge: Cambridge University Press, 1999.

Khomyakov, Aleksei. *L'Eglise latine et le protestantisme au point de vue de l'Eglise d'Orient.* Lausanne: B. Benda, 1872.

Kireevsky, Ivan Vasil'evich. *Pol'noe sobranie sochinenii.* Edited by M. O. Gershenzon. Moscow: Tip. Imp. Moskovskago universiteta, 1911.

Lawrence, D. H. "Preface to Dostoevsky's The Grand Inquisitor." In *Dostoevsky: A Collection of Critical Essays.* Edited by Rene Wellek. Englewood Cliffs, N.J.: Prentice-Hall, 1962.

Leatherbarrow, W. J., ed. *The Cambridge Companion to Dostoevskii.* Cambridge: Cambridge University Press, 2002.

———. *A Devil's Vaudeville: The Demonic in Dostoevsky's Major Fiction.* Evanston, Ill.: Northwestern University Press, 2005.

Leontiev, Konstantin. "On Universal Love." In Strizhev and Sechina, 261–97.

Linnér, Sven. *Starets Zosima in The Brothers Karamazov: A Study in the Mimesis of Virtue*. Stockholm: Almquist and Wiksell, 1975.

Lossky, Nikolai. *Dostoevskii i ego khristianskoe miroponimanie* [Dostoevsky and his Christian World-view]. New York: Izdatel'stvo imeni Chekhova, 1946.

Lossky, Vladimir. *In the Image and Likeness of God*. Crestwood, N.Y.: St. Vladimir's Seminary Press, 1974.

———. *The Mystical Theology of the Eastern Church*. London: J. Clarke, 1957.

Mihailovic, Alexandar. *Corporeal Words: Mikhail Bakhtin's Theology of Discourse*. Evanston, Ill.: Northwestern University Press, 1997.

Mochulsky, Konstantin. *Dostoevsky: His Life and Work*. Princeton: Princeton University Press, 1967.

Morris, Marcia A. *Saints and Revolutionaries: The Ascetic Hero in Russian Literature*. New York: SUNY Press, 1993.

Morson, Gary Saul. "Conclusion: Reading Dostoevskii." In Leatherbarrow, 212–34.

———. "Introductory Study." In Dostoevsky, *Writer's Diary*, 1–117.

Ollivier, Sophie. "Icons in Dostoevsky's Works." In Pattison and Thompson, 51–68.

Ouspensky, Leonid, and Vladimir Lossky. *The Meaning of Icons*. 2nd ed. Crestwood, N.Y.: St. Vladimir's Seminary Press, 1982.

Pattison, George. "Freedom's Dangerous Dialogue: Reading Kierkegaard and Dostoevsky Together." In Pattison and Thompson, 237–56.

Pattison, George, and Diane Oenning Thompson, eds. *Dostoevsky and the Christian Tradition*. Cambridge: Cambridge University Press, 2001.

Pullman, Philip. *The Amber Spyglass*. London: Scholastic, 2000.

Pyman, Avril. "The Prism of the Orthodox Semiosphere." In Pattison and Thompson, 103–15.

Riou, Alain. *Le monde et l'église selon Maxime le confesseur*. Paris: Beauchesne, 1973.

Robinson, Marilynne. *The Death of Adam: Essays in Modern Thought*. Boston: Houghton Mifflin, 1998.

Rose, Gillian. *Judaism and Modernity: Philosophical Essays*. Oxford: B. Blackwell, 1993.

————. *Mourning Becomes the Law: Philosophy and Representation.* Cambridge: Cambridge University Press, 1996.

Rose, Seraphim. *Letters from Father Seraphim.* Richmond Springs, N.Y.: Nikodemos Orthodox Publication Society, 2001.

Salvestroni, Simonetta. *Dostoevski et la Bible.* Paris: Lethielleux, 2004.

————. "Fedor Dostoevskii, Silvano dell'Athos, Simone il nuovo teologo e la voluntaria disceso agli inferi." *Studia Monastica* 45 (2003): 61–72.

————. "Isaaco il siro e l'opera di Dostoevskii." *Studia monastica* 44 (2002): 45–56.

Scanlan, James. *Dostoevsky the Thinker.* Ithaca: Cornell University Press, 2002.

Seduro, Vladimir. *Dostoevski's Image in Russia Today.* Belmont, Mass.: Nordland, 1975.

Shestov, Lev. *Dostoevsky, Tolstoy and Nietzsche.* Athens: Ohio University Press, 1969.

Solovyov, Vladimir. *Lectures on Godmanhood.* Poughkeepsie, N.Y.: Harmon Printing House, 1944.

Stanton, Leonard J. *The Optina Pustyn Monastery in the Russian Literary Imagination: Iconic Vision in Works by Dostoevsky, Gogol, Tolstoy and Others.* New York: Peter Lang, 1995.

Steiner, George. *Tolstoy or Dostoevsky.* 2nd rev. ed. Harmondsworth: Penguin Books, 1967.

Strada, V. "Il diavolo di Dostoevskij tra metafisica e metapolitica." In *L'autunno del diavolo*, Edited by E. Corsini and E. Costa. Vol. 1. Milano: Bompiani, 1998.

Strizhev, A.nandnV. Sechina, ed. *F. M. Dostoevskii i Pravoslavie* [Dostoevsky and Orthodoxy]. Moscow: Izd-vo "Otchii dom," 1997.

Sutherland, Stewart. *Atheism and the Rejection of God: Contemporary Philosophy and The Brothers Karamazov.* Oxford: Blackwell, 1977.

————. *Faith and Ambiguity.* London: SCM Press, 1984.

————. *God, Jesus and Belief.* Oxford: Blackwell, 1984.

————. "Language and Interpretation in *Crime and Punishment.*" *Philosophy and Literature* 3 (1978): 223–36.

————. "The Philosophical Dimension: Self and Freedom." In Jones and Terry, 169–85.

Sutton, Jonathan. "'Minimal Religion' and Mikhail Epstein's Interpretation of Religion in Late Soviet and Post-Soviet Russia." Paper presented at the School of Slavonic and Eastern European Studies. London, December, 2003.

———. *The Religious Philosophy of Vladimir Solovyov: Toward a Reassessment.* Basingstoke: Macmillan, 1988.

Tarasov, Oleg. *Icon and Devotion: Sacred Spaces in Imperial Russia.* London: Reaktion Press, 2002.

Terras, Victor. *A Karamazov Companion.* Madison: University of Wisconsin Press, 1981.

———. "The Art of Diction as a Theme in The Brothers Karamazov." 193–205. In *Dostoevsky: New Perspectives.* Edited by Robert Louis Jackson. Englewood Cliffs, N.J.: Prentice-Hall, 1984.

Thompson, Diane Oenning. "Problems of the Biblical Word in Dostoevsky's Poetics." In Pattison and Thompson, 69–99.

Thurneysen, Eduard. *Dostojewski.* Munich: Chr. Kaiser, 1921.

Turner, Denys. *The Darkness of God: Negativity in Christian Mysticism.* Cambridge: Cambridge University Press, 1995.

Vallière, Paul. *Modern Russian Theology. Bukharev, Soloviev, Bulgakov: Orthodox Theology in a New Key.* Grand Rapids: Eerdmans, 2000.

Vetlovskaya, Valentina. "Ob odnom iz istochnikov Brat'ev Karamazovykh" ["On One of the Sources of *Brothers Karamazov*"]. *Izvestiya Akademeii Nauk; seriya literatury i yazyka* 40 (1981): 436–45.

Walicki, Andrzey. *Legal Philosophies of Russian Liberalism.* Oxford: Clarendon, 1987.

Wasiolek, Edward. *Dostoevsky: The Major Fiction.* Cambridge, Mass.: M.I.T. Press, 1964.

———, ed. and trans. *Fyodor Dostoesvky: The Notebooks for The Idiot.* Chicago: University of Chicago Press, 1967.

———, ed. *Fyodor Dostoevsky: The Notebooks for The Possessed.* Translated by Victor Terras. Chicago: University of Chicago Press, 1968.

Weil, Simone. *Gravity and Grace.* London: Routledge and Kegan Paul, 1952.

———. *Notebooks.* Translated by Arthur Wills. London: Routledge and Keegan Paul, 1956.

———. *Waiting on God.* London: Routledge and Keegan Paul, 1951.

Weiner, Adam. *By Authors Possessed: The Demonic Novel in Russia.* Evanston, Ill.: Northwestern University Press, 1998.

Williams, Charles. *The Descent of the Dove: A Short History of the Holy Spirit in the Church.* London: Religious Book Club, 1939.

Williams, Rowan. "The Necessary Non-existence of God." In *Simone Weil's Philosophy of Culture: Readings toward a Divine Humanity.* Edited by Richard H. Bell. Cambridge: Cambridge University Press, 1993.

————. *Sergii Bulgakov: Toward a Russian Political Theology.* Edinburgh: T&T Clark, 1999.

Wiseman, Wendy. "The Sophian Element in the Novels of Fyodor Dostoevsky." *St. Vladimir's Theological Quarterly* 49 (2005): 165–82.

Wittgenstein, Ludwig. *Lectures and Conversations on Aesthetics, Psychology and Religious Belief.* Edited by Cyril Barrett. Oxford: Blackwell, 1970.

Young, Sarah, and Lesley Milne, eds. *Dostoevsky on the Threshold of Other Worlds.* Ilkeston, Derbyshire: Bramcote Press, 2006.

Zakharov, V. N., ed. *Evangel'skii tekst v russkoi literature XVIII–XX vekov.* Petrozavodsk: Izdatel'stvo Petrozavodskago universiteta, 1994.

————, ed. *Novye aspekty v izuchenii Dostoevskago.* Petrozavodsk: Izdatel'stvo Petrozavodskago universsiteta, 1994.

Zedergol'm, Kliment. *Zhizneopisanie optinskogo startsa, ieromonakha Leonida (v skhime L'va)* [The Life of the Elder of Optina, Priest-monk Leonid (in the Great Habit, Lev)]. Moscow, 1876.

Ziolkowski, Eric. "Reading and Incarnation in Dostoevsky." In Pattison and Thompson, 156–70.

INDEX